D0787817

ANALYSING FOR AUTHORSHIP

ANALYSING FOR AUTHORSHIP

A Guide to the Cusum Technique

JILL M. FARRINGDON

With contributions by

A. Q. MORTON, M. G. FARRINGDON and M. D. BAKER

CARDIFF • UNIVERSITY OF WALES PRESS • 1996

British Library Cataloguing in Publication Data

A catalogue record for this book is available from the British Library.

ISBN 0-7083-1324-8

Typeset at the University of Wales Press
Printed in England by Bookcraft Limited, Midsomer Norton, Avon

CONTENTS

PREFACE

Identifying the authorship of human utterance, whether selected literary quotations or items taken from the mass media, has long been a feature of entertainment programmes – variations on a prototype, with titles like *Who Said That*, or *Quote, Unquote*. Such games are enjoyable pastimes, but they are also a reminder of the fact that there is general consciousness of the act of recognizing differences in ways of speaking and writing.

Beyond such diversion, however, attributing disputed utterance of any sort is sometimes a matter of legal urgency or of fierce scholarly debate. It is then that a scientific method of exact attribution – one which is objective – becomes desirable. It should be understood, however, that such a science would have nothing to do with 'style' in any literary sense. This will reassure professionals in the literary field whose skills and expertise are directed towards quite other ends and aims in the realm of literary value.

As a literary critic by inclination and training, and a former literary academic, I address this book to fellow professionals in the humanities who have little or no interest and experience in either mathematics or statistics. It cannot be repeated too often: in order to attribute disputed texts by QSUM (that is, the cumulative sum technique), there is no need to be even an amateur statistician.

QSUM will interest anyone with a genuine attribution problem. It is not easy to accept the idea of such an exact science being possible in the field of human utterance: it can seem suspiciously too good to be true. However, such misgivings are fully addressed by the author(s) in the pages which follow and demonstrated to be both misguided and groundless.

QSUM can be mastered by anyone with the interest, time and motivation to learn the technique. Modern computers remove both the hard graft of counting by hand, and also the need for sophisticated statistical computation by the individual.

When learning to drive a car, it is easy to become mechanically proficient without knowing anything of what goes on under the bonnet (i.e. hood). This book is for non-mechanics who can, with sufficient practice, become the equivalent of 'proficient drivers' in the presentation and interpretation of QSUM graphs and charts. All you need is time, application and the right computer program.

ACKNOWLEDGEMENTS

Saul Bellow, the American novelist and Nobel prize-winner, began his novelistic career as an anthropologist whose research notes kept turning into novels. As Joseph – the central character in his first novel (*Dangling Man*) – says, 'The world comes after you. It presents you with a mechanic's gun, it singles you out for this part or that . . .'. In writing this book, I have felt in a similar situation: a literary critic presented with a mechanic's tool – the computer – and singled out for an uncharacteristic part. This transformation (or transmogrification!) has been effected by a small circle of colleagues.

My greatest debt is owed to Andrew Morton, who asked me to take part in the earliest tests of attribution by cusum analysis in 1988, thus arousing the fascinated curiosity which eventually led to my undertaking several subsequent projects. I am grateful for his patient explication in response to my initial (and very basic) queries, and for his enthusiastic endorsement of the idea of an introductory book, an idea born from my accumulation of collected results. Andrew Morton contributes in Part IV a comprehensive account of his development of the technique, with copious examples, expanding the briefer account given in earlier chapters and recapitulating the salient points essential for beginners.

To assess a book which is cross-disciplinary and which focuses on several different aspects of a pioneering technique, as the present volume does, calls for special abilities. In this respect, my debt to Sir Kenneth Dover, who acted as the official 'reader', is incalculable: given his early familiarity with the technique and his experience in the field of statistical stylistics, his unique capacity to address the book's subject-matter was a matter of my great good fortune. He deserves special thanks from all the book's contributors for agreeing to act as the official reader despite his own pressing commitments, and for the scrupulosity with which he undertook this chore, as well as for many helpful suggestions during the process of writing.

A large debt is owed to Professor Martin Battestin, both for his open-mindedness when first encountering the field of statistical attribution and for his continuing faith in the technique's efficacy in the face of wide scepticism. He generously acted as the 'ideal' uninitiated reader of my exposition of the Method in Part I, and later commented on other literary chapters: his advice and pertinent remarks on work in progress have been invaluable. Martin and Ruthe Battestin deserve special thanks, too, for initiating a visit (in 1992) to introduce QSUM to Faculty members of the University of Virginia, Charlottesville, and for so ably organizing a memorable and enjoyable occasion.

Professor John Worthen should be acknowledged as the first literary scholar to ask for a specific attribution, and I am grateful for the cheerful interest with which he confronted QSUM-charts without any of the defensive hostility often encountered in humanities faculties. In requesting the analysis of a story, 'The Back Road', which had been recently attributed (1992) to D. H. Lawrence, John has been, if not the 'onlie begetter' of this book, one of its most significant ones.

I have profited, too, from the advice of Professor A. F. ('Derek') Bissell, who read the whole of Part I in draft. Derek's statistical expertise – especially in producing a sophisticated variant on the technique, which has been published as a monograph – has proved most enlightening, and his interest has served to enhance the confidence with which we have all been able to proceed.

My periodic discussions with M. David Baker, who writes in Part III on his use of the technique for legal work, have been always enlightening. David has given generously of his time in commenting on most chapters in draft, and his professional experience has often clarified obscurities puzzling to a computing novice.

I am especially grateful for the chance to analyse children's written utterance from material supplied by friends and family, and I thank the children (now grown into adolescents or adults) for allowing me to examine their early writing.

My husband, Michael (who writes in Part III on using QSUM in court and also rebuts its various critics) first introduced me to literary computing, and so is primarily responsible for this book's existence. Without his efficient computer program for undertaking cusum analysis, it would have proved impossible to produce this volume in a comparatively short time.

And to all our friends, who have borne with such a strange (and recurrent) subject of conversation over the past three years, I can only offer apologetic thanks.

Jill Farringdon, Swansea, 1996

PART I

Introduction and history:
The method of cusum analysis; and a test case

Chapter 1

INTRODUCTION

What is the Cusum Technique?

The cusum (cumulative sum) technique – or **QSUM** – is a recognition system applied to human utterance, whether written or spoken. ('QSUM' is the term coined for the application of this system, and used since 1990 by those involved in the field.) It is based on analysing sequences of language units by a cumulative sum method of counting, the normal unit being *the sentence*. The second stage of the analysis counts, by cumulative sum, recurrent kinds of language-use within each sentence.

The resulting data obtained will produce one or more graphs, and, subsequently, **QSUM-charts.** These charts will show, by visual inspection, whether the sample of utterance being analysed comes from one source or more than one, i.e. is of mixed utterance. A sample may be compared with other samples of unknown or doubtful origin, to test whether they both come from the same or from different sources: in effect, as would more commonly be said, are by a single author, having been written or spoken by the same person.

It is as well to say from the outset that any technique, proposed with reasonable confidence as able to attribute utterance, is bound to attract criticism. Even those eager to find answers to problems in their field of scholarship, and thus willing to be convinced, have been apt to say that, in common parlance, 'It looks too good to be true'. Attempts at serious criticism of QSUM have, in fact, been relatively few: no more than four or five academics have, since 1990, attempted to disprove the method.[1] Where these critics have been very successful is in publicizing their disagreement with analysis by the method of QSUM, a disagreement which has given the impression (to the uninitiated) of positive disproof.[2]

The misgivings of critics and the issues they have raised have always been addressed with care by those using the technique. Full and detailed replies, dealing with every point of contention, have been produced (and have been published as legal reports) by professionals using the technique in a forensic setting. Critical comment is best dealt with as the relevant and particular issues arise, but one general point needs to be made at the outset:

  • **Most criticism has been based on misunderstanding, both of how the cusum technique works and of what it claims to be able to do.**

Hence, the most important road which any interested party must travel is to make sure that he or she has a full and clear understanding of the proper procedure when undertaking cusum analysis; and further, understanding of what it claims to show and – equally important – of what it does *not* claim (i.e. its limits: for example, one frequent misapprehension is that the technique claims that all and every sequence of sentences uttered in speech or writing by an individual must automatically prove attributable to that individual).

This book will thus, in Part I, explain first how the technique came into being; then, what its methodology is, suggesting a trial analysis by interested enquirers of their own utterance; and, finally, look in detail at a test case of authorship attribution. Only then, when some familiarity with the whole process has been gained, can queries and doubts be raised and rebutted as the learning process proceeds.

To show how easy it is for the newcomer to the technique to understand the charts by visual inspection, the reader will find little difficulty in scrutinizing some simple illustrations of the end-product, the **QSUM-chart** (as the two superimposed graphs have been named), before the stages by which the charts are made is outlined in detail in the next chapter.

Below, therefore, are given three illustrations.

Reading a QSUM-Chart

The basic method of reading is easy enough to follow. But there are some people who will 'freeze' at the sight of graphs, unsure of what is being represented – and, therefore, unsure of what they are being called upon to understand. For any reader who suspects such a reluctance, it is salutary to recall that marks on a page are only communications which can be translated into musical sound (by notation) or language (by printed words, mathematical symbols, or graphs).

Every chart represents a sample of utterance (**spoken or written**) counted in sentences: a letter, extract from conversation or other oral form, part of an essay or novel – in fact, any type of human utterance. The **title** describes what the sample represented in the chart is. The object of the exercise is to see if the sample is all the utterance of one person or not.

Figure 1 is a combined sample of sequential sentences of text from four letters by Helen Keller, written when she was aged seven to eight, selected from letters written over the period of one year, between January and December, 1888.[3] The total number in the sequence of sentences (which you can count along the horizontal axis, or bottom line) is **seventy sentences**.

In the middle of the graph, on either side, you will see the figures 0 and 0.0. This represents the movement from the average for the quantitative analysis: for the number of words per sentence, and the feature being analysed *within* each sentence.

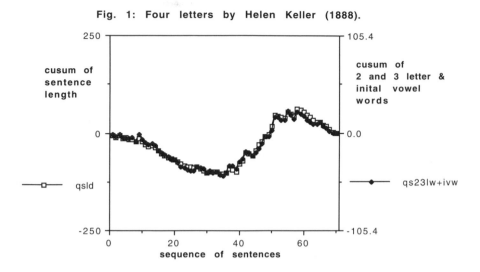

Figure 1: The habit of using two and three letters and words beginning with a vowel in a combined analysis of text from four letters by Helen Keller written over the period of one year, 1888.

If every sentence were identical in these two respects, the two graph-lines (representing the cusum of sentence length and of the feature, or 'habit', in the sample) would be straight lines from one side (0) to the other (0.0).

In fact, an individual's habitual utterance normally deviates around an average number of words per sentence. Some sentences will be longer, and some shorter, than the average. The **empty square** plots the line of the sentence deviations by cumulative sum (**qsld**).

The **black square** plots the average use of the language habit by cumulative sum (in this particular analysis, of words of two and three letters together with words starting with a vowel, **qs23lw+ivw** – at this early stage, the reader is asked to accept the validity of choice of the recurrent habit, and explanation will follow when 'The Method' is outlined in the next chapter).

If the two lines track each other closely enough, it is scientifically accurate to say that the writer of one sample cannot be distinguished from the other sample. In effect, this is taken to mean that the samples – in this case, text from four letters – are by the same writer, i.e. are **homogeneous**.

If the two lines separate markedly, two or more people are responsible (mixed utterance). You will note that the **two lines on this graph hardly diverge at all**, proving what was already known – that the four samples of writing which have been subjected to a combined cumulative sum analysis were by one and the same person, Helen Keller.

Figure 2 is an example of a chart showing mixed utterance. This QSUM-

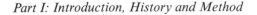

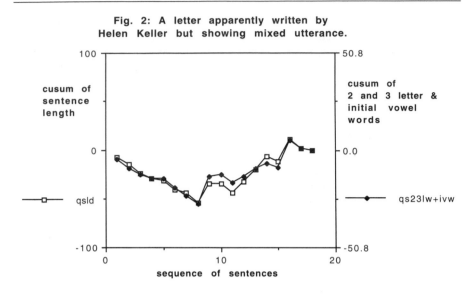

Figure 2: The habit of using two and three letters and words beginning with a vowel in a sample of writing by Helen Keller written in December, 1888.

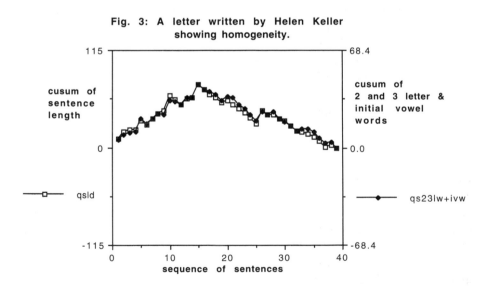

Figure 3: The habit of using two and three letters and words beginning with a vowel in an analysis of thirty-nine sentences of a letter by Helen Keller written on 10 November 1890.

chart is an analysis of a letter of eighteen sentences supposedly composed by a single author, Helen Keller. The first eight and the last three sentences track each other well; however, the two lines diverge markedly from sentences 9 to 15, which is clear evidence of its being mixed utterance. What we have here is a borrowing, or an insertion, from another source within the text of this particular letter.[4]

By contrast, Figure 3 shows a single sample, another letter, where the utterance is seen to be completely homogeneous. Figure 3 is a sample of sentences from a letter by Helen Keller, written when she was aged ten, selected from letters written during the year 1890. The total number in the sequence of sentences (which you can count along the horizontal axis) is **thirty-nine sentences**.

Here two lines track each other closely enough to be able to say that the text of the sample cannot be distinguished. In effect, this is taken to mean that the sample – in this case, text from a single letter by Helen Keller – is indeed by the one writer, i.e. it is **homogeneous**.

The reader should now have a basic idea of how cusum analysis is graphically illustrated, and can proceed to examine the method of arriving at a QSUM-chart.

But first, further background information on the technique will aid the serious enquirer. Language analysis by cumulative sum is a simple method developed in 1987–8 by Andrew Morton.[5] It was then extensively tested on a wide variety of textual material by Morton and a small group of co-researchers.[6] By 1990, it was capable of being used in legal cases as a forensic test of authorship, and has since been offered in evidence several times, in the UK and Northern Ireland, and in the Republic of Ireland. It has also been withheld from evidence where an analysis proved to be of no value to the defence solicitor who had requested it but rather would have aided the prosecution case. (This does not mean, of course, that the defendant in such cases was never convicted on other grounds.)

Although recently developed, the idea of using cumulative sums for testing authorship was not so much a sudden flash of inspiration as the end-result of many years of scholarly research into authorship attribution by Morton. His work in this field was itself based on earlier approaches by other academics into what has become known as 'quantitative stylistics': that is, the use of mathematical models as a basis for examining the periodic, or recurrent, nature of language use.

The attribution of authorship by a system of counting – statistical or quantitative analysis – has a long history whose development has been one of ever-increasing refinement of method, and this should be acknowledged as the basis of the present state of the methodology.

This history is next outlined.

The Search for an Objective Method of Authorship Attribution by Statistical Means: A Short History

There is a distinction to be made between literary criticism and literary scholarship, the latter being the discipline usually concerned with establishing textual authenticity, by historical examination and research. Criticism, on the other hand, is most fruitful when it concentrates on interpretation of a text of known authorship.

This scholarship/criticism distinction is perhaps crude and by no means absolute – it is, of course, possible to be both a scholar and critic; but it is generally true that painstaking scholarship has been the route to establishing textual integrity. Literary criticism – sensitive apprehension of a text – is less demonstrably fruitful when attempting to solve authorship problems beyond doubt, and this is particularly true when the text to be authenticated is one of recent or contemporary date. For example, when a book of stories and fictional fragments attributed to C. S. Lewis was posthumously published in 1977, debate as to its authenticity ensued.[7] Critics are entitled to such debates based on literary qualities in particular texts: this is perfectly legitimate. However, without an *objective* test of authorship – one capable of verification by experiment – even the most reasoned arguments for X or Y being the author of a work are endlessly open to dispute.

Professional criticism apart, it is part of general common awareness that individuals have language habits, ourselves included. Favourite words and phrases recur in a person's habitual speech and writing. The success of the catch-phrase as a comic device comes from the fact that people use such favourite phrases unconsciously, as victims of habit: it is amusing because it is unwitting self-revelation, and comedians capitalize on this by inventing catch-phrases for their comic personae. (In Wales, there is a tradition of identifying people by such comic tags.)

However, language habits like catch-phrases, which are so obvious that they can be easily recognized, are unlikely to be of use in statistical examination. A sophisticated analysis of language for attribution purposes must be based on regular and recurrent usage which is both very frequent while being unconscious to the user.

An example of the unreliability of a noticeable literary trait came to light when it was found that the phrase 'to say the truth' had been called a favourite habit of, and one able to identify, the eighteenth-century English author, Henry Fielding. Yet a concordance showed that it occurred only eight times in his first novel *Joseph Andrews,* a text of 128,271 words – and not at all in the anonymous *Shamela*, a satire usually attributed by critics to Fielding. Such a so-called habit is useless as a discriminator.

What has always been needed is a method simple and reliable both to use and to understand.

The first serious proposal for an objective test occurred almost a century and a half ago, when a professor of mathematics at London University, Augustus de Morgan, outlined his ideas for quantifying stylistic habits of language in a statistically reliable manner. The occasion for his suggestion was the dispute over the authorship of the Epistle to the Hebrews. He wrote that it might well be that if the number of letters in every word was recorded, and the average length of word in every epistle was calculated, then the same writer would have much the same average length of word in all his letters, and also differ in this respect from others. So if Hebrews had much the same length of word as the other Epistles, it would be by Paul; if it differed, it would be rejected as a valid Pauline text.[8]

This criterion of word-length, put forward for the first time in 1859 as an index of identifying a writer, may seem bafflingly mechanical to the traditional literary intelligence. Hostility to the idea of the mere length of a word being a useful discriminator must surely be because such an idea ignores semantics, the actual meaningful communication and purpose of utterance, rather than being an objection to counting in itself.[9] Moreover, words and their length are related to linguistic development, and thus have a connection with the history of the language at the time of writing. For instance, at one stage in the history of writing, the use in English of an alphabetical character for the sound 'th' – *thorn* – which later lapsed into disuse, meant that words like 'that', and 'then' (i.e. four-letter words in modern English) were then three-letter words.

De Morgan's suggestion commendably anticipated those twentieth-century studies which went on to explore whether word-length was indeed an index of authorship. For instance, focus on such an index (word-length) formed part of a study by the Cambridge statistician G. Udny Yule, in 1938, of Thomas à Kempis's *The Imitation of Christ*. This investigated word-distribution: how many words were used, what sort of words, and where they occurred. It was a major pioneering contribution. Yule went on to investigate the general assumptions and the problems of measuring word-distributions in general, specifically focusing on noun distribution.[10] Such a focus suggested an examination of word function, a fruitful area for future development.

In the 1960s, there were four major statistical studies of authorship, which together laid the foundations for most of what has followed, namely:

Alvar Ellegård's examination (1962) of the *Junius Letters:*
* *A Statistical Method for Determining Authorship: The Junius Letters, 1769–1772*

Mosteller and Wallace's study (1964) of the *Federalist* papers:
* *Inference and Disputed Authorship: The Federalist*

Louis Milic's analysis (1967) of Swift's prose:
* *A Quantitative Approach to the Style of Jonathan Swift*

Andrew Morton and James McLeman's work (1966) on the Pauline Epistles:

• ***Paul, the Man and the Myth: A Study in the Authorship of Greek Prose***
In most such work, the questions being asked have been relatively straightforward. Was it *this* author, **A**, who wrote *this* text, **X**? Such a simple question provided the test case which forms the **QSUM** attribution example in Chapter 2: was it D. H. Lawrence who wrote the newly discovered story, 'The Back Road', or not? This is the simplest kind of test on which to obtain a good result: **A** did, or did not, write **X**.

Another fairly simple question goes further: was it either author **A** or author **B** who wrote text **X**? This can be the focus of a legal investigation: for example, did the dead person who signed a suicide note write it, or was it written by the another specific person who was in a position to have done so, suggesting that there may be a crime of murder?

The fewer the potential authors, the greater the probability of producing a positive identification. In the study cited above on the *Federalist* papers, the task which fell to Mosteller and Wallace fell within fairly simple parameters. It was known, on external evidence, that twelve papers where the authorship was disputed were written either by Alexander Hamilton or by James Madison. These two writers were known to have written other essays in the *Federalist* series – Hamilton was the author of forty-three and Madison of fourteen of these essays.

Using these known works as control texts, Mosteller and Wallace experimented with different kinds of statistical test. They tried simple sentence length, for which both these authors proved all too similar; then word length, but this again was an unreliable indicator, proving more variable in the known than in the unattributed texts by these two authors. Eventually, they had more success with a large group of *function* words (that is, those words like conjunctions, prepositions, pronouns, adverbs, which connect and qualify the *content* words, i.e. all the subject-dependent words denoting what any communication is about). Using these, they were then able to credit the disputed papers with varying degrees of probability. (A more recent study returns to the most doubtful of all the twelve attributions, an essay which Mosteller and Wallace had attributed jointly to Hamilton and Madison. Using **QSUM**, it has been possible to attribute specifically the sections in the paper written by each writer, including identifying a single aberrant sentence by one of these two authors in the middle of a passage by the other.)[11]

Where there is no such small potential range of authors, the chances of making a positive identification are, of course, much slimmer, or even impossible. Ellegard's study of the *Junius Letters* was complicated by the number of possible authors being so large. There was one suspected author, Sir Philip Francis – *but on no external evidence*; so, theoretically, the potential range of authors extended to all the literate English men or women living at the time. A similar problem would arise in the case of positively attributing the story 'The Back Road', in the test case already mentioned. If the author was not D. H. Lawrence, who was it? Without a range of possible suspects, compiled from suitable considerations, there would be no chance of finding the actual author.

Ellegard decided to compare *Junius* (157,000 words) with Francis's other texts (231,300 words). He extended this comparison to other eighteenth-century works, involving a total of over a million words. Such a vast pool of words immediately suggests the usefulness of using a computer for all the counting involved; but in fact Ellegard proceeded by hand, counting his own selection of vocabulary, much of which comprised 'content' words, and using a computer only to tabulate and calculate the statistics. Ellegard found that his subjective testing did indeed result in favouring Francis as author, since his selected vocabulary items provided the best fit with the *Junius Letters*. His claim, though, must remain an uncertain identification since it lacks the objective demonstration which would be independent of the subjective choice of content words – an objective demonstration now capable of being provided by cusum analysis.

Louis Milic, a literary scholar in eighteenth-century studies, produced a significant study in his analysis thirty years ago of the prose of Jonathan Swift. Milic assumed that, in the search for identifiers, it was grammatical categories that would best reflect linguistic habits of mind in a writer. His resulting book on Swift was an in-depth study of a writer's language use which was based on syntax, possibly the least conscious aspect of word-choice and in some degree (always allowing for the demands of the simple or complex) less dependent on subject or genre. However, such a large project, involving not only Swift but four of Swift's contemporaries for comparison, was highly labour-intensive. It took a considerable amount of time to process such information by hand before turning to the computer for analysing the vast quantity of data produced. This project undoubtedly bore some fruit, resulting in the observation of particular patterns of Swift's writing that were not noticeable during the normal reading process, even by scholars familiar with this writer.

Milic's work was pioneering in the field of literary computing scholarship, and it deserves all credit for enthusing fellow-scholars to follow his lead in applying his method to other writers.[12]

Andrew Morton's work (with James McLeman) on the Pauline Epistles, though by no means his first scholarly work, brought him immediate media attention. Indeed, the present writer clearly remembers the occasion of his first television interview about this book during an early evening news magazine programme in the mid-1960s, long before a later acquaintance and academic association with Morton. Although New Testament criticism, in applying the new Higher Criticism of German scholarship, dates from the nineteenth century, the suggestion that Paul may not have written all the Epistles attributed to him still counted as 'news' in the mass media of the mid-twentieth century. Combined with the modern veneration accorded to scientific method – 'scientism' as it is sometimes called – the fact that this work had involved the use of a computer gave the television 'story' a new twist, or at least made it smack of the controversial.

The controversy which has often attached itself to Morton's work has been mainly based on this particular aspect of his scholarship. While New Testament criticism is not new, the detail of its speculations has usually been confined to small intellectual circles, and such speculations always lay open to the charge of subjectivism. Literary criticism is, to those who practise it, an art based on both a native talent for it and on experience: and as regards the New Testament, literary critical judgments, even when combined with scholarly research, always leave room for argument as regards specific textual attribution. Thus, Morton's aim in attribution studies has always been directed towards finding a test that satisfied two criteria: scientific objectivity and simplicity.

Paul, the Man and the Myth, Morton's co-authored work, created controversy by the very fact of its application of large computer-generated tables of cold statistics, rather than warm, sympathetic and sensitive reading, to Holy Writ. This was text regarded as sacred, 'God's Word'. Bernard Shaw was hardly the first to opine that the only way the Divine can 'speak to' humanity is through the imagination, a process otherwise known as inspiration.[13] This elevation of Imagination can hardly fail to appeal to writers. Nevertheless, even disallowing such an attitude, the significance of the Thing/Person/Event-in-time recorded in the New Testament writings need not depend upon a traditional veneration for an over-literal Gospel reading. For even with an exact attribution to various unknown 'X' and 'Y' writers of different parts of the four Gospels, the task of theological interpretation will remain what it always has been.

Controversy apart, a more serious criticism of Morton's work on the Pauline Epistles as well as on other early Greek writers, including Plato, was based on suspicion of his criteria (the variables of sentence length and the use of *kai*) and on doubt about the validity of his statistics. Therefore, Morton's continuing search for an ever more refined methodology was based on the need to satisfy fully some doubts voiced within the academic community. Nevertheless, by 1975, Morton's existing methods for attribution testing were respected enough for him to give evidence in the courtroom of London's criminal court, the Old Bailey, as an expert witness. He was able to satisfy the Court that a man serving a prison term, a prisoner who had heard of his work and approached him for help, had indeed been convicted on 'confessions' which, in terms of his habitual language use, could not have been made by him.[14]

Morton's eventual arrival at the development of cumulative sum analysis is next described.

The Development of QSUM: 1988–1995

Andrew Morton is now a retired Church of Scotland (Presbyterian) minister. He has combined pastoral care with a life-long interest in attributing human utterance, with the aim of making a significant contribution to New Testament scholarship. The main area of his attention has been the quantitative analysis of style, though the word 'style' is one which he finds unhelpful in seeking scientific attribution – unhelpful because he is aware that literary definitions of 'style', as applied to a particular author, cannot be made with any precision, however apt such literary descriptions as 'Lawrentian', 'Kafkaesque', 'Dickensian' may be – and *are* – to initiated readers. It is scientific precision that Morton has pursued in his development of a quantitative method of attribution.

For the pursuit of this aim, Morton is well qualified, combining an ability to read Greek with being also a scientific and mathematical scholar: he is a Fellow of the Royal Society of Edinburgh, an Honorary Fellow of Computer Science at Glasgow University, and also enjoyed many years of fruitful association with the late Sidney Michaelson, Professor of Computer Science at Edinburgh University.

Morton first suggested the idea of cumulative sum tests for language as long ago as the 1960s, carrying the idea over from its industrial setting: such tests are widely used in industry as a method of sampling averages. However, it was not until his retirement, and the arrival of the desk-top computer that the right conditions arose for his full attention to be directed to experimenting with its possibilities. By this time, he had for many years investigated the sound application of statistical principles to problems of attribution, and on these he could build. It is proper here to mention the body of New Testament studies he had already written, in association with others, based on a technical knowledge of such things as the development of the handwritten book before the era of printing, and the role of the scribe in the Ancient World, as well as on computational linguistic analysis.[15]

By 1987–8, Morton felt that his own cumulative sum tests on language use were encouraging enough for him to solicit the help of colleagues and friends in testing as wide a variety of texts as possible. My own tests were mainly in the field of modern and contemporary literature, in particular asking such questions as whether the claims Morton felt able to make for the method of QSUM would apply to the literature of modernism, or to poetry, or to a writer's own perception of difference or development of personal style – a concept more familiar to the literary than to the scientific approach.

This early testing, by as wide a group of people as then was practicable, provided a consolidation of the principles which formed the basis of Morton's first introductory book on the subject: *The QSUM Plot.* [16] My contribution to Morton's book came from suggesting a comparison of author Iris Murdoch's philosophical essays with her novels, since she had asserted a subjective awareness of deliberately changing her style for each kind of writing.[17] To the reader, she undeniably did change style: these different genres are certainly different kinds of writing; but Morton was able to show from analyses of samples of Murdoch taken from her novels and a philosophical essay that an author's deliberate and conscious change of style did not affect the habits which form the QSUM identification.[18]

Another discovery at this time came from my interest in the novelist and poet Muriel Spark. Spark had asserted not a consciousness of deliberately changing a style for a different purpose and audience, like Iris Murdoch, but an awareness of a crucial development in her writing career at a certain period of her life. She had used the concept – familiar and certainly valid in literary terms – of 'finding a voice', which is a profoundly important achievement for an author. The Spark project, interesting in itself, raised an unexpected question, that of someone editing an author's spoken words when uttered in an interview: whose QSUM 'fingerprint' would be revealed in textual material which had been edited by a third party? The answer to this question will be given later in this book.[19]

There is no suggestion, of course, that either Iris Murdoch or Muriel Spark was in any way deluded about the changes each perceived in their styles of writing, and this is a very important point to grasp when using QSUM for authorship identification:

• **It has nothing to do with 'style' in the literary sense.**

Testing carried out by other colleagues of Morton included all sorts of texts – detective novels, eighteenth-century writers, classical Greek texts, the poetry of Burns, to mention just a few. In all of these, QSUM survived the challenge, proving able to attribute authorship successfully in work where the authors were known and also in 'blind tests' carried out by Morton. At this time, those colleagues working on their own ideas for tests were carrying out all the work of counting samples by hand, the usual sample being 25–30 consecutive sentences. When supplied with the counted results, Morton then carried out the necessary computer work. Since then, computer programs for the analysis have been developed (subject to constant revision and up-dating), although no program is necessary for a modest simple experiment: a piece of graph paper will suffice for a reliable, if perhaps crude, result.

By 1990, the work proved acceptable enough for Morton to be able to use it in the appeal court. He appeared as an expert witness in that year and procured the release, through his evidence, of a convicted prisoner by satisfying the judges that a confession was unsafe. In the next three years, Morton's expertise was to be sought in many sensitive legal cases where 'confessions' or admission statements were at issue (cases like those of the 'Birmingham Six', the 'Guildford Four', the 'Armagh Four' and others). In 1991, he was joined in this legal representation as an expert witness by Dr Michael Farringdon.[20] The usefulness of QSUM for a wide variety of applications in law will be fully dealt with in **Part III** of this book.

Andrew Morton has in most recent years been engaged on applying the technique to his New Testament studies. A new book on the Pauline Epistles is already in print.[21] His latest publication, *The Making of Mark*, has just appeared.[22] Clearly, these will be seminal works of historical research, on which future generations of Biblical scholars will be able to build. His full account of the genesis of the cumulative sum technique, its development, and its application to Greek as well as English prose, appears later (as Chapter 11) and is a summary of principles and practice.

Now celebrated for his attribution expertise, Morton continues to receive requests for help from all sorts of sources (some of them rather unlikely – such as validating communications from spirit-guides).

It is now time to look in detail at what is actually involved in learning how to carry out a cumulative sum attribution. The Method will be the subject of the next chapter.

Chapter 2

THE METHOD

Learning to Make QSUM-Charts

The method of cusum analysis, or **QSUM**, aims to compare two aspects of habitual language use within a given text, segment of text, or combination of texts. This is done by counting the occurrence of these aspects by cumulative sum.

The first aspect is the length, that is the number of words, of the sentence, the basic syntactical unit used by a person providing a sample of language, spoken or written.[1] The cumulative sum is the sum of the deviations in length – whether more or less – of the sentences from the average sentence length in the sample under consideration, as the sentence lengths are added in sequence. This procedure produces the sentence length distribution (**sld**).

> **SAMPLE of language counted for**
> - **average sentence length**
> - **deviation from average of each sentence**

A second aspect counted will be the number of occurrences, within the sentences in the sample, of some feature (or 'habit') of language use. Again, the cumulative sum of the particular feature chosen will be the sum of the deviations from the average per sentence for the sample, as these differences are calculated sentence by sentence in sequence. A variety of features ('habits') have been used. The most common is the use of two- and three-letter words (**23lw**). Another is words starting with a vowel (initial vowel words, **ivw**), and a third is the combination of these two together (**23lw+ivw**), this having often proved the most useful identifier of consistency.

> **HABIT OCCURRENCE counted for**
> - **average occurrence per sentence**
> - **deviation of occurrence from average per sentence**

The initial counting, of the number of words in each sentence and the number of 'habit' words in each sentence, provides the primary data. Calculations are made of the averages of sentence length and of occurrences of the 'habit' words per sentence, then for both sentence length and habit of the deviations from these averages. A further counting (**by cumulative sum**) of these deviations for each sentence in sequence provides the final **data** necessary.

This **data** in turn will produce the **graphs**, and then the
> - **QSUM-chart**

which is a combination of the two graphs together. The QSUM-chart demonstrates in visual form the language use which has been analysed. The two overlaid graphs (making the QSUM-chart) allow the visual comparison of the cumulative sum of the sld (**qsld**) with the cumulative sum of one specific language habit (for instance, **qs23lw**, or **qs23lw+ivw**).[2] The two introductory charts in Chapter 1 have already illustrated such a comparison using, as the language habit within the sentence, the **qs23lw+ivw** test.

Starting with Yourself: Making a Graph of Your Own Writing or Speaking

Before attempting to use **QSUM** for any specific problem of attribution, it is always a useful – indeed a necessary – exercise to become familiar with how the technique works. If the method is to be used, the user needs to know exactly how a sample of utterance can be attributed, and how it can be differentiated from the utterance of other persons.

The first necessity is to obtain a sample of writing or speech whose origin is beyond dispute: *you*, the user, need to be sure of who wrote your sample, or uttered the spoken words of your sample, since

• **the integrity of the text**

is of first importance when making experimental use of QSUM. The most obvious source of such a sample for all of us is ourselves: letters, an essay or other written piece, a talk or ordinary recorded conversation, will all provide suitable material.

Although QSUM will work for short samples (even samples containing sentence-sequences of average sentence-length as low as eight to nine words), it does require practice to be able to 'read' the graphs and charts which are based on such samples. A more satisfactory result for the beginner requires a sample long enough to provide enough information for a graphic analysis which will prove easy to read. Twenty-five to thirty sentences will provide a good sample. The piece chosen should preferably comprise typical natural utterance – but please note that your choice *may* unwittingly contain an anomaly which may slightly affect your result. There are some factors which produce anomalies, defined as ab-normal utterance in quantitative terms. These can, from experience, be expected and explained: for example, a *list* creates an anomaly, since it is abnormal utterance – people do not regularly and repeatedly utter sentences comprising 'lists', where sequences of content words usually dominate the syntactic form. Such anomalies will be illustrated later.

Next follow the four stages by which the values of each QSUM test are calculated:

i.   counting the length of each sentence in the sample and the number of habit occurrences within each sentence;

ii. making a cumulative, or running, sum of these figures;

    iii.   finding the average and calculating how each sentence and habit within the sentence deviates from the average;

    iv.   making a cumulative sum of those deviations.

For scholars in the humanities – or for the general reader who has no mathematical or statistical expertise – it may help to know from the outset that a computer program may be written to carry out these stages quickly. Once created, there is no difficulty in learning how to use such a program on a computer – what is then needed is a clear objective, a good idea of how to proceed, and plenty of practice.

The Stages of Testing

Stage One

The first objective is to obtain the **qsld** of the length of sentences in the sample of utterance. The process is explained below, and the resulting data is destined to appear in a **Data Sheet**, where the calculations will appear in four columns.

i.   Column 1: **sld**

List the number of words in each of your sentences (words per sentence, or *wps*).

      e.g. Sentence   1:   14 words

                „   2:   8 words

                „   3:   23 words

ii.   Column 2: **Running total** of **sld**

Make a running total of the number of words per sentence by adding the *wps* of each sentence to those of the next.

      e.g. 1. Sentence 1:   14

                „   2:   14+8   = 22

                „   3:   22+23 = 45

iii.   Column 3: **Deviating averages**

Calculate the average *wps* by dividing the total arrived at in Column 2 by the number of sentences in your sample. For example, a sample of twenty-five sentences with a total of 402 words would give an average of 402/25 = 16.08 *wps*.

    Then calculate how each sentence differs from the average by adding or subtracting (remembering to respect the plus or minus sign). Each sentence will be either longer or shorter than the average, except for the rare instance of a sentence which exactly matches the average.

      e.g. Sentence   1:   14 words; difference from average

                                = 16.04 – 14 = **–2.04**

        Sentence   2:   8 words; difference from average

$$= 16.04 - 8 = \quad \mathbf{-8.04}$$
Sentence 3: 23 words; difference from average
$$= 16.04 - 23 = \quad \mathbf{+6.96}$$

iv.   Column 4: **Cumulative sum** of sld (qsld)
A running total (or cumulative sum) is then made for each of these values
(rounding off the decimal points).

e.g. Sentence 1: –2.04   = **–2** (rounded off)

    „   2: **–2** + (–8.04)   = **–10** (rounded off)

    „   3 : **–10** + (+6.96)   = **–3** (rounded off)

What you will end up with in your fourth and final column is your **qsld**, or the cumulative sum of the deviations from the average sentence length (cusum charts will always end at zero [0], and if they do not, something has gone wrong with your calculations – this point is more fully explained in Andrew Morton's later chapter [11]). This will show how in this particular sample of your utterance, your sentences have deviated from the average length, up or down (which will later appear on your chart as a graphic line moving up or down).

Stage Two
The next stage of the process is to determine which of several common language-habits within each sentence will remain consistent in the sample of language being tested. That is, which of these habits will best serve as the identifier: the particular test that yields the most consistent result, and, in combined samples, is able to act as the discriminator.

In this second stage, the steps outlined in Stage One are repeated for a number of common language habits within the sentence, in order to find which one(s) will remain consistent in the sample of language being tested. There are several characteristic features of language use within a sentence which may be analysed.

The steps outlined in Stage One are then repeated for these language features ('habits') within the sentences in the sample of utterance. The aim is to see how the deviations from the average occurrence of this particular feature, or 'habit', compare from sentence to sentence.

The final result of analysing the habit by cumulative sum will then be tested against the deviations of sentence length in the sample so that we can discover whether the utterance is homogeneous – the utterance of one person only – although in this case we already know the answer: *it is you*, testing whether the technique will work on utterance you know to be your own. (A word of caution here: one linguistics expert who was interested in analysing his language use found that a particular sample refused to match his other utterance. He then found that this sample, a dictated letter, had been significantly altered by his secretary. To repeat: **be absolutely sure of the integrity of the text.**)

As noted earlier, the most common features examined are

a)   two- and three-letter words (*23lw*);
b)   words starting with a vowel (initial vowel words, or *ivw*);
c)   a combination of both (*23lw+ivw*).

(The *23lw+ivw* test excludes any initial vowel words which already appear in the *23lw* list: in other words, do not count twice such words as 'and' or 'in', both of which start with a vowel but have already appeared in the *23lw* list).

A Note on Processing Text for Cusum Analysis

Any method which relies on counting individual 'sentences' and 'words' requires a definition of those terms. This is, of course, essential for the recognizing computer program. From the experience of the researchers who have been involved in working with QSUM since 1988, the following hints will prove useful.

• A sentence may be defined as any normal sentence ending in a full-stop, question mark, or exclamation mark. Speech should be punctuated by the analyst according to normal conventions. Care should thus be taken that such marks are eliminated if appearing within any sentence you intend to use. An obvious example would be *Mr.* or *St.* where the full stops indicate abbreviations for Mister and Street. It is quite easy to forget this: a way of checking your text-processing is to make sure your final computer results (at the end of the 'Results File') do not apparently include any sentences with one word – or no words – in them, as may happen if you include an abbreviation mark as a separate sentence by mistake.

• Half-sentences, like 'On Wednesday, perhaps, weather permitting' (a hypothetical answer to 'When will you come?') may be omitted – they can sometimes cause a distortion.

• Dialogue originating with the subject of the sample may be included, using quotation marks, so long as no distorting punctuation marks are used. For example, consider the following sentence.

'*Who is Sylvia?*' I said.

This would be word-processed without the question mark in the original, and would therefore comprise one sentence of five words, not two sentences of three and two words.[4]

• **Names** which appear in the text, of persons, places, or anything else, are obviously a problem for the analyst. Their length and spelling are a matter of pure chance, as are numbers and dates. The child who gives his name as

Rodney Aloysius Stewart Brown, The Elms, 198, Parkway Drive, Cola 19205, USA, The World, The Universe, The Cosmos

is only an example, familiar to us all, of name extension taken to absurdity. A researcher typing in a name of more than a single word need merely type **[name]** to show that a designation appears at that point. Otherwise the calculations may be distorted by the arbitrary inclusion, in the example just given, of fifteen extra words in the sentence. It cannot be stressed too strongly that QSUM has nothing at all to do with the *content* vocabulary, and with information otherwise vitally necessary. It is merely a statistical test of consistency with regard to function words.

• Similarly, **numbers** may be run together.

3.00 p.m., Wednesday, 31st March, 1986

can be typed in as one unit, remembering to omit the full-stops after '3' and 'p.m.', and without separating spaces or commas. It will appear in the data as a single 'word':

3pmWednesday31stMarch1986

• Contractions will also call for a decision. Frequent contractions, like 'I'm' for 'I am' will be counted by the computer program as a two-letter word. Such contractions do not cause a problem, so long as the analyst remains consistent in the text processing. You may decide to restore the full uncontracted form, or else to stick to the abbreviations, the latter being the practice of most QSUM analysts.

• Direct quotations by another person in the body of a text will obviously need to be deleted, as not being the utterance of the subject under analysis; but reported speech may be retained as paraphrase by the subject. For example, take the following sentence containing direct quoted speech in inverted commas:

When I saw him, he said 'I will see you at the usual place next Thursday morning'. [seventeen words]

This might be processed as

When I saw him he said [quote]. [7 words]

(Examples in later chapters will include the analysis of samples of dialogue from fiction, which is one author's utterance).

If a sentence contains reported speech, it may be treated as normal text, as, for example:

> When I saw him he said that he'd see me round at Joe's place probably on Thursday in the morning.

Here the original quotation has been loosely paraphrased, so all twenty words could be processed. However, there is always the problem that the analyst does not know how much of the paraphrase contains the original direct speech of another person, so in court work, reported speech may also be omitted.

• Anomalous sentences

The researcher will find that some sentences fall into the category of being anomalies: that is, sentences which have been genuinely uttered by the subject but are anomalous in terms of normal utterance. It should be stated at the outset that the ability to identify an anomaly comes with practice. In due course, it may be possible for the researcher to delete as necessary any *obvious* anomalous sentence prior to analysis. But this procedure is not recommended, especially for the novice. It is much more useful to analyse a sample, and then, if there is an apparent separation, to return to the text to examine the cause of the disturbance.

• Re-examination of the text is a crucial procedure

Only then will the sentence(s) be found to be either a true separation or anomalous.

An example of an obvious anomaly is the very short sentence of three or four words or less, which contains little information for processing. Such a sentence may be omitted, or more usually, added to the previous sentence (or the next one, depending on sense) by using a colon or semi-colon. Take the case of a two-word sentence:

> He was not sure of the exact nature of the problem. I am.

This could be processed as

> He was not sure of the exact nature of the problem; I am.

Sometimes such short units in text or speech are not really 'sentences' at all, in a syntactic sense. They may be exclamations:

> 'My word!' 'Oh yeah?' or 'Are you kidding?'

As such, they belong to the general idiom, part of cliché and convention, and do not constitute the characteristic syntactic habit(s) of the user which the analyst is seeking to identify. They may therefore be omitted as anomalous.

• Very long sentences may also be problematical. A much longer than average sentence will do no more than cause a large 'jump' in the lines of the two graphs on the combined QSUM-chart, which may look odd enough to worry the novice-reader, *but is not a separation.*[5]

Sometimes, however, a long sentence will constitute an illustrative list of examples to some main proposition: the *list sentence* is the most typical anomaly which will disturb a chart, and is best omitted. It is abnormal utterance, often offering a series of content words uninterrupted by function words. (Some lists could be said to be a form of 'shorthand' utterance, since the repetition of the function words is 'understood' by the listener.)

At other times, long sentences may actually be due to the compositional habit of an author (William Faulkner and Henry James are writers who come to mind in this respect); or else a long sentence may be a single anomalous instance within a given passage composed out of the need for a rhetorical effect; or it may belong to the prose conventions of the times – in which case it will not be anomalous, but may affect the length of the sample under analysis, as it does for the eighteenth-century authors in Chapter 5; or it may even result from a compositor's whim. (I have noted that the last explanatory sentence itself constitutes an illustrative list of examples.) It is perfectly permissible to break up very long sentences into smaller units which have simpler syntactic sentence structure.

For example, the following sentence (number 13) occurred in the forty-two sentence sample from Henry Fielding's *Joseph Andrews*, used as a control text for an attribution in a later chapter:[6]

Joey was now preferred from the Stable to attend on his Lady; to go on her Errands, stand behind her Chair, wait at her Teatable, and carry her Prayer-Book to Church; at which Place, his Voice gave him an Opportunity of distinguishing himself by singing Psalms: he behaved likewise in every other respect so well at divine Service, that it recommended him to the Notice of Mr Abraham Adams the Curate; who took an Opportunity one Day, as he was drinking a Cup of Ale in Sir Thomas's Kitchin, to ask the young Man several questions concerning Religion; with his Answers to which he was wonderfully pleased.

The number of words in this one sentence (taking the full-stop as marking the end of a sentence) is 107, where the average sentence-length of the sample was 48.1 words. There is an obvious break after 'Psalms', so replacing the colon by a full-stop would allow a new sentence to start with 'He behaved likewise . . .' (thus increasing the number of sentences under analysis by one).

Other very long sentences of over 80/90 words – almost twice as long as the average – occurred in the Fielding sample from which this sentence was taken. It is necessary to deal with such occurrences because they artificially enlarge the chosen sample, and this will increase the amount of information analysed to a point where the density will compress the result to an unacceptable degree – in other words, detail will be lost.

An unduly long sentence may be omitted, or repunctuated into smaller units. To omit a long sentence is not a deliberate distortion of the data. In the main, as already explained, such sentences (except for lists) do not cause separations but large jumps in the chart, so that nothing essential is being left out. What is desirable is the characteristic utterance of an author. If every other sentence were omitted as 'unsuitable', obviously sequence would be lost; but in practice such a situation does not arise.

Another anomaly could occur when a sentence has an artificially high, or low, number of occurrences of the habit being analysed. This is a freak result, occurring by chance on a rare occasion. A good example is given by Andrew Morton, in Chapter 11, which was actually uttered in a legal case:

No, it was not six of the ten of us, nor two of the six of us, it was one of the two of us.

This sentence has one hundred per cent *23lw* words, and was bound to cause an anomalous disturbance – which it did.

  • **It should be realized that QSUM as a recognition system does not propose that every single sequence of language and words uttered by a subject will automatically constitute that subject's unalterable habitual utterance. Allowance has to be made for the exceptions resulting from conventional features of speech and writing, and for unexpected anomalies, of which the above are only the main ones.**

Common sense will guide the user of QSUM. Such editing is marginal, affecting an insignificant percentage of any sample. What then remains constitutes the subject's normal utterance.

Completing the Test
Less common habit-usage has been the subject of experimental research. When using tests which rely on traditional orthography, it is well to remember that such standardization is relatively recent. Earlier language usage in English (Elizabethan English, for example) has been found to respond, under analysis, to other combinations of word-frequency. Again, some varieties of English as a foreign language deviate from common usage, and respond to the less habitual tests.

If the three common tests given as routine in the above instructions fail, unusually, to be discriminating, some other tests may be tried:

Use of • two-, three-, and four-letter words (*234lw*)
  • two-, three-, and four-letter plus ivw words (*234lw+ivw*)
  • three- and four-letter words (*34lw*)
  • three- and four-letter plus ivw words (*34lw+ivw*)
  • every word which is NOT 23lw (*not 23lw*)

The most satisfactory percentage of 'habit' words per sentence is between 45 and 55 per cent. The lower and upper limits for workability would be in the region of 35 per cent and 70 per cent. Below 35 per cent, homogeneity is hardly possible, and above 70 per cent, homogeneity becomes inevitable.

Stage Three

Once the calculations have been made, the results will appear on a **results file**, as illustrated below, the first word of each line being used to indicate which sentence it belongs to.[7] This gives a rough guide to its position in the text. (Short sentences – say, of only six words – may be *wholly contained* within a line starting with the previous sentence.)

The symbols which mark each habit being counted are easy enough to follow, marking two- or three-letter words, and words starting with a vowel; but the conventional symbols used here could be varied as desired by an analyst. Naturally, our computer program is constantly being up-dated, and the example given relates to the current version. A summary of the results, automatically counted, are given at the end of the textual display, followed by the necessary indications for the range and the QSUM-chart scaling.
  • **Note: using a specially designed program is not a difficult process**

Conventions used in the program:
  Sent# = sentence (with its sequential number)
  ^ = two- or three-letter words starting with a vowel
  # = two- or three-letter words not starting with a vowel
  v = any other word starting with a vowel

These symbols appear under the relevant words as per the number of letters in the word. Sentences 1 and 2 are reproduced here by way of explanation:


```
Sent# 1 (= sentence 1)
Welsh writers are also, as a group, concerned with their own
          ^^^ vvvv    ^^ v                              ^^^
```

```
Sent# 1
language. For them, the issue has a particular local urgency, but
            ###         ### vvvvv ### v                    vvvvvvv ###

Sent# 2
the principles underlying it are universal.
###               vvvvvvvvvv ^^ ^^^ vvvvvvvvv
```

Note that the first example of each class of word has been printed in bold: '**are**' is a 'two- or three-letter word starting with a vowel'; '**also**' is 'any other word starting with a vowel'; '**For**' is a 'two- or three-letter word not starting with a vowel'. All these words are marked by the symbol for that category beneath. Note, too, that the second sentence starts in the middle of the line with the words 'For them'; so that '**Sent 2**' is not so marked until the beginning of the next line, above the later words in that sentence '**the principles**'.

Marked Text from Data File JMF-88
(NB In accordance with the procedure for cusum analysis, quotations, names, abbreviations have been, in this sample, edited: thus, 'Ted Hughes' appears as 'TedHughes'; 'i.e.' appears as 'ie', without the abbreviation mark; and so on.)

```
Sent# 1
Welsh writers are also, as a group, concerned with their own
              ^^^ vvvv  ^^ v                              ^^^

Sent# 1
language. For them, the issue has a particular local urgency, but
            ###         ### vvvvv ### v                    vvvvvvv   ###

Sent# 2
the principles underlying it are universal. For Anglo-Welsh
###               vvvvvvvvvv ^^ ^^^ vvvvvvvvv   ### vvvvvvvvvvv

Sent# 3
poets, the issue of language might seem to be less crucial than for
       ### vvvvv ^^                    ## ##                    ###

Sent# 3
poets writing in Welsh, committed as these must be to
        ^^               ^^            ## ##

Sent# 3
the survival of the Welsh language and its culture. This is not at
###          ^^ ###                vvv ^^^ ^^^        ^^ ### ^^
```

Sent# 4
all the case. Apart from the fact than an increasing number of
^^^ ###   vvvvv   ###   ^^ vvvvvvvvvv   ^^

Sent# 5
Anglo-Welsh poets are deliberately electing to become bilingual
vvvvvvvvvvv   ^^^   vvvvvvvv ##

Sent# 5
(which, if nothing else, shows a sense of deprivation), there is also
      ^^   vvvv   v   ^^   ^^ vvvv

Sent# 5
the question of what kind of English the Anglo-Welsh poet will
^^   ^^ vvvvvvv ### vvvvvvvvvvv

Sent# 5
use to make poetry out of. In twentieth-century poetry,
^^^ ##   ^^^ ^^ ^^

Sent# 6
spoken language and conversational tones and rhythms have
              ^^^   ^^^

Sent# 6
marked the personal voice as a strong element. Auden called
      ###   ^^ v   vvvvvvv vvvvv

Sent# 7
poetry 'memorablespeech'. What kind of speech, then, will an
                              ^^   ^^

Sent# 8
Anglo-Welsh poet use?
vvvvvvvvvvv   ^^^

Sent# 9
The British Poet-Laureate, TedHughes, has described the
###

Sent# 9
Standard English of current educated speech as 'quote'. The
        vvvvvvv ^^   vvvvvvv   ^^   ###

Sent# 10
phrase 'team-calls' derisively raises the issue of class and of
                    ### vvvvv ^^   ^^^ ^^

27

Sent# 10
dialect as that which identifies social identity. This, too, then
              ^^   vvvvvvvvvv   vvvvvvvv   ###

Sent# 11
must be a consideration for the Anglo-Welsh poet in the struggle
     ## v   ### ### vvvvvvvvvvv   ^^ ###

Sent# 11
to speak in one's own voice (though the English class system, as
^^ vvvvv ^^^   ### vvvvvvv   ^^

Sent# 11
such, has never had an exact mirror image in Wales).
     ###   ### ^^ vvvvv   vvvvv ^^

Sent# 12
The choice of language also raises the issue of cultural
^^   vvvv   ### vvvvv ^^

Sent# 12
purity. Of all the major contemporary influences on speech, the
        ^^ ^^^ ###   vvvvvvvvvv ^^   ###

Sent# 13
most important, naturally, are the mass media, radio and
     vvvvvvvvv   ^^^ ###   ^^^

Sent# 13
television, especially the latter. The young, in particular,
           vvvvvvvvvv ###   ###   ^^

Sent# 14
encounter much spoken language directly on English and Welsh
vvvvvvvvv   ^^ vvvvvvv ^^^

Sent# 14
television, which includes a large component of American
               vvvvvvvv v   ^^ vvvvvvvv

Sent# 14
English.
vvvvvvv

Sent# 15
Clancy sees irony in the fact that saving the language
       vvvvv ^^ ###   ###

Sent# 15
involves children growing up on such mixed fare, summed up in
vvvvvvvv   ^^ ^^   ^^ ^^

Sent# 15
the cultural fusion of a word he has coined, 'Americymry'.
^^ v   ## ###   vvvvvvvvvvvvv

Sent# 16
Clancy's own remarks, as a writer, about adapting a Welsh verse
      ^^^   ^^ v   vvvvv vvvvvvvv v

Sent# 16
form, or drawing on his experience of living in Wales, while
    ^^   ^^ ### vvvvvvvvvv ^^   ^^

Sent# 16
remaining fully an American poet, are interestingly relevant to
              ^^ vvvvvvvv   ^^^ vvvvvvvvvvvvv   ##

Sent# 16
this discussion. In particular, his assertion that 'quote' (ie as
              ^^   ### vvvvvvvvv   ^^ ^^

Sent# 17
regards the homogenising effects of an international technology) is
       ###   vvvvvvv ^^ ^^ vvvvvvvvvvvvv   ^^

Sent# 17
to the point.
###

Sent# 18
Thus if the Welsh experience of television is one of
    ^^ ###   vvvvvvvvvv ^^   ^^ ^^^ ^^

Sent# 18
'Americymry', so, too, the Anglo-Welsh writer has to come to terms
vvvvvvvvvvvv ## ### ### vvvvvvvvvv   ### ##   ##

Sent# 18
with a degenerating language. DaveMillington's
     v

Sent# 19
'TheMacbethTragedy' is a humorous poem acknowledging the
              ^^ v   vvvvvvvvvvvvv ###

Sent# 19
tragicomic failure of a teacher attempting to put standard
                          ^^ v   vvvvvvvvvv ## ###

Sent# 19
Eng-Lit questions on Shakespeare to pupils reared on the illiterate
vvvvvvv   ^^   ##   ^^ ### vvvvvvvvvv

Sent# 19
trivialities of the modern media. It ends with the teacher
            ^^ ###   ^^ vvvv   ###

Sent# 20
answering his own questions to himself, with an ironic bow, as
vvvvvvvvv ### ^^^   ##   ^^ vvvvvv ###   ^^

Sent# 20
readers will note, in the direction of eecummings.
                ^^ ###   ^^ vvvvvvvvvv

Sent# 21
Some poets, including MikeJenkins, are willing to entertain
            vvvvvvvvv   ^^^   ## vvvvvvvvv

Sent# 21
the proposition that schools should return to a Welsh language
v

Sent# 21
'literature curriculum' as a means of putting the young in touch
                        ^^ v   ^^   ###   ^^

Sent# 21
with their own cultural heritage and history. Other
            ^^^   ^^^   vvvvv

Sent# 22
considerations apart (and they are formidable), such an effort
              vvvvv ^^^   ^^^   ^^ vvvvvv

Sent# 22
would seem doomed in the ubiquitous oral-aural media-culture
          ^^ ### vvvvvvvvvv vvvvvvvvvv

Sent# 22
that pervades twentieth-century life. MikeJenkins has written of
                                      ###   ^^

Sent# 23
being impressed by the fact that Welsh has no word for 'I', that
      vvvvvvvvv ## ###   ### ##   ### vvv

Sent# 23
capitalized ego which he associates with English imperialism, and
             ^^^   ## vvvvvvvvv   vvvvvv vvvvvvvvvv ^^^

Sent# 23
has written a poem ('I') on this subject. It is a neat point, yet to
v   vvv ^^   ^^ ^^ v   ###

Sent# 24
claim too strong a link between the conventions of language and
     ###   v   ###   ^^   ^^^

Sent# 24
national behaviour overlooks the imperial history, say, of other
                   vvvvvvvvv ### vvvvvvvv   ### ^^ vvvvv

Sent# 24
European nations with their uncapitalized first-person pronouns
vvvvvvvv   vvvvvvvvvvvvv

Sent# 24
(je and ich, for example). Nor was Rome, speaking the Latin
 ## ^^^ ^^^ ### vvvvvvv   ### ###   ###

Sent# 25
which also had no word for 'I', exactly non-imperial. *People* are
      vvvv ### ##   ### vvv vvvvvvv   ^^^

Sent# 26
imperial. Fascism is a state of mind, and to try to claim that some
vvvvvvvv   ^^ v   ^^   ^^^ ## ### ##

Sent# 27
people are better than others on linguistic grounds seems
       ^^^   vvvvvv ^^

Sent# 27
simplistic.

Sent# 28
The ability to make a true communication cannot depend,
vvvvvvv ##   v

```
Sent# 28
surely, even in Wales, on a knowledge of the Welsh language.
      vvvv ^^         ^^ v          ^^ ###

Sent# 29
Nowhere is this clearer than in PeterThabit-Jones's moving elegy
      ^^                    ^^                        vvvvv

Sent# 29
'Deathofason', where he observes his Welsh-speaking wife at the
                      ## vvvvvvvv ###                  ^^ ###
Sent# 29
graveside.


Sent# 30
What binds us at the deepest levels is not language at all but
      ^^ ^^ ###                  ^^ ###          ^^ ^^^ ###

Sent# 30
being able to recognise a shared humanity. Jones's 'Naagi', about
      vvvv ##           v                              vvvvv

Sent# 31
an old Arab dying in Swansea and cared for by two elderly Welsh
^^ ^^^ vvvv         ^^          ^^^      ### ## ### vvvvvvv

Sent# 31
sisters makes a similar point.
            v
```

After the marked text, the file goes on to summarize the information from this data, as follows:

```
OUTPUT FROM CUSUMCHART PROGRAM:
Program © 1992 M.G.Farringdon & A.Q.Morton
Version 1.5.1 of July 5, 1992.

Raw statistics for Cusum from text in data file "jmf/88"
(If tabs are out of alignment select OPTIONS on menu bar,
choose TABS..., change value to 12 and "OK".)
```

Sent#	sld	231w	ivw	231w+ivw
- - -	- -	####	vvv	^^^^^^^^
1: JMF/88	12	3	5	5
2: JMF/88	16	7	7	12
3: JMF/88	34	15	8	17
4: JMF/88	7	5	3	5
5: JMF/88	46	16	20	25
6: JMF/88	19	5	6	7
7: JMF/88	4	0	1	1
8: JMF/88	10	3	4	4
9: JMF/88	15	5	4	7
10:JMF/88	18	6	7	9
11:JMF/88	36	15	12	21
12:JMF/88	11	4	4	6
13:JMF/88	22	9	8	12
14:JMF/88	22	5	10	11
15:JMF/88	31	11	10	15
16:JMF/88	33	10	15	17
17:JMF/88	20	10	9	13
18:JMF/88	25	12	9	16
19:JMF/88	32	11	11	17
20:JMF/88	24	11	10	15
21:JMF/88	36	10	10	14
22:JMF/88	22	5	9	10
23:JMF/88	34	12	11	19
24:JMF/88	40	15	15	23
25:JMF/88	15	6	3	9
26:JMF/88	3	1	2	2
27:JMF/88	23	8	7	10
28:JMF/88	20	6	7	10
29:JMF/88	19	6	5	8
30:JMF/88	20	9	7	11
31:JMF/88	21	7	8	11

Below this results table, the average number of words in each class appears, with the percentages of the classes (of the total number of words).

Average number of words in each class and the percentages of the classes (of the total number of words).				
	sld	231w	ivw	231w+ivw
Averages:	22.258	8.	7.968	11.677
Percentages:	- -	35.9%	35.8%	52.5%

As can be seen, the average sentence length is 22.258 words, of which the average number of two- and three-letter words per sentence is 8.0; of initial vowel words, it is 7.968; and of the combined habit *23lw+ivw* , it is 11.677. Thus, the percentages are:

- for the number of two- and three-letter words in the sample displayed, 35.9% of the total number of words;
- for the number of words starting with a vowel, 35.8%;
- for the number of two- and three-letter words plus words starting with a vowel 52.5%.

Next is displayed the range of values of the cumulative sums, necessary for **scaling** the graphs and/or the QSUM-chart.

```
Range of each Cusum:


                    sld         23lw        ivw         23lw+ivw


        Max:         35          13          17           215
        Min:        -42         -16         -15           -26


        Range:       77          28          32            46
```

In this example, the values of cumulative sum of the sentence length distribution (**sld**) go from a maximum of +35 to a minimum of −42 (see **data sheet** at end of chapter, where the four columns ending in *qsld* are displayed), so that the *sld* range of values is 77. The habit values may be similarly calculated. Note that if the **sld** values had been from +35 to +42 (not −42), the range would have appeared as 7). It is necessary to know the range in order that the graphs may be drawn in a perspective which provides clear information by visual display on the computer in use.

   • **A note on scaling appears, with illustrations, in Appendix 2.**

In addition to the **JMF/88.res file**, the identical calculations are stored in another file, **JMF/88.CG**. The **CG** stands for 'Cricket Graph', and these calculations are in a computer-readable form for use on the computer's compiler, so that a data sheet may be produced in order to draw the graphs. The instructions as to how to do this (on an Apple Macintosh computer) are also displayed on the Results File:

```
To read the cusums into CricketGraph
open the CricketGraph application, then
from File menu choose Open,
click the "Show All TEXT Files" box,
and select the "88.CG" file name.
```

From these CG results, the data sheet is constructed and graphs and charts will be drawn. An illustration of a **data sheet** is given in Appendix 3.

Stage Four
Reading the charts which will result from your data is an acquired skill, and several observations need to be made.

A simple explanation of basic chart-reading has already been given in Chapter 1, and the reader is referred back to that for help in reading the illustrative QSUM-charts which will follow.

In that illustration, the Helen Keller graphs there displayed appear in the form of *double*-graphs, that is, the QSUM-chart. This is produced by the super-imposition of the *qsld* graph upon that of a chosen habit (e.g. *qs23lw*) so as to produce one single QSUM-chart.

However, the more sensitive way to compare the sentence-length and habit is to print out separate graphs for each, and to compare the movement of the sentence and habit deviations by the use of transparencies. Indeed, this method is *essential* for any serious project, and is the proper method for isolating either single-sentence anomalies or aberrant interpolations of passages which typically constitute mixed utterance (i.e. are by two or more authors).

For the purpose of demonstration, an analysis has been made of samples of the writer's own written utterance over a period of time. First, a single *qsld* graph (cusum of sentence length only), Figure JMF-1. Next, a single line

Fig. JMF-1: sld of a sample by the author (JMF).

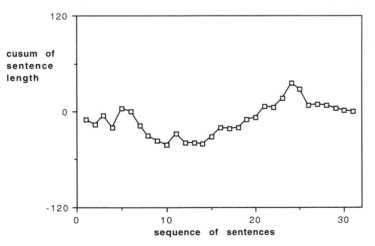

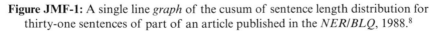

Figure JMF-1: A single line *graph* of the cusum of sentence length distribution for thirty-one sentences of part of an article published in the *NER/BLQ*, 1988.[8]

graph of the cusum of words of two and three letters, and those starting with a vowel (*23lw+ivw*), in Figure JMF-2.

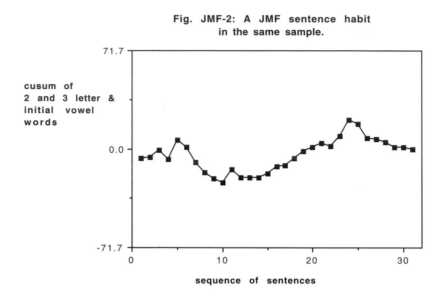

Fig. JMF-2: A JMF sentence habit in the same sample.

Figure JMF-2: A single-line *graph* of the cusum of words of two and three letters and starting with a vowel (*qs23lw+ivw*) in the same sample.

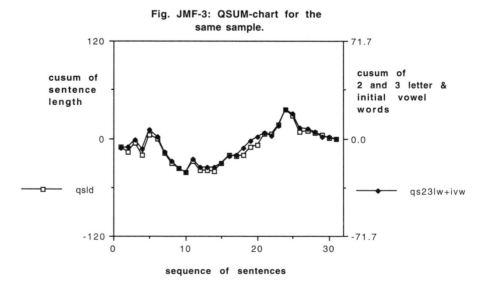

Fig. JMF-3: QSUM-chart for the same sample.

Figure JMF-3: A QSUM-chart showing the two separate line-graphs superimposed on each other to make a QSUM-chart.

Ideally, a transparency should be made of this second graph (of the habit under analysis, *qs23lw+ivw*), and it should then be laid over the first *qsld* graph for comparison. The use of tracing paper to trace the 'habit' graph is a substitute which will allow a reader to achieve a rough idea of the process and what it reveals. Transparencies for these two graphs would confirm homogeneity, but of course the chart method gives a quicker indication.

When the two graphs are run together to produce only one QSUM-chart, the result appears in Figure JMF-3.

What is here visible in the superimposed QSUM-chart is a consistent habit running through a reasonable sample of thirty-one sentences. To the experienced eye, this is a homogeneous chart. The two lines track each other quite smoothly, though some slight displacement appears around sentences 18–20, resulting in what QSUM-analysts usually call a '**blip**': this may be defined as a minor and temporary visual disturbance rather than a continuing separation – one which virtually disappears in a combined sample.

• **To find what causes a blip, it is necessary to return to the text.**

Usually, it will be an anomaly of the kind already examined; but sometimes a high degree of condensed information will vary the 'habit' averages too markedly. The sentences responsible here (18–20) constituted a short paragraph of critical information which summarized the form and content of a poem (from 'Thus if the Welsh experience of television . . .' to 'in the direction of e. e. cummings'). This had caused the habit variation.

At this stage, it is sufficient to understand that the QSUM-chart, Figure JMF-3, shows us what we know to be the case, single authorship.[9]

In order that the test habit chosen as the best identifier, *qs23lw+ivw*, may be compared with the other two popular tests, *qs23lw* and *qsivw*, these other two tests are given in comparison. First, the *qs23lw* test, Figure JMF-3a.

There is a some evidence of homogeneity in this chart (sentences 1–2, 5–11, 23–31), showing that there is a degree of consistency in the writer's use of two and three letters; but it is not a reliable enough indicator to act as the best positive identifier of attribution. As indicated above, the use of words of two and three letters was 35.9 per cent.

Next, the third most common test, that of using initial vowel words (*ivw*). Figure JMF-3b shows the result of testing this habit. There is a promising start in the chart by this test. The writer is indeed a high user of initial vowel words, which accounted for 35.8 per cent of this sample.

After the promising start, the central section, sentences 15–24, deviated as a group from the average consistency, and the habit is not a useful one as a discriminator for the writer. A comparison of the last two figures, JMF-3a and JMF-3b, with Figure JMF-3 shows that the combined habit is the most consistent (at 52.5 per cent of usage) and therefore is the best positive discriminator. As recommended above, in Stage 2, the most useful percentage

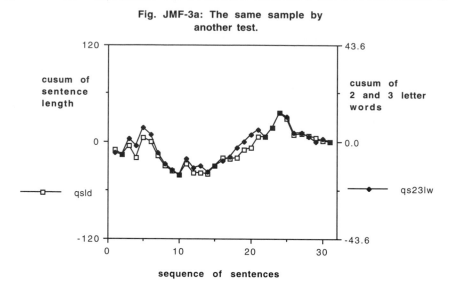

Figure JMF-3a: QSUM-chart of the same sample by another test (*qs23lw*).

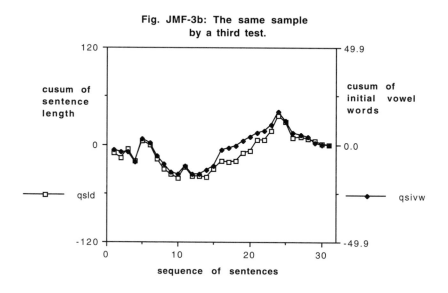

Figure JMF-3b: QSUM-chart of the same sample by another test (*qsivw*).

of habit words per sentence for discriminating authorship is between 45 and 55 per cent, so it is not surprising that a habit usage of 52.7 per cent resulted in the best evidence of homogeneity.

QSUM Testing Over Lengths of Time
The next examples show the writer's writing tested over different periods of time.

First, a sample from 1967, from a piece of arts criticism for the Welsh national newspaper, the *Western Mail*, combined with the thirty-one sentences from an article published in the American journal, *The New England Review and Bread Loaf Quarterly,* in 1988 – a difference of twenty-one years. This will

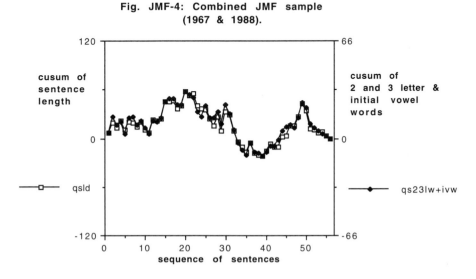

Fig. JMF-4: Combined JMF sample (1967 & 1988).

Figure JMF-4: Combined sample of twenty-five sentences of a newspaper theatre review by JMF, 1967, with the thirty-one *NER/BLQ* sentences from 1988, analysed by the *23lw+ivw* habit.

be seen to be an excellent match. The newspaper review article is consistent with the literary essay written twenty-one years later (the blip in Figure JMF-3 is still faintly visible, now appearing at sentences 44–6).

However, it is worth looking at the theatre review's QSUM-chart on its own, in Figure JMF-4a, for what it may indicate in terms of learning about reading charts.

At first sight, this chart seems to have unsatisfactory features. There is loose correspondence between the two lines at the beginning, as well as loss of directional consistency (that is, the *qsld* line moving in one direction while the 'habit' line, *qs23lw+ivw*, moves in another – for example, sentences 3 to 4); and there are clearly anomalous factors at work in the last five sentences. The fact that this chart appears to have a degree of actual distortion makes it useful as a learning exercise in how to assess results in charts.

Are these movements between the lines separations or anomalies? One way

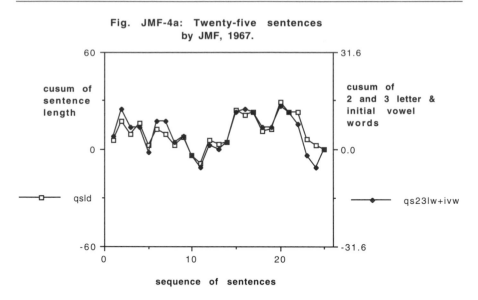

Figure JMF-4a: The same habit in the sample of twenty-five sentences of a theatre review by JMF, 1967.

of answering such a question is to combine them with another *authentic* sample by the writer under analysis. This has already been done, in Figure JMF-4. When combined to make a larger sample (totalling fifty-six sentences), the variations noted in the single chart vanish, showing that they are indeed anomalous. Appearing in combination with other writing by the writer, the twenty-five sentences of theatre criticism have lost virtually all apparent 'separations', and blend in smoothly as part of a combined chart.

So why did the single chart of twenty-five sentences produce a less satisfactory result?

• It is always necessary to return to the text to determine this question.

First, note that these twenty-five sentences had not been fully edited in terms of QSUM conventions – the first sentence of the review contained the unedited Shakespearean quotation 'the actors are come hither'.[10] But the slight looseness at the start is less obvious than the next blip, which was due to the fact that sentence 8 was a list sentence.

Much information in this theatre review was compressed into lists, and these lists occur at sentences 3, 4, 8, and 22.[11] At twenty-five sentences, and given the need for the compressed economical style inevitable in writing for a newspaper, with its constraints on space available, the chart (Figure JMF-4) has shown some of the effects of this requirement.

The final sentences (20–25) of the review, where there seems the greatest disturbance, included the list sentence 22; the long sentence 20 (at forty-two words, the second longest sentence in the sample – the average sentence length being 25.6 words); and sentence 23 (at nine words the shortest in the sample). All these anomalous features together have caused the observable blip.

This example conveniently shows the effect of anomalies described earlier in this chapter. The lists – which have caused by far the greatest anomalous movement in the chart – could, of course, be edited out and this QSUM-chart regularized; but note the tendency of the anomalies' effect to be cancelled in a combined sample by the same writer (Figure JMF-4). It is their compression into a short piece of writing which has caused the apparent problem in this single analysis.

As a further illustration, if this review by the writer is combined with a sample by a different person – say, author Aldous Huxley, using the same sample chosen for comparison with D. H. Lawrence in Chapter 3 – then the known different authorship emerges as a firm separation in the combined sample in Figure JMF-4b.

Fig. JMF-4b: Combined sample of JMF and another writer.

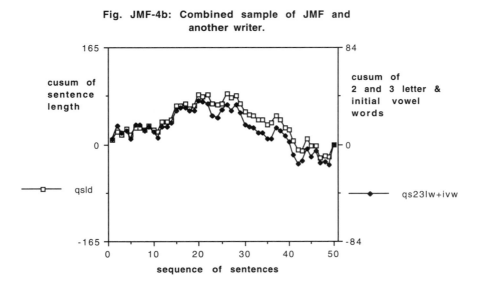

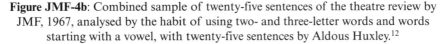

Figure JMF-4b: Combined sample of twenty-five sentences of the theatre review by JMF, 1967, analysed by the habit of using two- and three-letter words and words starting with a vowel, with twenty-five sentences by Aldous Huxley.[12]

This is a clear example of mixed utterance. Even before the actual meeting point of the two different samples at sentence 26, separation has begun to occur on the chart. This is a useful instance for advising readers that, in combined samples displayed on a QSUM-chart, a separation at the exact point where two texts join should not be expected. It sometimes happens – but it also happens that the *whole* of a combined chart will be visually disturbed (and examples showing this will appear in later chapters). The reader is reminded that while charts can easily show separation, the use of transparencies is a much more accurate determinant of where separation actually occurs.[13]

This particular chart of a combined sample demonstrates how QSUM is able to prove difference of authorship – even when one of the samples, JMF's theatre review, contains the few anomalies discussed earlier. Figure JMF-4b should be compared with Figure JMF-4, where my two texts written twenty-one years apart are shown to be homogeneous.

The next example (Figure JMF-5) is a 'sandwich', using the same two texts by the writer in the combined sample analysed in Figure JMF-4 but with an *insertion of twenty-five sentences* from the writer's earliest surviving piece of schoolgirl writing from 1953, thus ranging very widely over time from 1953–1988.[14]

Fig. JMF-5: Three JMF samples combined.

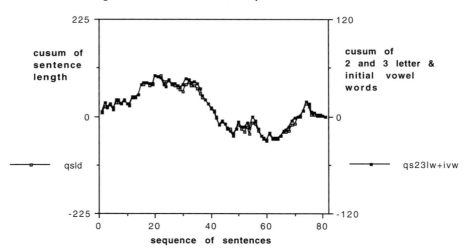

Figure JMF-5: Combined sample of the writing of JMF from 1967 and 1988, with a twenty-five sentence sample from a schoolgirl essay, 1953, inserted in the middle, analysed by the same habit.

As this combined sample totalled eighty-one sentences, finer points were used for the QSUM-chart in order to show greater detail: at more than sixty sentences, this is an advisable procedure.[15]

The inserted sample from 1953, an essay on the subject 'History is bunk: discuss', contained examples early in the text of both repetitious and 'list' sentences, including a quotation, which can be seen at work in sentences 29–31 of the combined sample ('The history of the world consists of an *unending succession of wars, counter-wars and yet more wars. Each war begins as the 'war to end all wars' and ends with another war already in the offing. The discomfort, misery, mutilation and sheer folly of war is only too clearly demonstrated in history . . .').*

Sentence 46 contained a list and sentence 47 has a list and is syntatically irregular, causing the slight slipping to be seen ('The panorama of the past as depicted by history cannot fail to attract, *so full is it of human interest, so full of pathos, splendour, glory, and colour.* Shakespeare's *great historical plays, and others – for was not Hamlet taken from history? – Shaw's SaintJoan, the Housman plays* – history must indeed be full of drama . . .').

Overall, however, this is a very satisfactory homogeneous chart. Having shown that JMF's later utterance is consistent with a very early piece of writing from 1953, the next chart, Figure JMF-6, replaces the 1953 extract with a sample from Chapter 1 of the present book – JMF's very recent utterance.

Fig. JMF-6: Two JMF samples with 25 sentences from this book inserted.

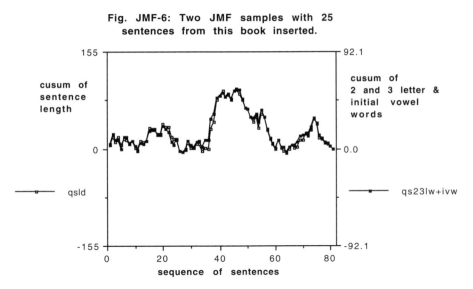

Figure JMF-6: The same habit in the combined sample of 1967 and 1988, analysed with twenty-five sentences from Chapter 1, 1994, inserted in the middle.

Again, finer points were used for the chart. This is a sound homogeneous chart with only sentences 34–38 calling for fresh comment.

It is sentence 38 which is chiefly responsible for the blip. At fifty-seven words, this sentence is the longest in the combined sample and is also a list (while sentence 34, at thirteen words, is among the shortest).

But surely it is the *consistency* which is the most striking feature of this chart, and which must impress itself upon an unbiased observer – compare this immediately visible homogeneity with the equally immediate confirmation of mixed utterance in the combined JMF/Huxley sample, Figure JMF-4b.

- **Visual consistency on the chart reveals same authorship.**
- **Separation on the chart reveals mixed authorship.**

The utterance of JMF is, in fact, consistent in the habit of using words of two letters or three letters and words starting with a vowel over a period of time from 1953 to 1994.

This is further demonstrated in the next chart, Figure JMF-7, where the first twenty sentences from each of the four samples already used above form one single combined analysis.

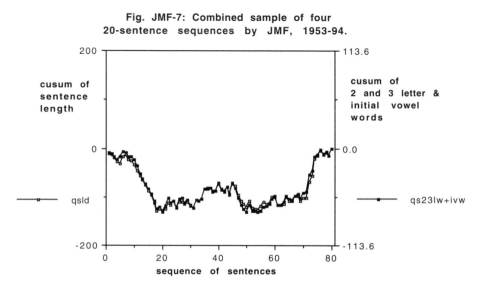

Fig. JMF-7: Combined sample of four 20-sentence sequences by JMF, 1953-94.

Figure JMF-7: The same habit in a combined sample of twenty sentences from each JMF sample, 1953–1994.

This is clearly a consistent combined sample, drawn again with finer points, indicating the single authorship which we know to be the case, and is an excellent demonstration of QSUM's ability to show homogeneity over time.

All the examples in this 'Starting With Yourself' section, except for the first two line-graphs, have been shown in the form of superimposed QSUM-CHARTS, but

- **remember that in most cases, it is necessary to check results by the use of overlaying a transparency** *as a matter of routine* **when establishing homogeneity or mixed utterance.**

That kind of intensive scrutiny, however, is not necessary for the novice learning how to use or understand the technique.

By referring back to the 'habit' chart JMF-3, all that need be grasped at this early stage is that we have found in this analysis a sound consistent habit, easily able to satisfy mere visual inspection. If it were necessary to attribute an unidentified sample suspected to be by the writer, but not admitted by her, the habit of *qs23lw+ivw* would be wholly suitable.

The next stage is to move on to an actual TEST CASE, which has used QSUM in an actual attribution project, and this will form the basis of Chapter 3.

First, though, a speculative note on the nature of the technique.

A Note on the 'Habit' and Linguistics

The idea of the number of letters in a word being discriminators of authorship often seems bizarre to literary critics and behavioural psychologists as well as to the lay person. Objections to words of two and three letters being counted for cusum analysis include a focus on *content* words of that number of letters: cross-examination in court drily queried whether 'a story about an ant and a bee' would throw the technique into confusion.[16]

In fact, of course, as any perusal of a crossword dictionary would reveal, there are very few words of that small size in use – a crossword dictionary of 471 pages needed only one page for two-letter words, and ten pages for three-letter words: of these, only a small proportion are *content* words, and usually these are words not in common everyday usage, such as 'ox', 'os', 'en', or not in *very* common usage, such as 'axe', 'fox', 'elm'.

The use of initial vowel words as a significant habit within the sentence has aroused even more incredulity: 'preposterous' was a comment by one expert witness.[17] To suggest that words starting with a vowel might play a part in being able to identify authorship is often, to the uninitiated, the most perplexing aspect of the technique.

A possible reason why *initial* vowel words are important in word-frequency, and therefore in discrimination, may well be that so many words in English begin with Latinate prefixes, some of which were originally two- or three-letter words starting with a vowel –

ab, ac, al, at, en, em, ex, in, im, inter, il, ov, ob, un, ub, uni –

it is a list which could be extended. A dismissal like 'preposterous' might not have been provoked so readily if the critic had cared to examine a QSUM 'results file' showing the use of initial vowel words being as high as 35–40 per cent of total usage in the analysis of utterance by a writer or speaker.

In attempting to understand why cusum analysis 'works' with the so-called 'filler' words, it is reasonable to consider individual lexis. Taking a person's vocabulary as being, say, 20,000 words, then it is useful to be reminded by a teacher's diagram for a child's reading scheme (for instance, the *Ladybird Key*

Words to Literacy) that this number may be divided into sections of equal frequency of usage.[18] Twenty-five per cent of language usage in English, according to this scheme, consists of the repetition of a mere twelve words :

a and he I in is it of that the to was

Notice, first, that two of them, 'a' and 'I' would count as initial vowel words; but the crucial fact is that these are the most syntactically significant words:

the indefinite and definite articles, **a** and **the**

three key pronouns, **I**, **he** and **it**

the most basic of the conjunctions, **and**, which joins two simple sentences

two forms of the basic verb 'to be', **is** and **was**

three of the commonest prepositions, **in, of, to**

• the only four-letter word, **that** (which would have been a three-letter word when the Anglo-Saxon character *thorn* was in use), occurs presumably since it doubles as a demonstrative pronoun (*that* car) and a frequent noun-clause conjunction, and for introducing indirect speech (She said *that* . . .).

It may be asked, how reliable are such lists of 'most frequent' words? The following comparisons may stand as an illustration. Taken from the concordances to Henry Fielding's novel *Joseph Andrews* (written 1741), and Dylan Thomas's *Collected Poems* (1950) and verse-play *Under Milk Wood* (1951), these lists give the most frequently used words:

• The first twelve words listed in the Fielding/Thomas concordances

Fielding's *J. Andrews* Thomas's *Poems | Under Milk Wood*

I*	The*	The
To*	And*	And
The*	Of*	In*
And*	In*	Of*
Of*	A*	A*
A*	To*	To*
You	My	His
My	I*	You
In*	On	I*
He*	With	On
Me	That*	Her
For	Is*	With

And the next four most frequent words:

As	His	Is*
It*	For	He*
That*	From	As
Have	As	My

The appearance (**starred**) of most of Ladybird's most frequent twelve words in the first sixteen most frequent words of literary works by these two authors, writing very different genres and separated by two hundred and fifty years, is a confirmation of the usefulness of using these vocabulary items for recognition of authorship.

If one extends the frequency list to cover the first thirty most frequent words given by the Ladybird scheme – that is, adding the next eighteen most frequent words in common use, most of which are two or three letters (**all as at be but are for had have him not on one said so they we with you**) – these will be seen to include more of the top sixteen high-frequency words listed in the Fielding and Thomas works. The remaining two words in the two authors – **from, my** – turn up in the list comprising the first *one hundred* frequent words, which are used 50 per cent of the time in normal discourse.

The *Key Words* scheme actually pinpoints a further 150 most frequent words. This makes a total of 250 altogether. This one-eightieth, or 1.25 per cent, of the hypothetical total vocabulary, comprises 66 per cent of habitual language usage, thus leaving a (hypothetical) remainder of 19,750 words (or 98.75 per cent) as selected vocabulary to convey semantics – content and meaning.

To illustrate the importance of this point, it is useful to consider a procedure now commonly used in teaching reading to schoolchildren aged seven to eleven. It is called 'cloze procedure', and involves a teacher using text from a children's book and deleting some of the words; the children then have to guess the missing words, an exercise which speeds up the process of learning to read by familiarizing children with the formal structure of syntax, collocations and the like: learning this kind of anticipation is called, in pedagogic terminology, 'acquiring the intermediate reading skills'.

A good method of explaining the use or misuse of this teaching aid to students in higher education who are training to be teachers is to provide the students with an example of cloze procedure where the extract chosen is heavily subject-dependant: say, a passage on biology, or on mechanics, where 'sets' of words associated with those particular subjects predominate. With many key content words deleted instead of the short filler-words, or syntactic elements, the students will find it impossible to guess the missing words associated with that special subject: a demonstration, surely, that speech, reading and writing depend on the acquisition of common structural elements (syntax) on which semantic words (meaning) may be strung.[19]

With this in mind, it is interesting to look again at the first ten sentences of text from **JMF/88.res file**, this time with every word except those of two-, three- or four-letter words deleted, in order to see the part syntactic structure might play in the success of QSUM.

Edited Results File JMF/88 (all except two- and three- and four-letter words deleted)

– – are also, as a – – – – own – . For them, the – has a – – – but the – – it are – . For – – , the – of – – seem to be less – than for – – in – , – as – must be to the – of the – – and its – . This is not at all the case. – from the fact that an – – of – – are – – to – – (– , if – else, – a – of –) – is also the – of what kind of – the – – will use to make – out of. In – – , – – and – – and – have – the – – as a – – .   – – – – . What kind of – , then, will an – – use? The – – , – , has – the – – of – – – as ' – '. The – ' – ' – – the – of – and of – as that – – – – .

This appears as a skeletal framework upon which the (deleted) meaning is strung.

The file may be edited even further to leave only the words of two and three letters, which is, after all, the basis of a common QSUM test and played a large part in this analysis.

Edited Results File 'JMF.88' (all except two- and three-letter words deleted)

– – are – , as a – – – – own – . For – , the – has a – – – but the – – it are – . For – – , the – of – – – to be – – – for – – in – , – as – – be to the – of the – – and its – . – is not at all the – . – – the – – an – – of – – are – – to – – (– , if – – , – a – of –) –   is – the – of – – of – the – – – – to – – out of. In – – , – – and – – and – – – the – – as a – – .   – – – – . – – of – , – , – an – – use? The – – , – , has – the – – of – – – as ' – '. The – ' – ' – – the – of – and of – as – – – – – .

In this re-editing, the syntactic framework is even more obvious. It is hard to avoid the conclusion that QSUM's success must be based on syntactic structure.

That it is capable of differentiating individuals is a fact to be explored by those competent in psycho-linguistics.

APPENDIX 1: PUBLISHED TEXTS BY THE WRITER USED IN THE SECTION 'STARTING WITH YOURSELF'

a) Thirty-one sentences* from 'Confessions of An Anglo-Welsh Reader' published in *New England Review / Bread Loaf Quarterly,* (already printed above as JMF.88 Results File).
 • **(the QSUM conventions of text processing affects the form of the text)**

Welsh writers are also, as a group, concerned with their own language. For them, the issue has a particular local urgency, but the principles underlying it are universal. For Anglo-Welsh poets, the issue of language might seem to be less crucial than for poets writing in Welsh, committed as these must be to the survival of the Welsh language and its culture. This is not at all the case. Apart from the fact than an increasing number of Anglo-Welsh poets are deliberately electing to become bilingual (which, if nothing else, shows a sense of deprivation), there is also the question of what kind of English the Anglo-Welsh poet will use to make poetry out of. In twentieth-century poetry, spoken language and conversational tones and rhythms have marked the personal voice as a strong element. Auden called poetry 'memorablespeech'. What kind of speech, then, will an Anglo-Welsh poet use? The British PoetLaureate, TedHughes, has described the Standard English of current educated speech as 'quote'. The phrase 'team-calls' derisively raises the issue of class and of dialect as that which identifies social identity. This, too, then must be a consideration for the Anglo-Welsh poet in the struggle to speak in one's own voice (though the English class system, as such, has never had an exact mirror image in Wales).

The choice of language also raises the issue of cultural purity. Of all the major contemporary influences on speech, the most important, naturally, are the mass media, radio and television, especially the latter. The young, in particular, encounter much spoken language directly on English and Welsh television, which includes a large component of American English.

Clancy sees irony in the fact that saving the language involves children growing up on such mixed fare, summed up in the cultural fusion of a word he has coined, 'Americymry'. Clancy's own remarks, as a writer, about adapting a Welsh verse form, or drawing on his experience of living in Wales, while remaining fully an American poet, are interestingly relevant to this discussion. In particular, his assertion that 'quote' (ie as regards the homogenising effects of an international technology) is to the point.

Thus if the Welsh experience of television is one of 'Americymri', so, too, the Anglo-Welsh writer has to come to terms with a degenerating language. DaveMillington's 'TheMacbethTragedy' is a humorous poem acknowledging the tragicomic failure of a teacher attempting to put standard Eng-Lit questions on Shakespeare to pupils reared on the illiterate trivialities of the modern media. It ends with the teacher answering his own questions to himself, with an ironic bow, as readers will note, in the direction of eecummings.

Some poets, including MikeJenkins, are willing to entertain the proposition that schools should return to a Welsh language literature curriculum as a means of putting the young in touch with their own cultural heritage and history. Other considerations apart (and they are formidable), such an effort would seem doomed in the ubiquitous oral-aural media-culture that pervades twentieth-century life. MikeJenkins has written of being impressed by the fact that Welsh has no word for 'I', that capitalized ego which he associates with English imperialism, and has written a poem ('I') on this subject. It is a neat point, yet to claim too strong a link between the conventions of language and national behaviour overlooks the imperial history, say, of other European nations with their uncapitalized first person pronouns (je and ich, for example). Nor was Rome, speaking the Latin which also had no word for 'I', exactly non-imperial. *People* are imperial. Fascism is a state of mind, and to try to claim that some people are better than others on linguistic grounds seems simplistic.

The ability to make a true communication cannot depend, surely, even in Wales, on a knowledge of the Welsh language. Nowhere is this clearer than in PeterThabit-Jones's moving elegy 'Deathofason', where he observes his Welsh-speaking wife at the graveside.

What binds us at the deepest levels is not language at all but being able to recognize a shared humanity. Jones's 'Naagi', about an old Arab dying in Swansea and cared for by two elderly Welsh sisters makes a similar point.

b) Twenty-five sentences* of a newspaper review-article, 'Actors on the Road', (*Western Mail*, August, 1967).
   *(parts in italic show the anomalous sentences indicated in respect of Figure JMF-4a)

If there was one thing that could rouse the brooding Hamlet out of his inner conflict and waken him to life, it was the news that *'the actors are come hither'*.

The idea of a troupe of actors moving around the country still has about it an air of romantic excitement, in these days of closed provincial theatres and instant drama at the flick of a television switch.

It recalls the theatre's ancient origins, bands of touring players performing in *inn courtyards, village squares, church porches.*

The Royal Shakespeare Company's 'Theatregoround' is the modern version of just such a travelling group of actors and directors who perform in *schools, colleges, community centres* and places where there is little or no theatre.

Its repertoire includes some Shakespeare, Pinter, Chekhov, and two demonstration programmes – 'xxxxxxx' and 'xxxxxxxx'.**

But its aims are anything but romantic or backward-looking; they are to interest a new audience in the RSC's mainstream work at Stratford and London, and to establish a closer link with the existing audience.

Audiences who do, in the main, watch the work of the professional theatre have come to expect a certain kind of dramatic experience. They tend to like their plays buttressed by *elaborate sets, decor, costumes and interpretations which are polished or rhetorical.*

Theatregoround would like to stimulate, by its visits and performances, a new approach and reaction which would concentrate less on the externalities and more on the human figures on stage. These, in themselves, should be enough to carry the real emotional tenor of the play.

Last week 'Theatregoround' held the first of two Drama Courses for teachers at Stratford, the second to begin on August 28.

Since teachers hold positions of key responsibility in developing the dramatic instincts and responses of children, the courses act as a kind of bridge between the professional theatre, and what it is trying to do today, and its potential audience.

Dominated by the canned clichés of the television screen, children are usually frightened off Shakespeare and the 'classical theatre' at a young age. The emphasis of the course was on mime and improvisation and the making of a play rather than on stage techniques for putting on actual written plays.

The techniques of professional acting are, after all, a matter of years of training, and it was felt that amateurs, especially children, might do better to make their own play, which would at least grow organically out of their own experience, rather than tackle complex masterpieces.

Improvisation, incidentally, can teach us a great deal about ourselves – total failure to improvise can show us just how other-directed our personalities are. The influence of this kind of thinking was discernible in the production of *Macbeth* which opened on last Wednesday night with Paul Schofield in the title role.

The severe simplicity of the set concentrated attention on the figures on the stage. The thick rust carpet, which served at once for the 'blasted heath' and, slightly modified, for the castle scenes, underlined one of the play's dominant images – blood.

Paul Schofield has been criticised for his staccato delivery; but the way the verse jerks forward in short, breathless bursts after his encounter with the witches suggests the force of inward pressure that shake the inward man with alternate audacity and fear.

The loss of control as his voice rises to a high off-pitch 'murther' takes us straight into the inward Macbeth.

This new emphasis on *creativity, natural rhythms, spontaneity, the inward*

**[deleted titles: 'The Actor and The Director' and 'The Director at Work'] *experience*, may have links with the general current trend towards breaking out of rigid traditional forms.

This side of dogmatism, it seems a valuable reassertion. Certainly 'Theatregoround' is a very worthwhile venture, which has already succeeded in arousing great enthusiasm in different parts of the country.

By going out into the community, and taking the theatre to the people, it can only enlarge the experience of all who see it.

c) The twenty-five sentences from Chapter 1 used in the combined sample **JMF-6** are from 'Morton is now a retired Church of Scotland minister' to 'It is not to be suggested, of course, that either Iris Murdoch or Muriel Spark were deluded about changes in their styles of writing'. (Note: text used was processed according to general processing rules).

APPENDIX 2: SCALING THE GRAPHS AND CHARTS

As explained in the section on the results file, it is necessary to know the range in order that graphs or charts may be drawn in a perspective which provides clear information by visual display. Graphs are scaled by using the range to calculate both the *sld* graph line and the *habit* line in the correct way for any specific computer screen. Take the illustration given in the chapter above:

```
Range of each Cusum:
```

	sld	231w	ivw	231w+ivw
Max:	35	13	17	21
Min:	-42	-15	-15	-25
Range:	77	28	32	46

The objective is that the graph show the line at about one quarter to one third of the vertical range of the sample in proportion to the horizontal space. Thus, if the range is multiplied by three and divided by two, the resulting figure gives the necessary vertical axis.

e.g. 77 x 3 = **231**
231 / 2 = 115.5

Rounding up the answer (115.5) to 120 will give a satisfactory display, as in Figure JMF-1a. Here the arrows show that the graphic illustration is about 25 per cent of the width of the graph.

If, however, the graphic illustration took up about 60–70 per cent of the

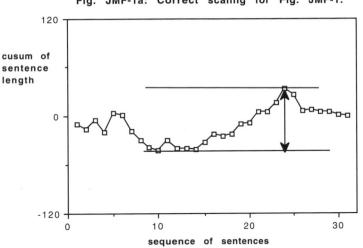

Fig. JMF-1a: Correct scaling for Fig. JMF-1.

Figure JMF-1a: Sample of thirty-one sentences of JMF, 1988, previously displayed in a single-line graph (JMF-1).

width, instead of a quarter, then the detail would be grossly exaggerated, as in Figure JMF-1b. This graph has grossly exaggerated peaks and troughs, giving far too much detail to be useful.

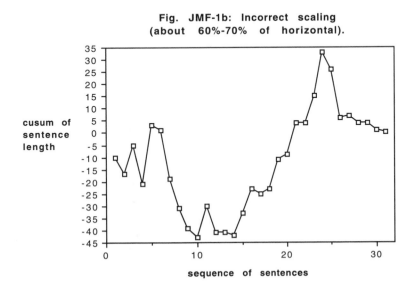

Fig. JMF-1b: Incorrect scaling (about 60%-70% of horizontal).

Figure JMF-1b: The same *sld* line-graph wrongly scaled.

Similarly, it would be possible to scale wrongly in the opposite way, where the graphic illustration took up only about 8–10 per cent proportional to the graph's width, as in Figure JMF-1c. Here the results have been so flattened as to produce a faintly waving line and so lose all detailed information.

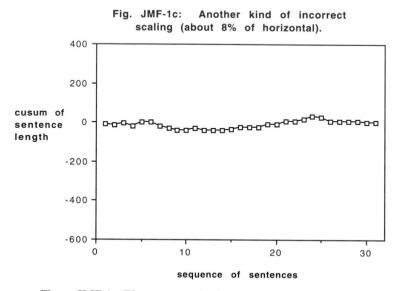

Fig. JMF-1c: Another kind of incorrect scaling (about 8% of horizontal).

Figure JMF-1c: The same graph with another sort of wrong scaling.

Scaling the range of the 'habit' results

Suppose the habit to be calculated is the *23lw+ivw* figure, as for Figure JMF-3 in the chapter. The range (see above) is 45. The objective is the same as for the *sld* calculation, but this time it is reached in the following way.

Multiply the habit range (46) by the *sld* graph **scale** (120) and divide by the *sld* **range**:

46 x 120 = **5520**
5520 / 77 = **71.688**

Referring back to Figure JMF-3, the reader will observe that this has been rounded up to 71.7.

With this example as a guide, it should be possible for the reader to calculate how the figures for the *23lw* and *ivw* scales, in Figures JMF-3a and JMF-3b have been reached.

APPENDIX 3: ILLUSTRATION OF A DATA SHEET (TO TEXT A, FROM DATA FILE JMF.88)

JMF88.data

	1	2	3	4	5
	Sent#	sld	Column 3	Column 4	qsld
1	1 :88ed	12	12	-10.258	-10
2	2 :88ed	16	28	-6.258	-17
3	3 :88ed	34	62	11.742	-5
4	4 :88ed	7	69	-15.258	-20
5	5 :88ed	46	115	23.742	4
6	6 :88ed	19	134	-3.258	0
7	7 :88ed	4	138	-18.258	-18
8	8 :88ed	10	148	-12.258	-30
9	9 :88ed	15	163	-7.258	-37
10	10 :88ed	18	181	-4.258	-42
11	11 :88ed	36	217	13.742	-28
12	12 :88ed	11	228	-11.258	-39
13	13 :88ed	22	250	-0.258	-39
14	14 :88ed	22	272	-0.258	-40
15	15 :88ed	31	303	8.742	-31
16	16 :88ed	33	336	10.742	-20
17	17 :88ed	20	356	-2.258	-22
18	18 :88ed	25	381	2.742	-20
19	19 :88ed	32	413	9.742	-10
20	20 :88ed	24	437	1.742	-8
21	21 :88ed	36	473	13.742	6
22	22 :88ed	22	495	-0.258	5
23	23 :88ed	34	529	11.742	17
24	24 :88ed	40	569	17.742	35
25	25 :88ed	15	584	-7.258	28
26	26 :88ed	3	587	-19.258	8
27	27 :88ed	23	610	0.742	9
28	28 :88ed	20	630	-2.258	7
29	29 :88ed	19	649	-3.258	4
30	30 :88ed	20	669	-2.258	1
31	31 :88ed	21	690	-1.258	0
32					

Here the computation can be seen displayed in the four columns corresponding to the four stages which end in the *qsld* of the sample under analysis.

Chapter 3

A TEST CASE FOR THE ATTRIBUTION OF AUTHORSHIP:

A Cusum Analysis of 'The Back Road', a short story newly attributed to D. H. Lawrence

In the late 1980s, an American researcher at Delaware University, Dr Jonathan Rose, was engaged in a routine examination of historical material: namely, issues for the year 1913 of *Everyman* (a magazine published by Dent, London during the early years of the twentieth century). In one of the issues, he discovered a short story entitled 'The Back Road' which had been printed with the initials 'D.H.L.' beneath it.[1] Since those initials famously belong to D. H. Lawrence, who is known to have published in *Everyman*, and whose early novels were published by Dent, it was easy – natural even – to believe that this was a previously unknown early story by Lawrence. The case for its being so has been made by Dr Jonathan Rose and need not be rehearsed here.[2]

The background to this QSUM project is that John Worthen (author of a biography of Lawrence, and then lecturing at the University College of Swansea) harboured serious doubts about Lawrence's authorship of the story.[3] Following a joint lecture on the QSUM technique by Michael and Jill Farringdon, arrangements were made to examine the story. This would be only the second time this technique had been used for attribution on a text involving a twentieth-century writer. The first time was for testing *The Dark Tower*, the posthumous attribution to C. S. Lewis, already referred to in Chapter 1.[4] Although Lewis was both a considerable scholar and writer, it offers him no disrespect to suggest that the Lawrence project would be the first QSUM attribution test of a major figure in modern literature.

Step One

The first task in any project of this nature is to prove that the author under dispute, in this case D. H. Lawrence, is no exception to the rule in having a QSUM 'fingerprint' (as it was beginning to be called by 1992). There would be no point in examining a disputed text if there were no satisfactory consistency for the writer to whom it had been attributed, and against which it could be tested. (In point of fact, no one tested to date has proved to be an exception to the technique.)

To establish this, analysis was made of four samples of Lawrence's writing, these being chosen by John Worthen, who also supplied the text of 'The Back

Road', not yet published at that time. Full texts of the samples are given in Appendix 1, and are briefly indicated below:

Le1: Letter to Edward Garnett, 1913.
Le2: Letter to Louie, 1907.
SL: *Sons and Lovers*, 1913.
NE: 'New Eve and Old Adam', 1913.
TM: 'German Books: Thomas Mann': a review article, 1913.
BR: 'The Back Road'.

All the Lawrence samples were selected by John Worthen.[5] As can be seen, they represent a range of genres – novel, short story, letters and literary criticism. It is noticeable that only one of his chosen texts (**Le2**, 1907) moves outside the period of the disputed story's publication date of 1913. In literary critical terms, basing judgements on internal evidence, a focus on the particular time of writing – especially for someone at the start of his career – would be the expected procedure, for the sake of comparison. The indifference to time demonstrated by QSUM is hard for the literary intelligence to grasp, relying as such apprehension does on sensitivity to quality, not quantity.

Thus, it was felt that basing the project on contemporaneous Lawrence texts might prove more persuasive to the literary members of the academic community who would naturally be new to QSUM. However, the inclusion of the earlier letter, dating from 1907, does demonstrate the technique's indifference to time, despite there being only a small gap of six years.[6]

These five samples were word processed and tested by QSUM, first individually and then in varying combinations. This involved analysing and cross-matching two, three, or four of the samples together, in totals of from 50 to 100 sentences. It would be tedious and irrelevant to show the full range of the many interesting results, and only those most pertinent are shown here, including those which would eventually be presented in the *D. H. Lawrence Review* as the basis of argument for the final conclusions of the project. The stages of the project are next outlined.

To begin at the ending – and perhaps to satisfy curiosity at the outset – the first QSUM chart, Figure DHL-1, shows the result of a combined analysis of four twenty-sentence samples from four of the samples listed above – **SL**, **NE**, **TM**, and **Le2**. This is a QSUM-chart confirming homogeneity in the writing of D. H. Lawrence over a cross-section of kinds of writing (or genres). The two lines, *qsld* and *qs23lw+ivw*, track each other consistently throughout the chart. However, before such a demonstration of consistency – in a combined text of ample size – could be reached, each sample had, in turn, first been tested for its own homogeneity.

As each sample by D. H. Lawrence was individually tested, typical QSUM

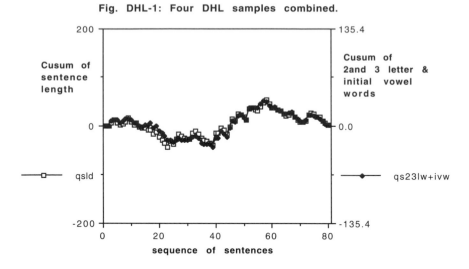

Fig. DHL-1: Four DHL samples combined.

Figure DHL-1: The habit of using two- and three-letter words and initial vowel words (*qs23lw+ivw*) in a combined sample of twenty sentences each from four genres of writing by D. H. Lawrence (**SL, NE, TM,** and **Le2**).

queries and choices appeared. All three of the most common tests (as in the **JMF** demonstration charts in Chapter 1) were tested on the textual samples, and the result was that, once again, the habit of using two and three letters and words starting with a vowel (*23lw+ivw*) proved to be the one most consistent and thus suitable to discriminate writing by Lawrence.

• **This is always the first step: to find the correct test for the author being attributed. Without that, an analyst cannot proceed**.

The first sample tested was the thirty-six sentences which end *Sons and Lovers* and Figure DHL-2 shows the first result. The habit of using two- and three- letter words and words starting with a vowel is consistent in this chart, but there are some apparent disturbances, especially at sentences 13–14, 18, and 28–32, which cause characteristic 'blips'. A return to the text shows that these have been caused by the usual anomalous features, and the last section has been strongly affected by the powerful rhetorical demands made by bringing the novel to its close.

The average words per sentence in this sample – and, interestingly, in most other texts by Lawrence tested in this project – was between thirteen and fourteen words. Sentence 13 is easily visible in the chart as a long upward 'jump', and was, at thirty-nine words, three times as long as the average for the sample ('Everywhere the vastness and terror of the immense night which is roused and stirred for a brief while by the day, but which returns and will remain at last eternal, holding everything in its silence and its living gloom').

Fig. DHL-2: A sample from SONS AND LOVERS.

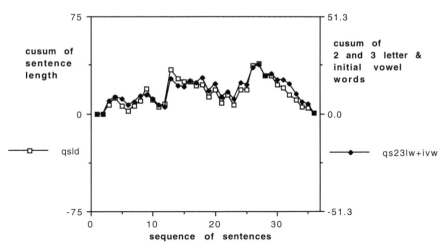

Figure DHL-2: The same habit in a sample of 36 sentences of D. H. Lawrence's novel, *Sons and Lovers*.

As indicated in the section on anomalies in Chapter 2, such 'jumps' can often cause startling visual disturbance. This long sentence has disturbed the regular pattern of the several following sentences, up to sentence 18: this was a very short sentence of three words and the result was similar, a temporary separation (observe how the habit line rises while the *qsld* line moves horizontally).

Sentences 28–32 may be quoted here:

[28] 'Mother,' he whimpered, 'mother!'
[29] She was the only thing that held him, up, himself, amid all this.
[30] And she was gone, intermingled herself.
[31] He wanted her to touch him, have him alongside with her.
[32] But no, he would not give in.

Sentence 28 is anomalous, a 'short sentence' below five words – with a repeated exclamation. Sentence 30 expands the previous thought ('And she . . .'), and structurally is scarcely a 'new' sentence (again, the two graph lines move in different directions). Sentence 32 is high in habit usage while being only half the average length. These features *coming in sequence* cause the discernible 'blip'.

As explained in the note on text processing in Chapter 2, the short sentences could be added on or deleted; however, in combination with longer textual samples, such effects tend to be cancelled out. The long sentence 13 would, however, continue to cause an upward 'jump' in a combined chart, and, for the sake of visual aesthetics (and no other reason), it was omitted from the first 20 **SL** sentences used in the first chart shown, i.e. the combined sample Figure DHL-1.

Fig. DHL-3: Two Lawrence letters combined.

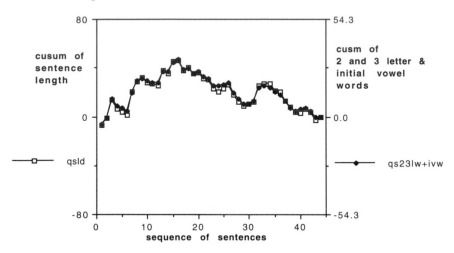

Figure DHL-3: The same habit in a combined sample of forty-four sentences from two Lawrence letters chosen by John Worthen, nineteen sents. (**Le2**) and twenty-five sents. (**Le1**).

Next, in Figure DHL-3, a combined sample of forty-four sentences from the two letters chosen by John Worthen, **Le2** (nineteen sentences) and **Le1** (the first twenty-five sentences of the letter). The chart for these two letters can be seen to be a very consistent QSUM result – and, it will be noted, for two letters written six years apart, which should be no surprise given the consistency over much longer periods of time for **JMF**, demonstrated in Chapter 1. This result calls for little comment, though the fact that there are no 'blips' in the combined-letters chart, while there are in the **SL** chart (Figure DHL-2), may perhaps be attributable to the rhetorical demands of fiction, as opposed to the free conversational style of letter-writing; but this is speculative, and, in any case, is by no means an invariable rule. Should the reader remain dubious as regards the blips in the **SL** chart:

• **it cannot be stated too often that the appearance of an occasional anomalous 'blip' never constitutes a demolition of the QSUM consistency.**

Such minor disturbance can be shown to be statistically insignificant by a more sophisticated statistical test.[7] But by the criteria of ordinary QSUM, further proof is that, when combined with enough authentic utterance by the subject (in this case Lawrence), such small 'blips' disappear as Figure DHL-1 has shown.

It would seem useful here to demonstrate the technique's indifference to both time and genre by a 'sandwich' test. If the 1907 letter is 'sandwiched' between two later samples of writing by Lawrence from 1913, of different genres, novel and criticism – **SL** and **TM** – the result remains consistent, as shown in Figure DHL-3a.[8] QSUM here shows that samples of writing by Lawrence spanning both time and genre are indistinguishable.

Fig. DHL-3a: Three DHL samples combined.

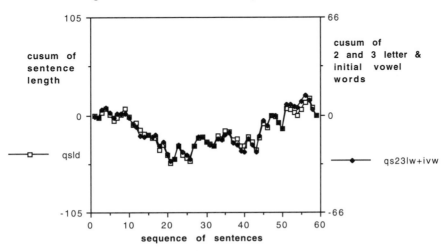

Figure DHL-3a: The same habit in a combined 'sandwich' sample of fifty-nine sentences: twenty sentences of **SL**, nineteen sentences of **Le1**, and twenty sentences of **TM**.

Next, in Figure DHL-4, the result of analysis of a sample from the short story selected, 'New Eve, Old Adam' (**NE**). This chart is visibly consistent apart from a regular displacement between sentences 4–15. These sentences match perfectly when overlaid on separate graphs, using a transparency. The displacement has occurred due to the length of sentences at the start of the sample. The average words per sentence is 13.2 words, but the first sentence is thirty-one words, and the third is three words, while the descending movement of the graph-lines indicates that *most* of the opening sentences are below average – sentence 5 is again only three words, as the reader may observe:

[1] 'After all' she said, with a little laugh, 'I can't see it was so wonderful of you, to hurry home to me, if you are so cross when you do come.'

[2] 'You would rather I stayed away' he asked.

[3] 'I wouldn't mind.'

[4] She burst into a jeering 'pouf' of laughter.

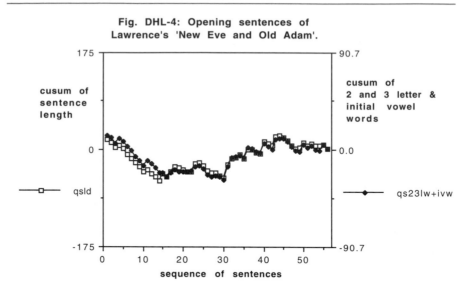

Fig. DHL-4: Opening sentences of
Lawrence's 'New Eve and Old Adam'.

Figure DHL-4: The same habit in a sample of fifty-six sentences from the opening of
Lawrence's short story, **NE**.

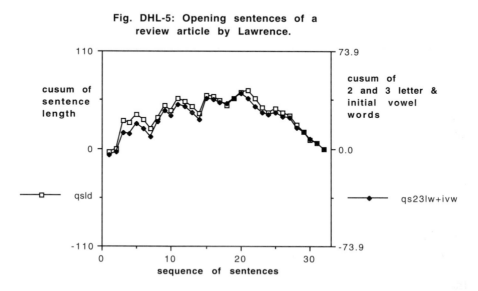

Fig. DHL-5: Opening sentences of a
review article by Lawrence.

Figure DHL-5: The same habit in thirty-two sentences of a critical review on Thomas
Mann (**TM**), written by D. H. Lawrence, 1913.

[5] 'You,' she cried.
[6] 'You and Parisian Nights' Entertainment!'

The last two 'sentences' are, structurally, exclamations. It is this anomalous sequence of sentences which has caused the slight, but statistically insignificant, displacement. Obviously, when making a combined chart (for Figure DHL-1), it was sensible to choose the twenty-sentence sequence, from the fifty-six sentences of 'New Eve and Old Adam', avoiding this anomalous opening sequence.

Lastly, the sample from the critical article entitled 'German Books: Thomas Mann' (**TM**), the result of which is shown in Figure DHL-5. This can be seen to be a homogeneous chart, but with a rather loose correspondence. This effect is due mainly to sentence 3 (see below). There is a later 'blip' due to anomalous sentence 19, (where the two lines move in different directions), which affects the following sentences up to sentence 23. (In a longer sample, this anomalous occurrence would cease to disturb consistency to any noticeable degree as it appears to do in this figure).

The review opens with three sentences in which Lawrence defines his subject and gives background information about contemporary German literature:

Thomas Mann is perhaps the most famous of German novelists now writing. He and his elder brother H. Mann, with Jacob Wassermann, are acclaimed the three artists in fiction of present-day Germany.

But Germany is now undergoing that craving for form in fiction, that passionate desire for the mastery of the medium of narrative, that will of the writer to be greater than and undisputed lord over the stuff he writes, which is figured to the world in Gustav Flaubert.

To the reader these are interesting and necessary introductory remarks, and the first two sentences, as can be seen above, present little problem for QSUM consistency.

The third long 'list' sentence is typical of Lawrence in his search for more exact meaning; but a look at the chart will show the upward leap sentence 3 occasions – its length is forty-eight words where again the average is a little over thirteen words. To the cusum technique, the 'list', or illustrative, sentence constitutes anomalous syntactic structure, as already explained, and it is this which is responsible for the apparent separation.

Thus, when twenty sentences from the article were used for the combined sample, the twenty sentences selected started at sentence four, so as to avoid the third sentence in the individual **TM** chart. As can be seen, sentences 4–23 blended smoothly in with the other three extracts in Figure DHL-1, despite the slightly anomalous nature of sentences 21 and 22 described above.

D. H. Lawrence has thus been shown to be no exception to the technique. In examples ranging across form and genre, his utterance has remained visibly consistent.

Step Two

Having shown that Lawrence was no exception to the technique, it was then necessary to show that he separated significantly from another person's writing. Who better to choose than Aldous Huxley, his contemporary, friend and the editor of *The Letters of D. H. Lawrence*, 1932?

Once again, it was necessary to analyse a sample of Huxley's writing alone to show its internal homogeneity. A sequence of twenty-six sentences from his 'Introduction' to his edition was chosen, and the first result is given in Figure AH-1.[9] As usual, the sample was analysed to see which test was suitable for indicating consistency in the author being tested.

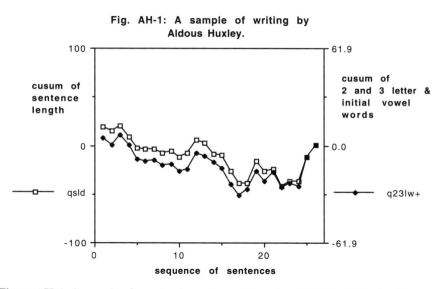

Fig. AH-1: A sample of writing by Aldous Huxley.

Figure AH-1: A sample of twenty-six sentences taken from Huxley's Introduction to his edition of *The Letters of D. H. Lawrence*, 1932.

Unlike D. H. Lawrence, Huxley proved homogeneous on two tests, which is always useful for later discrimination. Huxley was homogeneous by the habit of using two- and three-letter words (*qs23lw*), as well as the habit of using two- and three-letter words and words starting with a vowel (*qs23lw+ivw*). The latter conclusion may seem surprising in view of the chart shown above, where, at first sight, the analysis by this habit seem to show the lines separating.

The result is a useful example, however, for warning the novice that what may at first sight seem to be separation (and thus inconsistency) may be due to the chance of a few anomalous sentences.

If comparison of the two graph-lines is made not by the single superimposed QSUM-chart method, but by using a separate transparency, they will be seen to be mainly consistent, and thus to indicate homogeneity. For reading convenience, the separate graphs are reproduced below, but for the fullest understanding a transparency of the *qs23lw+ivw* graph should be overlaid on the *qsld* graph so as to observe both consistency and deviation when laid over the other. In effect, the reader would discover the sentence(s) responsible for the apparent separation in the QSUM-chart Figure AH-1 printed above.

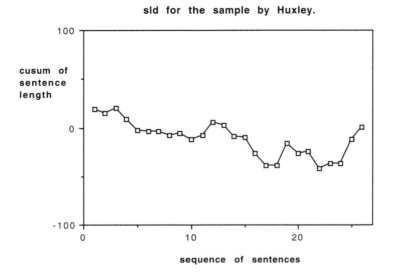

Single-line *qsld* **graph** of the 26-sentence sample by Huxley, shown above in the QSUM-chart AH-1.

It is useful to look at the sentences which caused the apparent separation in Figure AH-1, which were the following:

[Sentence 1] Here, in a parenthesis, let me remark on the fact that Lawrence's doctrine is constantly invoked by people, of whom Lawrence himself would have passionately disapproved, in defence of a behaviour, which he would have found deplorable or even revolting.

This sentence is long in terms of the sample (at forty words, where the average w.p.s. is twenty words, and has a habit usage slightly below average), and this has caused the lines at the start of the chart to start off apart from each other.

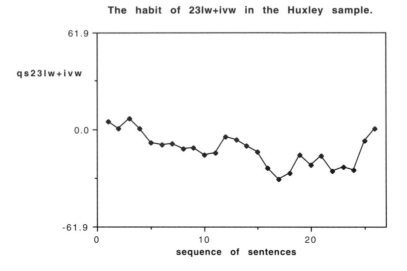

The habit of 23lw+ivw in the Huxley sample.

Single-line graph (*qs23lw+ivw*) of the same sample.

[Sentence 22] Not so Lawrence.

At three words, this is obviously a short sentence – more an afterthought to the previous sentence than a new sentence.

When sentence 22 is added on to sentence 23, using a semi-colon, and sentence 1 is removed completely, then the result of the re-processed Huxley sample, now twenty-four sentences, shows a remarkable difference, in Figure AH-1a.

• **The consistency that was there all the time is now visible in the QSUM-chart illustration.**

Thus, without the need for a transparency, the new chart reveals this to be a homogeneous sample of utterance by Aldous Huxley.

It should be remarked here, with regard to the reprocessing of this text and the previous Lawrence examples, that many newcomers to the technique are uneasy about what they may see as unwarranted 'hacking about' of a result to 'make it fit'. What needs to be clearly understood is that there is no actual *need* to remove anomalies, which fall into clearly defined examples – the long sentence, the short sentence, the repetitious or the list sentence. The reprocessing of these two sentences in this example has been carried out in order to show that what may seem like apparent inconsistency is perfectly explicable; and to show that removal of the anomalous sentences results in a well-nigh perfect chart.

However, there are two points to make:

• **The first** is that if the original twenty-six sentences of Huxley were added

Fig. AH-1a: The same sample after editing.

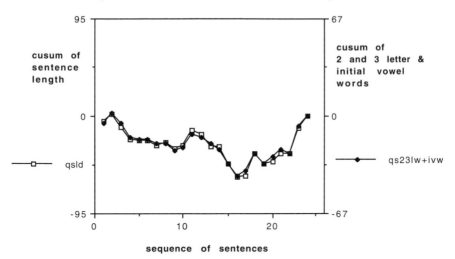

sequence of sentences

Figure AH-1a: The same sample re-processed as twenty-four sentences.

to further Huxley samples, to make total samples of fifty, or seventy-five, or 100 sentences, then the anomalies would reduce to visible insignificance, and would be hardly noticeable, since the greater the number of single-authored sentences being analysed, the greater the overall consistency and homogeneity by visual inspection.

• **The second** is that if the Huxley sample is combined with utterance of a different author, it will separate. This combination with a different author, Lawrence, constitutes the next stage of the enquiry.

Step Three
Four examples will be shown in Figures **AH-2**, **AH-3**, **AH-3a** and **AH-4**.

In the first combined sample, Figure AH-2, an equal number of sentences by Lawrence and Huxley, twenty-five sentences each, are analysed together to make a total of fifty sentences. Note the smooth consistency of the first twenty-five sentences by Lawrence, and the separation that follows the addition of the Huxley twenty-five sentences. Once again, it should be reiterated that the *kind* of utterance used in the combined sample is irrelevant – we have already seen different genres consistent for Lawrence in Figure DHL-1, and the fact that this sample combines part of a letter and of an essay is not a factor affecting the outcome. Figure AH-3 is interesting in showing not only a separation but also a cross-over of the *qs23lw+ivw* 'habit' line: this moves from being on top to being beneath the *qsld* sentence-length line, this taking place at around sentence 44 where the Huxley sample joins the Lawrence material.

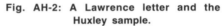

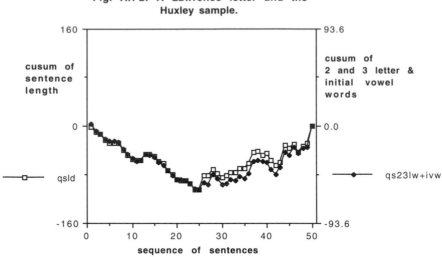

Figure AH-2: The habit of using two and three letters and words starting with a vowel in a combined sample of twenty-five sentences from a letter by D. H. Lawrence (**Le1**) followed by an equal number of sentences from the Huxley sample.

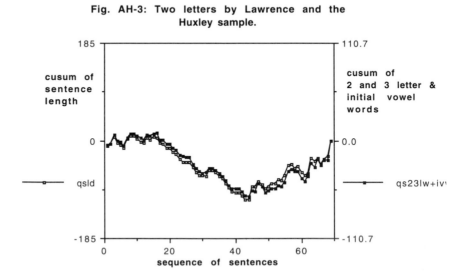

Figure AH-3: The same habit in a combined sample of forty-four sentences from letters by D. H. Lawrence (**Le1 and Le2**) followed by twenty-five sentences of Huxley.

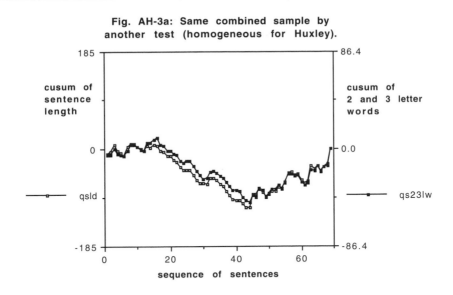

Figure AH-3a: Same combined sample by another test (homogeneous for Huxley).

Figure AH-3a: Another habit in the same combined sample of forty-four sentences from letters by D. H. Lawrence (**Le1** and **Le2**) followed by twenty-five sentences of Huxley.

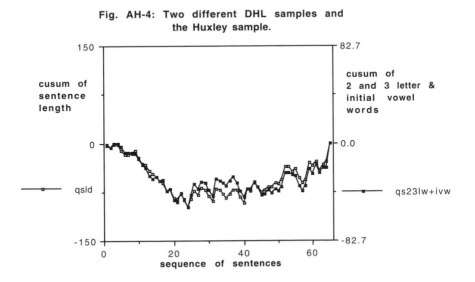

Fig. AH-4: Two different DHL samples and the Huxley sample.

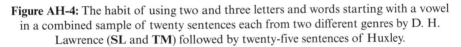

Figure AH-4: The habit of using two and three letters and words starting with a vowel in a combined sample of twenty sentences each from two different genres by D. H. Lawrence (**SL** and **TM**) followed by twenty-five sentences of Huxley.

It makes a useful comparison here to show the same combined sample analysed by the second habit by which Huxley was found to be homogeneous, the *23lw* habit, and this is shown in Figure AH-3a. Here, there is again separation; but the second test by which Huxley is consistent, that of using two- and three-letter words, clearly reveals its homogeneity from shortly before the point at which the Huxley passage joins the Lawrence material, at sentence 45.

The reader should not expect that separation will always occur at the exact point of the intrusion of the alien material; there may often be displacement by a sentence or two – and sometimes much of the chart may be distorted. It is impossible to predict in advance the course the separation will take. Sometimes there will be an almost exact visible separation, in terms of sentences by the two authors; the reader is referred back to the early chart, **Figure 2**, shown in Chapter 1, where the inserted material in the letter by Helen Keller can be precisely pinpointed: cf. Figure AH-4.

Here the combined chart is disrupted in another way. The **SL** sample remains fairly undisturbed, but the middle and end of the chart show clear mixed utterance, with the cross-over of the habit line, *qs23lw+ivw*, this time coming at virtually the point when the Huxley sample joins the **TM** sample at sentence 40.

Whatever form the separations may take, the importance for the reader is to recognize what QSUM reveals, i.e. the visible separation of utterance previously homogeneous, which will be apparent even to the novice chart-reader.

- **This visible separation is the evidence of mixed authorship.**

Step Four
Now it was possible to move on to 'The Back Road'.

The first step was to see if the story was itself homogeneous, by one writer alone. It is a short story of only twenty-two sentences, rather a small sample; but fortunately it provided satisfactory homogeneous consistency, as seen in Figure BR-1. This is a homogeneous chart, apart from a 'blip' at sentence 7, a typical list-sentence:

> [vii] He raced express trains, he sprang backwards across the river, he felled the rector with his right, the janitor with his left, and, not so improbable, he butted Farmer Heeltap's bull to the scathe of the latter.

This sentence causes mild disturbance, but the chart over-all reveals single authorship for this newly found story, by the most consistent test for the unknown author – the *qs23lw+ivw test*.

The question is, was that single author D. H. Lawrence? To discover the

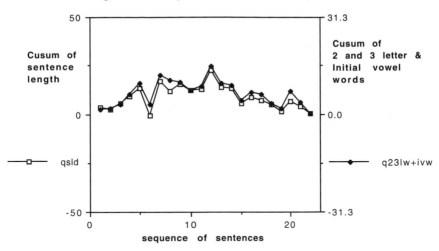

Figure BR-1: Sample of the twenty-two sentences of 'The Back Road' analysed by the *23lw+ivw* test

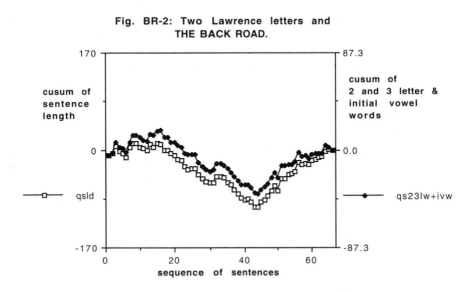

Figure BR-2: The habit of two- and three-letter words and words starting with a vowel in a combined sample of forty-four sentences from two Lawrence letters, followed by the twenty-two sentences of 'The Back Road'.

answer to this question, it was then necessary to test the story with all the Lawrence texts chosen, in combinations of two, three or four samples, placing 'The Back Road' in varying positions – at the beginning, middle, or end of the test. This was exhaustive testing, and by no means always necessary for an analyst confident of the accuracy of **QSUM**, and who has acquired competence, and thus confidence, in the analytic procedure. As this was a test case, however, it was essential that no doubt should remain.

    • **In each case, no matter where it was placed, the result of the analysis was a separation from the Lawrence material.**

Of these results, only a few are shown here.

    Compare Figure **BR-2** with Figure **AH-3,** where 'The Back Road' follows the two Lawrence letters in the same way that the twenty-five sentences of Huxley had done.

    • **The separation here clearly indicates that 'The Back Road', combined in the same way as the earlier combined Lawrence/Huxley sample, is distinguishable and must be by a writer other than D. H. Lawrence.**

Note that the form taken by the separation of the disputed story is quite different from that taken by the Huxley sentences. This confirms that different usage of habits by different writers will give a different kind of separation in a combined sample with the author who is under analysis, in this case, D. H. Lawrence.

    For readers new to the technique, which must mean most of the literary/linguistic world, the natural question may again recur: can sentences from letters and from a short story – different genres and varieties of writing – be compared linguistically? Literary habits of apprehending texts are so ingrained that it is hard to grasp that this scientific technique ignores one of the cardinal rules of literary criticism: comparing like with like. By now, however, growing familiarity with QSUM should have convincingly demonstrated to the reader that this technique is indifferent to value and therefore to genre; what it measures is quite other than what will interest the literary critic.

    First, then, in Figure BR-3, a combined test of 'The Back Road' with twenty sentences of a Lawrence novel and critical essay, **SL** and **TM** (cf. Figure AH-4, for a similar test with the Huxley sample). This is a dramatic separation, where the normal consistency for the Lawrence sentences has been totally disturbed by the addition of the twenty-two sentences of 'The Back Road'.

    However, 'The Back Road' is a short story and, for completeness, it remains to be tested in a combined sample with the short story selected by Professor Worthen, **NE.** It is an easy matter to answer any critical misgivings about genre by providing a QSUM-chart showing 'The Back Road' analysed with the Lawrence short story, 'New Eve, Old Adam'. Figure **BR-4** shows the result of such an analysis. Here the result is a striking separation. The opening twenty

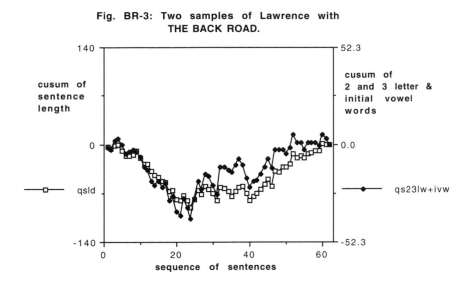

Figure BR-3: The habit of using two- and three-letter words and words starting with a vowel in a combined test of twenty-two sentences of 'The Back Road' following twenty sents. each of **SL** and **TM**.

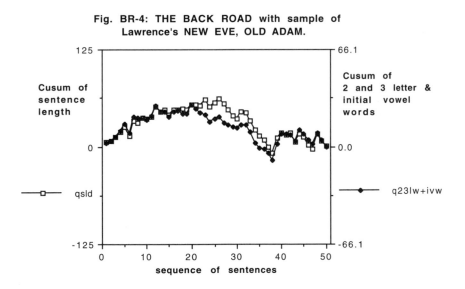

Figure BR-4: The habit of using two- and three-letter words and words starting with a vowel in a combined sample of 'The Back Road', followed by twenty-eight sentences of **NE**.

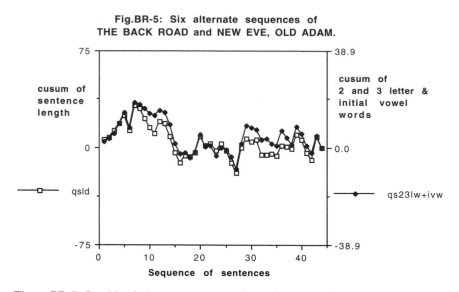

Figure BR-5: Combined alternate sequences from the two stories: eight sentences of 'The Back Road' followed by eight sentences of 'New Eve and Old Adam'; and then **BR,** eight; **NE,** eight; **BR,** six; **NE,** six.

sentences show very clearly the homogeneity of the disputed short story **BR**; but the addition of **NE** starts to disturb the chart from that point, just before the Lawrence sentences are added. This new story is obviously no QSUM fit with D. H. Lawrence, despite those initials under it. The separation is most pronounced.

There is, finally, another way to treat samples so as to show mixed authorship beyond doubt, even though that has surely been accomplished in the charts already shown. The sentences from the two texts, the Lawrence story and 'The Back Road', can broken up into short sequences so as to produce six small *alternate* samples of each text. When this is done, separation occurs almost at the point the first eight-sentence sample from 'The Back Road' joins the first eight sentences from the Lawrence text, the whole then becoming a very disjointed chart – see Figure BR-5. This is conclusive evidence of mixed authorship.

Anyone still wishing to attribute 'The Back Road' to D. H. Lawrence should be prepared to indicate why this particular story is the one and only exception to which the cusum technique need not apply.

However, there is a coda to this project which, given the amount of time involved in carrying out the QSUM attribution, qualifies as what Thomas Hardy might call one of *Life's Little Ironies*. After QSUM had established to the satisfaction of those involved that the utterance of D. H. Lawrence was clearly distinguishable from the utterance comprising 'The Back Road' by every test made, my literary critical faculty, until then dormant, suddenly noticed that two of the words in the story were used in a way that was abnormal for English usage.

The story mentions the Saline Hills, which are in Scotland. As used in the story, the words 'janitor' and 'rector' are *Scottish* vocabulary, not English vocabulary. In English usage, a 'janitor' would be a 'porter'; and 'rector' in Scotland means a 'headmaster', not a cleric, as in England.

Thus, a case would have to be made out for D. H. Lawrence not only writing a school story set in Scotland but using distinctively Scottish vocabulary – not impossible, but, it goes without saying, highly unlikely.

APPENDIX 1: DETAILS OF LAWRENCE TEXTS SUPPLIED BY JOHN WORTHEN TO JILL FARRINGDON

a) The thirty-six final sentences of *Sons and Lovers*
This sample is readily available to readers from any edition of the book.

b) Two letters by D. H. Lawrence
As indicated in the Notes, these were from the standard edition of the *Collected Letters of D. H. Lawrence* (Cambridge University Press). The first, to Edward Garnett, 19 May 1913 (forty-four sentences), starts, 'I am relieved when you put me in my place with a quiet hand' and ends '. . . I had hardly the energy to walk out of the house for two days.'

The second, to Louie Burrows, 20 October 1907 (nineteen sentences) starts, 'I have a request to make' and ends 'But I will post your note to her.'

c) Critical article 'GERMAN BOOKS: Thomas Mann', 1913
The first thirty-two sentences start 'Thomas Mann is perhaps the most famous of German novelists now writing' and ends 'Speaking of one of his works he says [quote].'

d) 'New Eve and Old Adam', 1913
The sample of fifty-six sentences starts 'After all', she said, with a little laugh . . .' and ends 'The city was far below.'

  • **The combined sample from four Lawrence texts, twenty sentences each used for Figure DHL-1:**

a) Sentences 1–21 from final thirty-six sentences of *Sons and Lovers* (omitting sentence 12), starting 'He shook hands and left her at the door . . .' to 'They seemed something.'

b) Sentences 12–31 from 56-sentence sample of 'New Eve Old Adam', starting 'He drank his tea in silence . . .' to '. . . and spinning it as if she would spurn it'.

c) Sentences 4–23 from opening sentences of the review, 'German Books: Thomas Mann' starting 'It is as an artist rather than as a story-teller that Germany worships Thomas Mann . . .' to 'He is physically ailing, no doubt.'

d) First twenty sentences from a letter written in 1913 to Edward Garnett, starting 'I am relieved when you put me in my place with a quiet hand . . .' to 'We might stop a week at the sea side.'

APPENDIX 2: THE 26-SENTENCE SAMPLE FROM THE INTRODUCTION, pp. XIII–XIV, BY ALDOUS HUXLEY IS FOUND IN *LETTERS OF D. H. LAWRENCE*, EDITED BY HUXLEY IN 1932

The sample starts 'Here, in a parenthesis, let me remark on the fact that Lawrence's doctrine . . .' and ends '. . . but there is also the pure and powerful illumination of the disinterested scientific intellect.'

APPENDIX 3: FULL TEXT OF THE NEWLY FOUND STORY 'THE BACK ROAD'

The gravel crunched, and a boy, moving slowly along, passed the janitor's house and stood for the first time in the Back Road. His eyes grew moist, and he sniffled softly to himself as he strove to hold back the eager tears. He felt somehow the charm of the green hills and the tall trees, and, so comforted, he wandered on between the leafy giants.

That night in the dormitory he overheard a conversation of absorbing interest – three boys discussing the deeds, actual and potential, of the captain. The voices sank to thin sibilants, growing thinner and fainter in the new boy's ears as he floated away into the land of dreams. The captain was there but changed. He raced express trains, he sprang backwards across the river, he felled the rector with his right, the janitor with his left, and, not so improbable, he butted Farmer Heeltap's bull to the scathe of the latter.

The end of school life had come, and the boy's last days wore to evening. The roar of the river rose louder with the falling shadows, and a huge orange moon swung slowly up from the Saline Hills. The boy and the girl were seated beneath the kindly tree that bore their initials cunningly entwined. She was silent, his own lips were sealed; but he drew closer to her, and drew her closer to himself. Her eyes flashed softly in the golden moonlight, a shining mist whirled around him, and in that enchanted haze he kissed her with the ineffable tenderness and self-forgetfulness of youth.

October, with a shrill wind driving a thin rain before it. The gravel crunched, and a man bronzed and bearded passed the janitor's house, and stood in the Back Road. He turned mechanically to the left, and stopped before a mighty tree. High up he saw what had once been a cunning device of interwoven letters, but the swelling bark had writhed and sundered them.

He fumbled with his stick and moved uneasily with his feet, and his mouth twitched at the corners. A vociferous band of schoolboys strolling past fell silent for a moment to gaze curiously at the stranger. The stranger glanced at them in his turn, murmured a few half-audible words, and turned away. One of the boys declared he had heard something about 'all gone' and 'familiar faces', but the others laughed and told him to shut up.

And the stranger walked dully onward, the black current of his thought running through dead rainbow hopes. And before and behind stretched the black ribbon of road between gay ridges of withered leaves.

PART II

Literary and linguistic attributions:
The range of QSUM

Four chapters of problems in Attribution:
Editing, Translations, Plagiarism,
Children's Language, and other
Literary Illustrations

Chapter 4

FINGERPRINTING AUTHORS

> '. . .Trying to learn to use words, and every attempt
> Is a wholly new start, and a different kind of failure,
> Because one has only learnt to get the better of words
> For the thing one no longer has to say, or the way in which
> One is no longer disposed to say it.'
>
> (T. S. Eliot, 'East Coker', *Four Quartets*)

Muriel Spark, Finding a Literary Voice and the QSUM-chart

In Chapter 2, the **test case** for an actual case of authorship attribution focused on a short story alleged to be by D. H. Lawrence.

It was a member of the editorial board of the *D. H. Lawrence Review*, in which the results of that Lawrence project were initially published, whose instinctive response it was to describe the analysis by QSUM as 'scientific mumbo-jumbo'.[1]

Others have expressed fears about the intrusion of science into those areas of knowledge and practice traditionally within the province of the humanities. For example, a university lecturer in the Republic of Ireland, who was interested in the attribution of a ship-board 'diary' (allegedly written by an Irish emigrant *en route* to Canada at the time of the mid-nineteenth-century potato famine), wrote of QSUM's involvement in this dispute:

> Going by Morton's published book on the subject, these [stylistic features] may be nothing more than the frequency of three and four letter words. Many historians and literary critics more used to working from a combination of instinct, experience and trained observation will be troubled by the intrusion of this latest scientific discipline into their own scholarly preserve.[2]

This particular critic's misgivings are typical of the reaction of literary scholars. But such reactions are based on a misunderstanding of QSUM's claims and acknowledged limits. Traditional approaches when used responsibly have often proved valid; they are not under threat of being superseded by this new technique. Where literary responses and instincts are sound, scholarship and the scientific attribution of utterance can only be mutually supportive (see later Fielding studies, where literary scholars and quantitative analysts have worked together).[3]

Popular press reporting has often – indeed, *usually* – given a simplistic account of QSUM, or misrepresented it altogether, leading to the notion that authorship can be attributed by a simple count of the number of words used of two and three letters. This has occasioned bafflement, and excuses for ridicule – for example, it seems to the lay person an occasion for quoting, with amusement, the opening of Shakespeare's most famous soliloquy (with its 100 per cent *23lw* usage): 'To be or not to be' – which was the headline in a student newspaper article ridiculing the method.[4] (A more interesting cavil would have been to wonder how to count, in cusum analysis, neologisms like Shakespeare's 'be-all and end-all', coined from two- and three-letter words but now constituting nouns – they would be counted as such, if necessary.)

The use of initial vowel words as a significant habit within the sentence has aroused even more incredulity: the comment 'preposterous' was one verdict by one expert witness.[5] To suggest that words starting with a vowel might play a part in being able to identify authorship is often, to the uninitiated, the most mysterious aspect of the technique, and speculative reference has already been made in Chapter 2 to this aspect of the technique.[6]

Such scepticism is understandable. The arts are nothing if not explorations, and celebrations, of quality and value; and professionals in the arts today – sometimes swimming against the tide of a popular, if unexamined, faith in 'science' – are likely to be defensive about scientific application in fields where their own accomplishment, confidence and expertise has always prevailed.

Most literary academics are instinctively hostile towards the use of quantitative analysis for settling whether a particular author has written a disputed text or not. (Indeed, I count myself among their number.) By sympathy and by training, anyone who has made a study of literature for the love of it is used to apprehending a literary text for what it is: a human communication directed towards human readers.[7] What matters to the literary specialist is familiarity with the rhetoric of literary device, sensitivity to tone, pace, rhythm, lexis, to subtle changes in point of view. In seeking to identify an author, the most important factor is attention to the achievement of that whole enterprise which authors call 'finding a voice'. In a disputed text, the question for most of us is whether or not we hear that living 'voice' to which ordinary, if intensive, reading has sensitized us.

This point is worth labouring for readers who have little experience of literary judgements, and who are mystified by this whole concept of 'finding a voice'. Is it merely craftsmanship, a question of using words to say something the way one wants, or is 'disposed to say it', as Eliot put it in the epigraph to this chapter?

A comment in a newspaper review is useful here:

Poets are often said to 'find their voice' rather as if it had been hidden under a gooseberry bush and merely needed the right person to walk past at the right moment. What *W. H. Auden: Juvenilia* traces is a long hard, non-stop-process, not of finding a voice but of constructing it. [8]

It is a critical commonplace to observe that a writer usually begins in imitation of earlier writers ('ventriloquism', as it is sometimes called) before acquiring an individual 'voice'.

Such an authorial 'voice', however, is what makes a text *recognizably that of a particular author*. This process may be the labour of many years, and certainly the achieved voice is the means by which authors are enabled to express their own particular vision. The Nobel prize-winning novelist William Golding has written,

> The writer watches the greatest mystery of all. It is the moment of most vital awareness, the moment of most passionate and unsupported conviction. It shines or cries. There is the writer, trying to grab it as it passes, as it emerges impossibly and heads to be gone. It is that twist of behaviour, that phrase, sentence, paragraph, that happening on which the writer would bet his whole fortune, stake his whole life as a *true* thing.[9]

This description of the distinctive truth of an author's writing is qualitative: it implies that it is by apprehending the quality of utterance that we learn to know writers.

This is not to imply that each work by a writer 'sounds' the same. There are special 'voices' to be found for different books too. As Walker Percy put it while waiting to start a new novel, 'All I know . . . is not to write the first sentence until the tone or voice is right'; and also, 'I have been working for months on one sentence, and I have finally got it . . .' (the first sentence of his next novel).[10]

One of the simplest and most useful accounts of the intimate relation between the individual voice and what we call 'literary style' is given by science-fiction writer Ursula LeGuin: 'Style is how you as a writer see and speak. It is how you see: your vision, your understanding of the world, *your voice*'[11] (my italics).

No literary critic would dissent from these definitions of recognizing an authorial voice by parameters of quality, not (linguistic) quantity. Therefore, when invited in 1988 to take part in the experimental work on the development of QSUM, it was my confident belief – born of many years of recognizing *difference* among literary 'voices' – that the limitations of the technique were soon to be exposed.

Early Applications of QSUM to Literary Texts

It was in that spirit of dissent that I prepared a collection of samples from a variety of styles and stylists suitable for testing cusum analysis. At that time (1988) A. Q. Morton was preparing a book on his findings, and was especially interested in testing samples of work by writers who were themselves conscious of writing 'differently' at different times.[12]

Two writers immediately came to mind in this connection: Iris Murdoch and Muriel Spark. Murdoch, novelist and philosopher, has claimed that she is conscious of deliberately writing in a necessarily different style for her essays and her novels. At one level, this is both true and comprehensible: reading philosophy, i.e. following a train of thought and discussion of ideas, is not the same exercise as reading a novel, i.e. experiencing a work of art. Nor can writing in these two modes be the same.

However, from analysis of the passages supplied to him taken from three novels and a philosophical essay by Iris Murdoch, Morton was able to show that her underlying **QSUM** pattern of language-use is totally consistent.[13] Whatever cumulative sum language-patterns exist, they are clearly very subtle: despite the differences everyone undoubtedly recognizes between genres and 'registers', such as fiction and philosophy,

- **the use of these unconscious linguistic habits does not change.**

For the literary and linguistic scholar, this very first result on Iris Murdoch raised all sorts of questions. If there is consistency across time and across genre, at what age does such consistency begin?[14] Are there any implications for the whole literary enterprise, based as it is on drafting and re-drafting, and for the process just discussed, of 'finding a voice'? To refer back to the Eliot epigraph, a writer's conscious *disposition* to say anything was beginning to seem the very opposite of what QSUM reveals.

QSUM and the Writing of Muriel Spark

QSUM's exploration of writers who were aware of a difference of style in their own writing continued with a study of poet and novelist, Muriel Spark, who had become conscious of a change in her writing at a certain stage of her literary career.

In 1961, Muriel Spark had been asked to contribute to an issue of *Twentieth Century* to be called 'The Gods', which would feature contributions by many famous names of the century – Arnold Toynbee, Julian Huxley, Simone Weil and others. An article entitled 'My Conversion', by Muriel Spark, appears in this issue.[15] In it, she discusses her writing before and after she became a Roman Catholic. She says: '. . . I think there is a connection between my writing and my conversion, but I don't want to be too dogmatic about it. Certainly all my best work has come since then.' That would be between 1954 and 1961, during which time she had established her reputation by writing five novels, all well-received.[16] There had also been volumes of short stories and poetry.[17]

Since 1961, she has written a further twenty novels, more short stories, poems, and a play. Much of her writing prior to her conversion in 1954 is self-described in this article as 'just critical work', although in 1951 she had won a short story competition in the Sunday newspaper, the *Observer* with her story 'The Seraph and the Zambesi', and had also published poetry.

Continuing on the theme of achieving a 'voice', and its connection with her religious belief, she goes further, saying:

> I take this attitude to Catholicism because it's really a Christian thing to me conducive to individuality, to finding one's own individual point of view. I find I speak far more with my own voice as a Catholic, and I think I could prove it with my stuff. Nobody can deny I speak with my own voice as a writer now, whereas before my conversion I couldn't do it because I was never sure what I was . . . I was talking and writing with other people's voices all the time.

Furthermore, in discussing style and her admiration for good stylists, Spark makes the assertion 'I didn't get my style until I became a Catholic because you haven't got to care, and you need security for that.'

There are several interesting ideas here about the nature of writing in connection with the individual literary 'voice', and about 'style'. Muriel Spark differentiates between her earlier and later writing. She believes she has developed a style that can be recognized. If this is true – and most admirers of Muriel Spark would accept that it is true – then it is, of course, a style to be apprehended by the qualitative recognition and judgement we have briefly touched on.

Its truth, however, does not negate the application of QSUM, with its statistics for identifying writers through analysis of recurring language-habits, and with its claim that everything written by the same author remains consistently identifiable whether it is written early or late and regardless of genre.

As expected, cusum analysis of Muriel Spark's writing over forty years was indeed able to show a remarkable consistency; but before looking at the charts which demonstrate this, it should be properly acknowledged that the results in no way conflict with her own awareness of achieving an individual voice and a 'style' just as she has stated in her 1961 article, and as perceptive readers will be able to recognize.

A. Q. Morton accepts that 'we are all aware of differences in our speech and writing' in different situations (what modern linguistics would describe in terms of 'varieties' of language and the 'appropriateness' of language use in social situations). However, Morton continues: 'Literary people talk much of style; they never say, with any precision, what the word covers.'[18] It is tempting here to recall what novelist/scientist C. P. Snow once called 'the two cultures' (though that description begs many questions). In literary culture 'what the word covers' cannot be defined by the mode of scientific precision, or in numerical terms. To put it in terms of linguistics, it is 'inappropriate' to talk of such a mode with regard to style.

It is relevant that Muriel Spark goes on to discuss style in her article, remarking,

> Anybody with a good style, a good technique, is worth reading to see how far he can persuade you. He might have the most wonderful message under the sun to preach, but it's not a bit of good unless you [*sic*] can persuade and give delight and pleasure.[19]

Those qualitative aspects of human communication, giving delight and pleasure, are not aims or ends in the factual world of scientific precision.

Despite the QSUM consistency of Muriel Spark's work over more than forty years, she was in no way deluded in saying that her post-conversion work was for the first time 'in her own voice'. That there is such a thing as 'style' is evident from commonly-used descriptions like 'Lawrentian', 'Dickensian', 'Shakespearean', as I have already noted in an earlier chapter.[20]

In his text of the Herbert Read Memorial Lecture the writer Salman Rushdie accurately describes achieved individuality in the novel:

> But the most wonderful of the many wonderful truths about the novel form is that the greater the writer, the greater his or her exceptionality. The geniuses of the novel are those whose voices are fully and undisguisably their own, who, to borrow William Gass's image, *sign every word they write*. What draws us to an author is his or her 'unlikeness', even if the apparatus of literary criticism then sets to work to demonstrate that he or she is really no more than an accumulation of influences.[21]

What anyone new to QSUM attribution needs to realize from the outset is that there are obviously two truths about this matter of 'signing every word' one writes.

First, there is difference and development in a professional authorial life, recognizable to the author and readers, and this difference constitutes a 'voice' and a literary style, to do with language use and authentic individuality. But second, this real difference does not affect an underlying permanent structure of unconscious language usage, to do with identifying utterance scientifically by QSUM.

QSUM attribution will seem irrelevant to the artist, to whom the difference is the only significant thing. It is the authentic, truth-telling, artistic voice that Muriel Spark found coming into existence in the post-1954 period. She does not, after all, say she did not write her earlier work, only that she had not been using 'her own voice'. Just as its counterpart, a physical 'voice', is more than the vocal chords it makes use of, a 'style' is more than the habitual language patterns and structures each person has developed and uses unconsciously (and which – we may only speculate – *may* perhaps have a neuro-cortical base?).

To state the obvious, cusum quantification cannot recognize literary attributes and therefore cannot recognize art. A style needs to be recognized in encounter, and so requires an attentive reader (or listener). If we want to know who Muriel Spark is, to hear the authentic voice of the artist, we must read – or come to be capable of reading – the imaginative work, the fiction and poetry. It is through the English language that she speaks, using her consistent QSUM 'fingerprint', but it is through her art that she communicates her vision, and there is no objective technique for apprehending that.

The Spark QSUM-charts

Muriel Spark's Writing Pre-1954
The first stage in looking at Muriel Spark's work was to make a cusum analysis of her work prior to 1954, the period before her conversion. So the first three samples were taken from

- her book of literary criticism, *John Masefield* (1953).
- 'The Ballad of the Fanfarlo', a narrative/dramatic poem, twenty-two pages in length (1952).
- *Observer* prize-winning story 'The Seraph and the Zambesi' (1951).[22]

The first task, as usual, was to apply the most common three tests – *23lw*, *ivw*, and *23lw+ivw* – to these samples (usually abbreviated hereafter to *Masefield*, *Ballad*, and *Seraph*).

Muriel Spark showed remarkably good consistency on all three common tests, and was found to be homogeneous, in combined samples, by all three. But, after exhaustive cross-testing, the discriminating test proved to be the habit of using two- or three-letter words.

As an example of a single sample, however, two charts will be shown for comparison purposes in Figures MS-1 and MS1a. This demonstration of a single sample shows that satisfactory regularity can be observed in the analysis by both tests. It is always useful if a writer is homogeneous by more than one test, as will be seen in the second part of this chapter.

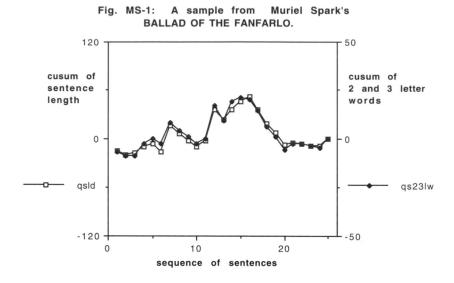

Figure MS-1: Sample of twenty-five sentences from Muriel Spark's 'Ballad of the Fanfarlo', analysed by the habit of using two- and three-letter words.

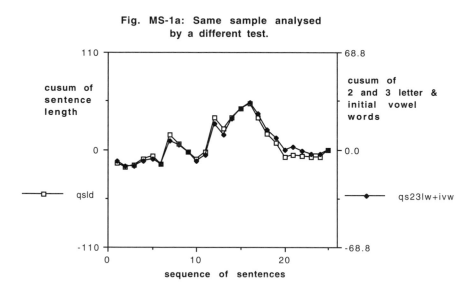

Figure MS-1a: The same sample of twenty-five sentences analysed by another test (*23lw+ivw*).

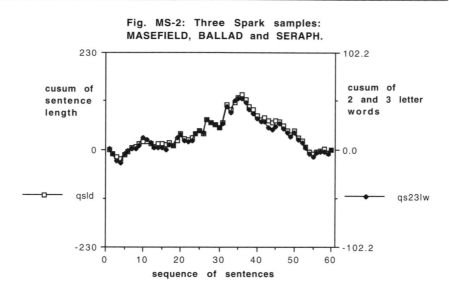

Figure MS-2: Combined sample of twenty sentences each from *Masefield*, Ballad, and Seraph, analysed by the habit of using two- and three-letter words.

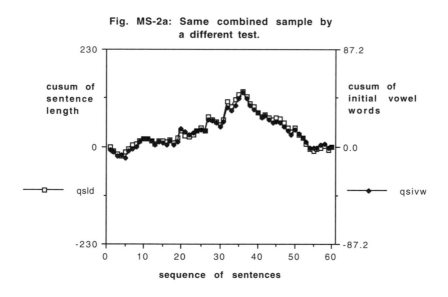

Figure MS-2a: The same combined sample analysed by the habit of using initial vowel words.

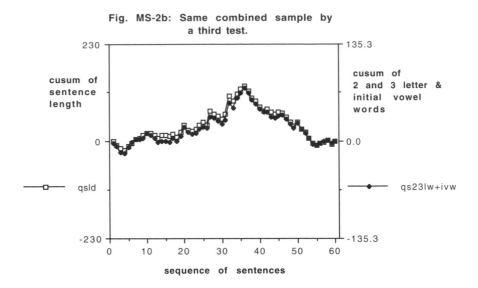

Figure MS-2b: The same combined sample analysed by the habit of using two- and three-letter words, and words starting with a vowel.

When a combined sample of the three texts was analysed together, the result appears in Figure MS-2. This is a sound consistent QSUM-chart, showing that the combined sample of twenty sentences each from a critical work, a long narrative ballad, and a short story, is visibly homogeneous. Muriel Spark is not an exception to the technique.

Relatively consistent charts resulted also from the habit of using initial vowel words, and of using two- and three-letter words and words starting with a vowel: see Figures MS-2a and MS-2b. This result in Figure MS-2a is a consistent QSUM-chart. Figure MS-2b is slightly looser, but not to any significant degree. These three charts all demonstrate the assertion made at the start of this section on Muriel Spark, that her linguistic habits are consistent and homogeneous by the three tests used. As already stated, however, the discriminating test was found to be the habit of using two- and three-letter words.

The next step was to move on to her later writing.

Muriel Spark's Writing Post-1954
The significant question for A. Q. Morton was whether her post-conversion writing – or, ultimately, her work up to the present time – has stayed consistent with these early samples, despite her consciousness of a significant change of direction in her writing ('I didn't get my style till I became a Catholic'). It is an author's personal awareness of difference, something recognizable to an

**Fig. MS-3: The same combined sample plus
31 sentences from THE COMFORTERS.**

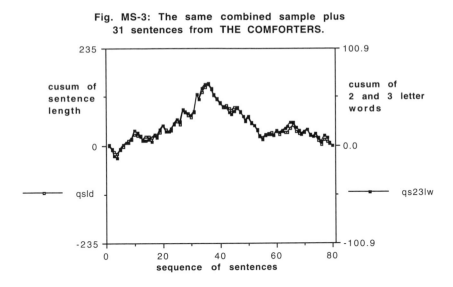

Figure MS-3: The habit of using two- and three-letter words in twenty sentences each
from the first three samples (pre-1954) followed by thirty-one sentences from *The
Comforters* (1957).

intelligent reading public, that was the focus of his interest, the important
point being to show that what is measurable in the QSUM 'fingerprint' has
nothing to do with genuine changes in literary style, but nevertheless remains
consistent throughout a writer's career.

The findings in relation to this question are shown above. If a sample of
thirty-one sentences from her first novel, *The Comforters*, 1957, is added on to
the first three samples analysed above, the result may be seen in Figure MS-3.
There is a slight anomalous 'blip' at sentences 61–4, but this is insignificant.

Clearly, Muriel Spark's QSUM-habits(s) remain totally consistent. As
Morton was then able to point out '. . .conscious changes in style do not affect
the types of habits used in this analysis.'[23]

This point is supported by the further analyses of Muriel Spark's writing
which I have undertaken. Two more charts will suffice as a demonstration.

Figure MS-4 is an analysis of two samples: twenty-five sentences from a
short story published in 1975, 'The First Year of My Life', combined with
twenty-five sentences from Muriel Spark's novel, *A Far Cry From Kensington*,
1988.[24] The regularity is of almost perfect spot-on-spot quality, except for a
slight displacement somewhere between sentences 5 and 10. (This is due to a
sequence of three sentences where the frequency of occurrence deviated too
exaggeratedly from the average: 'These careless women in black lost their

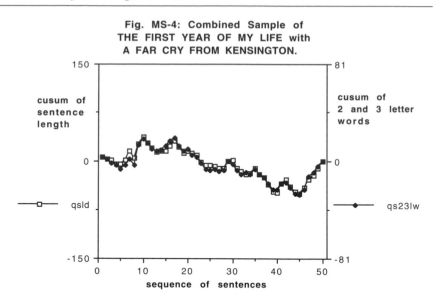

Figure MS-4: Combined sample of twenty-five sentences each from a 1975 story and a 1988 novel, analysed by the habit of using two- and three-letter words.

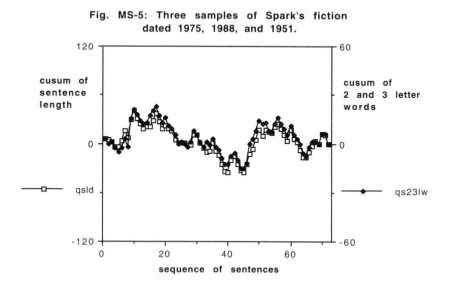

Figure MS-5: Combined sample of twenty-five sentences each from the 1975 story, the 1988 novel, and the 1951 short story, analysed by the habit of using two- and three-letter words.

husbands, and their brothers. Then they came to my mother and chuckled and crowed over my cradle. I was not amused.' The first two sentences here have between 16 per cent and 18 per cent habit usage (average 55%), while the last sentence in this sequence has 100 per cent – and is, in any case, a literary joke governed by the form of the original, Queen Victoria's well-known comment, 'We are not amused'.

When a 22-sentence sample from Muriel Spark's 1951 story, 'The Seraph and the Zambesi' is added to the above combined sample, the result appears in Figure MS-5. This 'sandwich' test establishes that Muriel Spark's writing remains consistent over the period 1951–88 when analysed by the use of her habit of using words of two and three letters.

Thus far, the project on Muriel Spark had proceeded much as expected, offering a good opportunity for distinguishing between literary criteria ('finding a voice') and quantitative criteria (QSUM) in the field of authorship attribution.

But there was more to be discovered yet.

The Editing of Muriel Spark

At this stage of the investigation into Muriel Spark's writing, when the project seemed ready for completion, events took an unexpected turn. In an attempt to add another genre of writing to the four kinds already sampled (literary criticism, novel, narrative poem, short story), it seemed a good idea to analyse a sample from the very article in which the author's remarks on her style appear, thus adding Muriel Spark's authentic conversational utterance to the other genres of her utterance which had been analysed.

This article appears to be a first-person account by Muriel Spark of her conversion to the Roman Catholic faith and its relation to her development as a writer.

But a sample of the first thirty-four sentences from the article immediately appeared as markedly deviant, in terms of analysis, and at variance with all the other Spark samples already yielding homogeneous QSUM-charts, examples of which we have seen above.

When a sample of the first thirty-four sentences from 'My Conversion' (abbreviated hereafter to 'Conversion') was added to the combined *Masefield*-Ballad-Seraph sample used for Figures MS-1 to MS-3, the result is shown in Figure CONV-1. If this were Muriel Spark's spoken (recorded) utterance, it should have remained homogeneous with the written samples, since spoken language has been successfully tested and combined with written text many times. However, the addition of the new thirty-four sentences has completely disturbed the previous homogeneity (Figure MS-2). The resulting separation starts at about sentence 50, breaking well into the known homogeneous text by Muriel Spark.

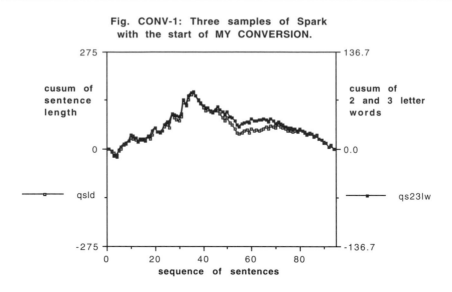

Figure CONV-1: Combined sample of sixty sentences of Muriel Spark followed by the thirty-four opening sentences of 'My Conversion', analysed by the habit of using two and three letters.

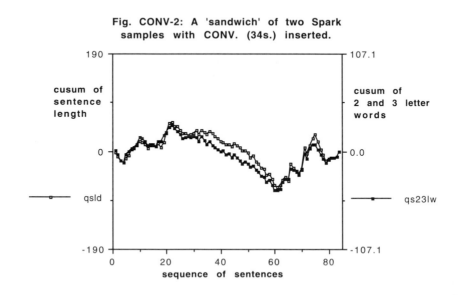

Figure CONV-2: The same habit (*23lw*) in a combined sample of fifty sentences of *Masefield*/Ballad with the thirty-four sentences of Conversion inserted at sentence 26.

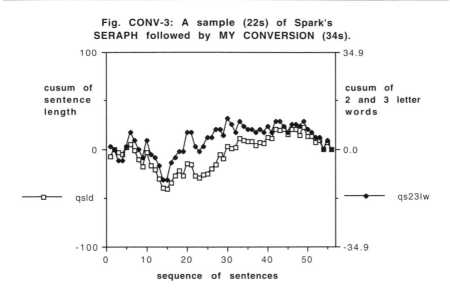

Fig. CONV-3: A sample (22s) of Spark's SERAPH followed by MY CONVERSION (34s).

Figure CONV-3: The same habit in a combined sample of twenty-two sentences of Seraph followed by thirty-four sentences of Conversion.

To explore this separation further, two more charts were made combining the thirty-four sentences with smaller Spark samples.

Figure CONV-2 shows a 'sandwich' of a combined sample of twenty-five sentences each of *Masefield* and Ballad, with the thirty-four sentences of Conversion inserted; and Figure CONV-3 shows the result of combining twenty-two sentences of Seraph with the thirty-four sentences of Conversion. In Figure CONV-2, the insertion of the sentences from the article has produced an even more marked separation starting shortly before sentence 26. In Figure CONV-3, where the sentences from the article outnumber the sentences from the short story, the separation is dramatic.

The separations in these combined sample charts show an increasing divergence as the authentic number of Spark sentences decreases until the last analysis shows a very wide distortion. This confirms that the article is not homogeneous with Muriel Spark's own writing. As we would now say, what we have here are mixed samples of utterance by more than one person.

How could this be explained? At that early stage of our QSUM testing in 1988, such a result disturbed more than the Muriel Spark charts – A. Q. Morton's first book (*The Qsum Plot,* with the late Professor Sidney Michaelson) was being prepared for printing. Could this unexpected new result cast doubt on the technique's reliability?

To reiterate, the crucial point when reading charts which give an apparently negative result is that the analyst:

- **must always go back to the text.**

Misunderstanding of this elementary basic rule has misled several of QSUM's critics, who have concluded that the technique 'does not work' because they have failed to grasp that an apparently non-homogeneous chart must always be compared with the text(s) represented.

A re-examination of the article in the issue of *Twentieth Century* revealed that this first-person article, beginning 'I was born in a very peculiar environment . . .', had actually resulted from an interview of Muriel Spark by the American journalist and editor W. J. Weatherby. A brief introduction preceding the article provided some comments by Weatherby on the content of the ensuing article.

Perhaps, then, W. J. Weatherby had *edited* his material from the interview, himself putting together the substance of Muriel Spark's replies to his questions so as to form a coherent whole? A re-reading of the opening sentences in this light, paying attention to the form of article in terms of the sentences which opened paragraphs, began to suggest a series of possible interviewer's questions:

Where were you born?
When did you begin to take an interest in the Catholic faith?
How did your conversion come about?
What writing had you done up to this point?

Suddenly, it seemed that this routine analysis may have served to enlarge our understanding of how the technique worked: when an editor compiles the spoken utterance of someone who has been interviewed the finished text may well show that the subject's habitual QSUM language use has been seriously disturbed by the interviewing editor's QSUM language habits, depending on the amount of editing carried out.

The question then became: if the thirty-four sentences of interview text were not homogeneous with Muriel Spark, do they form a homogeneous sample in themselves? And if they do, were they homogeneous with W. J. Weatherby, or were they an awkward hybrid of the two?

To find the answer to this, the first step was to analyse the thirty-four sentences alone. The results are given in the Figures CONV-4, -5, and -6.

It must be remembered that the two- and three-letter word test is the one which is able to discriminate Muriel Spark's writing, although she shows homogeneity by three tests. This result clearly shows that the Conversion sample is non-homogeneous by the discriminatory test, although some consistency begins to appear on the chart at about sentence 26.

Analysis by the other two tests homogeneous for Muriel Spark's writing then followed, resulting in Figures CONV-5 and Figure CONV-6.

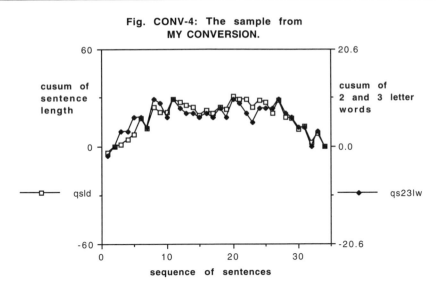

Figure CONV-4: Sample of thirty-four sentences of 'My Conversion' analysed by the habit of using two- and three-letter words.

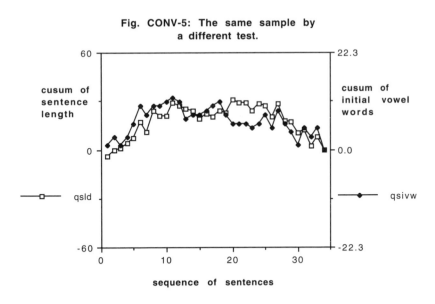

Figure CONV-5: The same sample analysed by the habit of using initial vowel words.

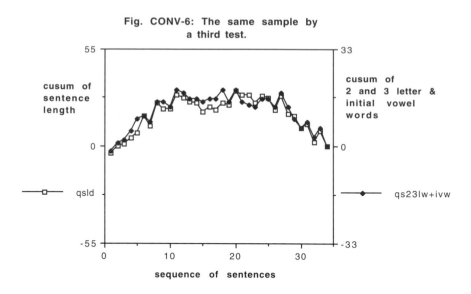

Fig. CONV-6: The same sample by a third test.

Figure CONV-6: The same sample analysed by the habit of using two- and three-letter words and initial vowel words.

The discord in Figure CONV-5 is even more marked. There is no homogeneity in the sample of thirty-four sentences from the article by the *ivw* test, although we have seen that Muriel Spark is quite homogeneous by this habit (see Figure MS-2a above).

Finally, turning to the *23lw+ivw* test, in Figure CONV-6, it can be seen that this habit, also, is non-homogeneous in the sample, though not as badly disturbed as the first two 'habit' tests. It can easily be seen that none of the three tests gives a satisfactory homogeneous graph, although all three charts do begin to show some regularity from about the twenty sixth sentence onwards.

This evidence of editing is not surprising. The beginnings of texts, whether of articles or books, are usually subject to constraints and are often edited: the need to supply information, set a scene, indicate the subject of the piece – all these will tend to dictate the form of organization of material.

Despite this indication that the piece was basically mixed utterance, A. Q. Morton decided that it would be worthwhile finding further writing by Weatherby to carry out more tests on his utterance, to analyse with the thirty-four sentences from 'My Conversion'. Even though these sentences proved so irregular, combined tests making a larger sample might indicate the controlling language structure at work.

Three short samples by W. J. Weatherby were found, comprising a total of forty-seven sentences: firstly, the seven sentences used in his Introduction to the Conversion article; then a further fourteen sentences from his Introduction

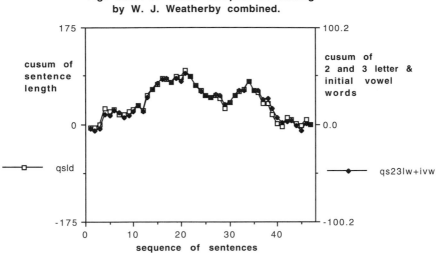

Fig. CONV-7: Three samples of writing by W. J. Weatherby combined.

Figure CONV-7: The habit of using two- and three-letter words, and initial vowel words in forty-seven sentences of utterance by W. J. Weatherby.

to his book *How the Draft Was Edited* (itself including pertinent remarks on the process of editing); and lastly, another twenty-six sentences from his book *Breaking the Silence*.

As always, the first step was to confirm that W. J. Weatherby is no exception to the technique; his combined forty-seven-sentence sample was tested for homogeneity, in Figure CONV-7. This result shows that W. J. Weatherby is no exception to the technique, and is consistent by the *23lw+ivw* test.

The next question was, could he be found to separate by this test from the undisputed utterance of Muriel Spark?

Figure CONV-8 shows the result of a combined test of the two writers. A very clear separation can be observed, almost throughout. These two samples, of writing of comparable length, are clearly not by one person, which confirms what we already know, of course.

But what happens if an analysis is made of combining the thirty-four sentences of Conversion with the first thirty-four sentences of W. J. Weatherby's combined sample utterance? Analysed by the test by which Weatherby was found to have a consistent habit, the *23lw+ivw* test, this is a statistically homogeneous chart. The 34-sentence sample is not homogeneous with Muriel Spark's writing (Figures CONV-1, 2 and 3)

• **but it is homogeneous with W. J. Weatherby**

as Figure CONV-9 shows us.

So this first-person account cannot have been actually composed in its

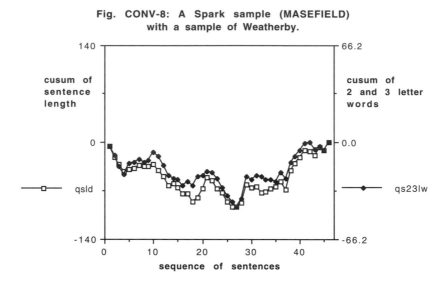

Figure **CONV-8**: Combined sample of utterance by Muriel Spark and twenty-one sentences of Weatherby (7 + 14 of his first two samples), analysed by the habit of using two- and three-letter words.

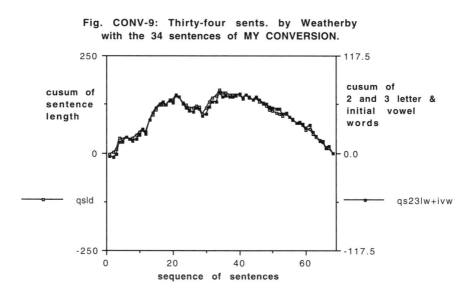

Figure **CONV-9**: A combined analysis of thirty-four sentences of the article published in *Twentieth Century* as 'My Conversion' by Muriel Spark, followed by thirty-four sentences of W. J. Weatherby (*23lw+ivw* test).

present form by Muriel Spark, although – paradoxically – Spark admirers will recognize the authentic literary voice. Since Muriel Spark had, presumably, agreed to the article's publication under her name, it faithfully represented her thoughts and sentiments.

The ironies of this exercise rebound upon us all, in that 'My Conversion' should have discussed 'finding a voice' in literary terms, that the second Weatherby sample discussed the process of editing, and that the focus of this investigation should have been the connection between the consistent QSUM 'fingerprint' and the unique literary voice.

APPENDIX 1

An opportunity for extending the investigation into Muriel Spark's writing came with the publication of the first volume of her autobiography, *Curriculum Vitae*, 1992, in which she mentions that some early articles worked on by her 'after the war' had been published under someone else's name.[25] This would be the editor of the magazine *Argentor* (journal for the National Jewellers' Association), for which Muriel Spark worked at that time .

I have trace one of these articles mentioned, and discovered it to be signed by William Llewellyn Amos – this was the one entitled 'The Goldsmith Painters'.[26]

It seemed an interesting exercise to analyse an extract from the article with Muriel Spark's writing. Accordingly, forty-one sentences from 'The Goldsmith Painters' were analysed in combined samples with Muriel Spark's utterance.

As shown in this chapter, Muriel Spark is homogeneous by the three main tests, but is able to be discriminated by the *23lw* test. Analysis of the article on its own showed evidence of some editing, since one of the tests – the *23lw+ivw* test – showed greater consistency of results than tests by the *23lw* habit, and very poor results for the *ivw* habit. But combining samples from Muriel Spark's published work and this article showed that the degree of editing must have been minimal, since consistency can easily be shown by the first two tests.

First, in Figure ARG-1, forty-two sentences from 'The Goldsmith Painters'

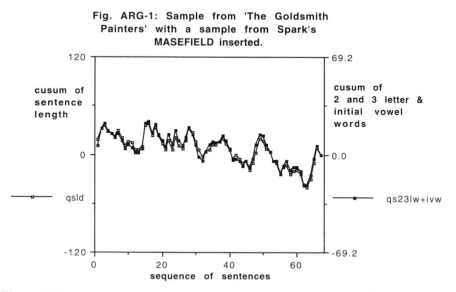

Fig. ARG-1: Sample from 'The Goldsmith Painters' with a sample from Spark's MASEFIELD inserted.

Figure ARG-1: A combined sample of forty-two sentences taken from 'The Goldsmith Painters', with twenty-five sentences from JOHN MASEFIELD inserted at sentence 28, analysed by the *23lw+ivw* test.

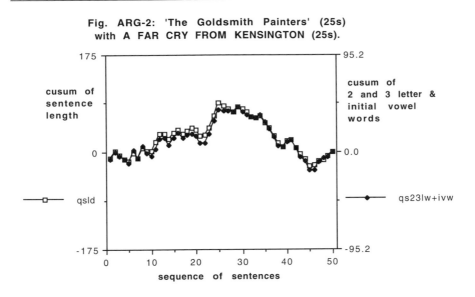

Fig. ARG-2: 'The Goldsmith Painters' (25s) with A FAR CRY FROM KENSINGTON (25s).

Figure ARG-2: The same habit in a combined sample of twenty-five sentences taken from 'The Goldsmith Painters', followed by twenty-five sentences from *A Far Cry From Kensington*.

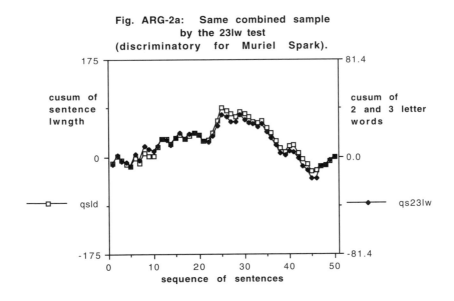

Fig. ARG-2a: Same combined sample by the 23lw test (discriminatory for Muriel Spark).

Figure ARG-2a: The same combined sample by another test (*23lw*, discriminatory for Muriel Spark).

were combined with twenty-five sentences from her critical book, *John Masefield*, written close to the time of the article's composition (late 1940s).[27] The result by this 'sandwich' test is sound: the two samples are indistinguishable by this test, which reveals the homogeneity which Muriel Spark asserts was the case.

A sample which combined two samples of the same number of sentences from the article and from a late Spark novel, *A Far Cry From Kensington*, produced the two following charts, Figures ARG-2 and ARG-2a.[28]

Apart from one small explicable blip at sentences 20–21, Figure ARG-2 demonstrates once again a consistent result from the *23lw+ivw* test.

The next chart, ARG-2a, shows consistency by Muriel Spark's discriminatory habit. The blip at sentences 20–21 has disappeared: this is because the culprit sentence 21, a short sentence truncated by the deletion of a quotation ('In 1487 his father describes Botticelli as being [quote]'), has a low proportion of two- and three- letter words but no additional initial vowel words at all, which caused the original blip. There is slight displacement of the second half of the chart owing to the three long sentences in the middle, which disturb the exact correspondence of the second half of the combined sample.

These results are a gratifying endorsement of QSUM. It is clear is that there is no marked QSUM separation by combining the article by 'William Llewellyn Amos' with the writing of Muriel Spark. Her language habits then were, and have remained, consistent.

APPENDIX 2

Samples Used in Muriel Spark Analysis

1. The 20–25 sentences from *John Masefield*, are taken from Chapter Four (87–89), starting at 'First, the poems were made to be spoken, and so, if possible, they should be read aloud . . .' to '. . .We should be aware of this fact when we read them'.
2. Twenty-five sentences from 'The Ballad of the Fanfarlo' , taken from *Collected Poems I* (19–22), starting at 'O where am I you slender sleepers? . . .' to '. . . where there was/The new moon like a pair of surgical forceps/With the old moon in her jaws.'
3. Twenty-five sentences from 'The Seraph and the Zambesi' (the *Sunday Observer* prize-winning story) in *The Go-Away Bird and Other Stories*, (159–60), starting at 'The performance was set to begin at eight' to 'This was a living body'.
4. Twenty-five sentences from *The Comforters*, 1957, (77–9), starting at 'For after dinner at a restaurant in Knightsbridge they had been to Soho . . .' to '. . . Then Laurence found out definitely – he finds out everything, of course.'
5. Twenty-five sentences from 'The First Year of My Life', in *The Secret Self*,

ed. Hermione Lee (London, Dent), 267–8, starting at 'I was born on the first day of the second month of the last   year of the First World War, a Friday . . .' to '. . .They're not supposed to smile till they're three months old'.

6.   Twenty-five sentences from *A Far Cry From Kensington*, Constable, 1988, (115), from 'Tom came on leave again, for a weekend, and asked me to marry him. . .' to '. . .and VIs, for which there were air-raid warnings'; and 116–17, from 'After supper downstairs he left me and I went up to bed . . .' to '. . . I don't know how he got transport; probably he got a lift.'

Texts of Other Utterance Used as Samples

W. J. Weatherby's Introduction to 'My Conversion' in *Twentieth Century*, (Autumn 1961).

> The fear of writers committed to a religious or political faith is that it will blot their writing. Muriel Spark provides a lesson in how to make your faith help you as a writer without letting it hinder you: commitment without a price. Her galloping reputation as one of the freshest of British satirists since the war dates from her conversion: it gave her, as she says, 'a norm' from which to work. It would be easy to guess from much of her work where her personal faith lies – *Memento Mori* is not only the title of one of her novels but the thought that haunts so many of her characters, haunts them because death is so clearly not going to be the end. Equally well, she catches people who are really more dead than alive and she understands the waste of it. But none of the Catholic undertones blot the surface of her writing: her clear, pointed style is a delight and her angle on life entirely her own. And the sparkle she puts into her books is obviously there, too, in the person.

Sample taken from W. J. Weatherby's 'Preface' to *How the Draft Was Edited* (xii–iii), starting 'The pile of manuscript in the Schomberg collection is the third prefinal draft . . .' to '. . . and to Mr Wendell Wray for their help in turning the manuscript into a book, and one trusts, a permanent part of Negro literature and American history.'

Forty-seven sentences from W. J. Weatherby's *Breaking the Silence*, (Penguin Original, 1965), 47–50, starting 'I am left no choice now as to how to begin my own story . . .' to '. . . A sacrificial offering of experience as an argument against the haters: [quote], perhaps I was.'

Thirty-four opening sentences of 'My Conversion' starting 'I was born in a very peculiar environment, which is difficult to locate . . .' to '. . . Certainly all my best work has come since then.'

Extract from 'The Goldsmith Painters', *Argentor*, 147–510, from 'During the fifteenth and sixteenth centuries, when the influences of the Renaissance were sweeping across Europe . . .' to '. . . Finally, having decided to become a painter, Sandro was apprenticed to the master, Fra Fillipo Lippi.'

APPENDIX 3

The practitioner of QSUM will become used to editing out anomalies, as discussed in Part I. As they are usually of a predictable nature, they can often be identified, with enough practice, even at the processing stage.

The samples of Muriel Spark used in this chapter provided typical examples of anomalies which needed to be eliminated from the final texts used in the analyses shown.

For instance, in the *Masefield* samples, the following sentences were removed as anomalies:

> When I say that there still exist vast audiences who listen to stories, I am thinking of those many thousands (many thousands more than listen to broadcast novels) who listen to broadcast commentaries on national events, cup-ties, The Derby, State processions.

This is a typical 'list' sentence, as is the following half-sentence:

> . . . see the close of the race in 'Right Royal', the account of the fight in 'The Everlasting Mercy', the last lap of the fox's fight in 'Reynard The Fox'.

There were two sentences, comprising a verse each, which were eliminated as anomalies from 'The Ballad of the Fanfarlo'. These are given below:

> Then each one cried, 'You false witness,'
> And each one sat up to testify
> In Manuela de Moneteverde's name,
> And each one said, 'You lie'.

> 'You lie, you lie,' cried each to each,
> And each to each arose,
> And they had fallen all on all
> And felled them with bitter blows.

The *repetitions* here are the obvious source of the anomalous nature of the verses when analysed. (On the other hand, it is interesting to point out that, from the point of view of the poem, these verses form a dramatic climax, crucial verses, rising into the rhetoric of the ballad-form.)

As an example of a list sentence, the following deleted sentence from *The Comforters* could hardly be bettered:

In the second pub, where a fair fat poet said to Caroline, 'Tell me all about your visions, my dear'; and another poet, a woman with a cape and a huge mouth, said 'Is there much Satanism going on within the Catholic Church these days?'; and another sort of writer, a man of over fifty, asked Caroline who was her psycho-analyst, and told her who was his – at this pub Caroline collected, one way and another, that the Baron had been mentioning this and that about her, to the ageless girls and boys who dropped in on him at his bookshop in Charing Cross Road.'

In the rhetoric of the novel, the list of comparisons and sequence of scenes contributes to the satiric effect, and to Caroline's perception of what is happening to her; but in terms of cusum analysis, it is an anomalous sentence.

A similarly long list sentence was deleted from 'The First Year of My Life':

Apart from being born bed-ridden and toothless, unable to raise myself on the pillow or utter anything but farmyard squawks, or police-siren wails, my bladder and my bowels totally out of control, I was further depressed by the curious behaviour of the two-legged mammals around me.

This brilliant story turns on a new-born baby's ability to speak in ironic tones and with satiric disgust about the helpless situation it finds itself in, so that the sentence is, in context, extremely funny. It is Muriel Spark's oblique commentary on the insanity of the First World War, which should be obvious to a new-born baby let alone to the adults equally helpless in the situation. The other satiric elements – the parody of scientism, of New Age-ism, of academe, of artistic rivalry ('poets and philosophers have got there first'), and of regal displeasure ('I was not amused') – all these are part of the individual authorial voice found by Muriel Spark, as opposed to her QSUM 'fingerprinting' habits.

In *A Far Cry from Kensington*, repetition is again at work making necessary the following deletion:

I had met Tom Hawkins at a dance, then we met again. Then, when he went back to his unit, we wrote to each other, at first every week, then twice a week, then every day.

The narrative, economically showing the rapid pace of events by the linguistic rapidity of the sequence of 'then' phrases, creates a novelistic effect – but it causes a QSUM anomaly.

Chapter 5

HENRY FIELDING AS TRANSLATOR OF GUSTAVUS ADLERFELD'S *THE MILITARY HISTORY OF CHARLES XII*

The translation of a text from one language into another inevitably places translators under various kinds of restraint. The most difficult variety of writing a translator can attempt is obviously that of imaginative writing, born so intimately from the living language – hence the notorious 'untranslatablity' of poetry. Some would amend that to the untranslatability of all literature: Sir Kingsley Amis wrote that he had refrained, in a conversation with the Russian poet, Yevtushenko, from 'doing my piece about an interest in the paraphrasable content of literature being an anti-literary interest' when recalling his reason for not having read *Dr Zhivago* despite its having been translated into English.[1] Many would agree that nothing replaces a reading in the original language.

Such an attitude, paradoxically perhaps, leaves the translator of a poem relatively free to deviate from exact wording in an attempt to render the spirit of the poem. Translators know this: the sub-titles of many poetic translations acknowledge it – for instance, the Australian poet, Vicki Raymond, has published *'versions of'* Horace, Muriel Spark has published poems *'after'* Catullus, while a book of poems recently reviewed by the writer contained translations from the Welsh in 'a style of translation designed not at all to be a literal rendering, but an attempt to recreate the progressions of imagery with something of the energy they have in the original'.[2] Obviously, the aims of translators will differ.

A factual document, on the other hand, must be very faithfully rendered from the original: it can be argued that the translator is more constrained by the nature of such material. In terms of the writing, a military history is just such a limiting work, crammed full of the details of campaigns, exact dates, place-names and military names. What such a work has to be, first and foremost, is an accurate record. There is hardly scope for much free translation in a historical account.

However, from the point of view of attributing authorship, the necessity of scrupulously following a given text would make even more meaningful an anonymous translator's retention of any stylistic traits known to be habitual. The use of favourite words and phrases, of characteristic positions of words (like habitual sentence openers), or even of interpolations into the original by the translator – all these would all provide evidence for probability of authorship.

Gustavus Adlerfeld's *The Military History of Charles XII* (abbreviated hereafter to *Charles XII*) is a three-volume work in French published in 1740, and translated, anonymously, into English in the same year. It is a tedious work to read, consisting of the monotonous narrative of military campaigns and their outcome. The ordinary reader is likely to be reminded of the nursery rhyme 'The Grand Old Duke of York' ('He marched them up to the top of the hill/And he marched them down again'), which at least has the literary virtue of rhythmic interest, conspicuously lacking in *Charles XII*. A sample of the text – the first few lines of the first sample, illustrated in Figure MH-1 – will give the flavour of the whole:

The 15th, in the morning we saw there three ladders, which the enemy had abandoned. We gave one sol a day more to every man, on account of their being obliged to work night and day. The enemy forbore firing; but took possession of the side of the WARTA, both with foot and horse, and drew a line of eighty paces round about the bridge, among the ruins of the suburb, which had been burned down. This line they furnished with gabions, and we observed they had begun a battery against the great gate of the city. In the mean while they fired almost without intermission, from their small arms on that gate, and the MUHLENSCHANTZ; notwithstanding which, we had but one dragoon wounded.

Early this century, the anonymous translation of this history was tentatively attributed by scholars to Henry Fielding, on the grounds of external evidence.[3]

In the 1970s, the use of computer-generated concordances of texts by Fielding had eventually yielded a list of favourite words and phrases, sometimes linked to favoured positions, which promised to be helpful indicators for any doubtful works attributed to this author. The most obvious candidate for a positive identification was the anonymous *Shamela*, long thought to be by Fielding, and results for this work were very positive.

But it was the case for Fielding's translation of *Charles XII* which seemed to offer unique possibilities for examining the validity of attribution of authorship by quantitative methods of analysing language: here was a text where faithful translation was essential, so that any linguistic traits characteristic of Fielding found in the translation would be important in attributing authorship. An examination of the work was undertaken, and this project, carried out in 1977–8, and based on statistical probability of selected usages of language, did indeed offer some positive conclusions. The results supported the suggested authorship by Fielding.[4]

Following this, further work on Fielding continued in the 1980s, leading to collaboration with the distinguished Fielding scholar, Professor Martin Battestin, of the University of Virginia. The project involved the attribution of forty-one pseudonymous essays mainly published in the eighteenth-century journal *The Craftsman* and attributed by Professor Battestin to Henry Fielding, on internal evidence, i.e. literary grounds. After some years of collaborative effort, significant statistical probabilities were established in support of Professor Battestin's claims for most of these essays, and in 1989 the results were published in a book.[5]

However, the development of QSUM since the date of that publication means that work on attributing anonymous works to an author can now achieve a degree of probability so overwhelming that it is likely to satisfy any remaining doubts. Some critics were reluctant to accept the sound – but inevitably less sensitive – statistical tests which had supported the attribution of *New Essays by Henry Fielding*. It is gratifying to report that none of those pseudonymous essays which has since been analysed by QSUM has failed the positive attributions made by those earlier statistical methods, and in due course, all the essays will be tested.[6] It has also now become possible to go back to *Charles XII* to see whether conclusive proof can be provided by new QSUM tests. This would, after all, be an especially interesting case.

The example of Muriel Spark and the dominant editorial 'fingerprint' suggested that a translator's 'fingerprint', too, would survive in a translation. Although a piece compiled by an editor in the same language after an interview is different from the task of translating a given text from another language, yet there are comparable features. Another person's actual utterance is being partly paraphrased, whether by an editor or by a translator, and the original utterance, in re-presentation, is being 'filtered through' someone else's language habits, and thus subtly and unconsciously altered (*formally*, not in substance).

The first thing to do, as usual, was to establish that it was possible to obtain a homogeneous graph for a sample taken from the translation. Figure MH-1 gives the first result of twenty-nine sentences from the English translation of *Charles XII*.

• **All Figures which include samples from *Charles XII* are coded Figures MH-, for 'Military History'.**

As the reader should by now be able to judge, Figure MH-1 is a consistent chart by the *23lw* test, indicating homogeneous authorship.

Another habit also produced a useful result shown in Figure MH-2. This chart is equally encouraging, giving another homogeneous result, this time by the *23lw+ivw* test. In both these charts, analysed by different habits, this sample of the work is clearly the work of one translator.

Before proceeding further, it is proper here to consider what constitutes a sentence in an eighteenth-century text. Leaving aside the problem of

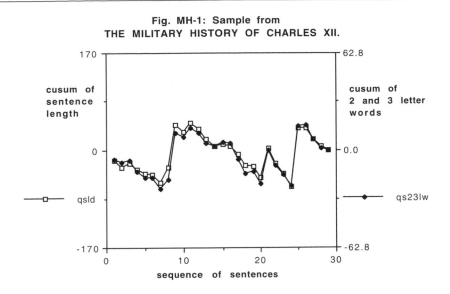

Figure MH-1: The habit of using two- and three-letter words in twenty-nine sentences from the translated text of *The Military History of Charles XII* taken from Vol. II (94–97), beginning 'The 15th, in the morning, we saw three ladders . . .' to '. . . and killed them by the waterside.'

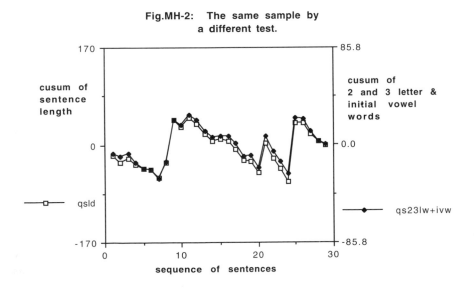

Figure MH-2: The habit of using two- and three-letter words and initial vowel words in the same twenty-nine sentences.

compositors' eccentricities (no small matter in early publishing, where type-setters introduced colons and semi-colons at will), prose writing in the eighteenth century tended anyway towards lengthy sentences. The above sample from *Charles XII* has an average sentence length of thirty-three words, and in fact some of the sentences were much longer than that. When the analyst sets out to work with routine samples of text of the recommended length of twenty-five to thirty sentences, care must be taken that any one sample should not be so overwhelmingly long that fine detail will be ironed out. (A useful reminder is that the longer the textual material, the less sensitive the resulting test is likely be.)

A sample which is 958 words long can be as long as some published articles or essays – a modern reviewer often works to a brief of 800 to 1,000 words. Accordingly, four of the longer sentences in the above sample (totalling 388 words) were deleted from the text, and the remaining sample of twenty-five sentences newly analysed. The result is given in Figure MH-3. The occasional 'blips', for the usual reasons, make the resulting chart look ragged, but it is a homogeneous sample of utterance (as later combined charts will confirm).

Fig. MH-3: The same sample edited to a smaller length.

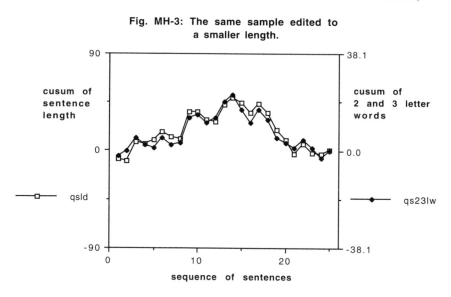

Figure MH-3: The habit of using two- and three-letter words in the same sample reduced from twenty-nine to twenty-five sentences (570 words).

The next task was to obtain a homogeneous sample from a text by Henry Fielding. His novel *Joseph Andrews* (Wesleyan text) was chosen as a control, and several samples were tested by QSUM, all samples being homogeneous by the method. Figure HF-1 is a representative chart for Fielding's utterance. In this very regular QSUM-chart, the reader's attention needs to be drawn to the

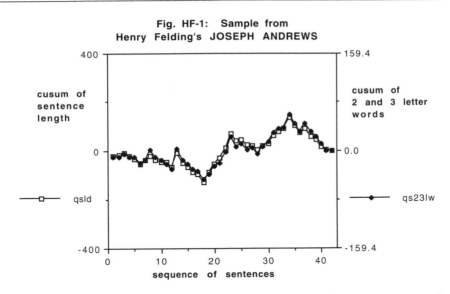

Figure HF-1: The habit of using two- and three-letter words in forty-two sentences of Henry Fielding's *Joseph Andrews*, Book I (21–6), starting 'To wave a circumstance . . .' and ending '. . . Perseverance in Innocence and Industry'.

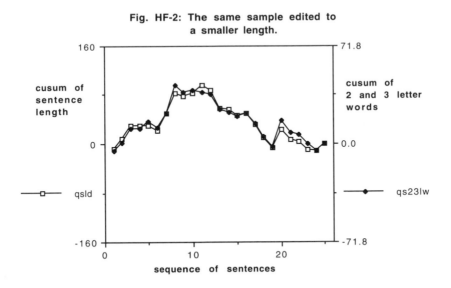

Figure HF-2: The same habit in the same sample reduced to twenty-five sentences totalling (881 words of the original.)

number of sentences, forty-two, relative to the number of words, 2,035. A sample of 2,000-plus words can be the length of a complete essay (for example, of one of the *New Essays* discovered by Professor Battestin). This is, in other words, a very long sample. That in itself does not invalidate the excellent result, but the same stricture applies as to the earlier sample from *Charles XII:* the larger the sample, the more detail is lost.

The reduction of the sample from forty-two sentences to the conventional sample number of twenty-five sentences more than halved the number of words to a total of 881. It has been pointed out by members of an academic audience on different occasions that sentences in various QSUM examples displayed need not be sequential, and that they would produce the same consistency if analysed in random order. This is true, and the twenty-five selected sentences were not chosen sequentially but in two segments from the original sample: seventeen sentences from the beginning (sentences 1–18, but omitting sentence 13, at 107 words, an abnormally long sentence); and another eight sentences from the end of the sample, sentences 35–42.

This produced the chart shown as Figure HF-2. This is a satisfactory homogeneous sample of Fielding's utterance. The 'blip' at sentence 11 is insignificant and is caused by sentence 13, which had only seven words. Such a short sentence, so well below the average for this particular sample, has begun to drag the *qs23lw* line downwards (the average sentence length is 35.14 words for the reduced sample).

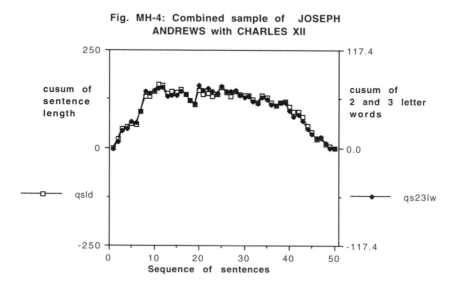

Fig. MH-4: Combined sample of JOSEPH ANDREWS with CHARLES XII

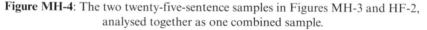

Figure MH-4: The two twenty-five-sentence samples in Figures MH-3 and HF-2, analysed together as one combined sample.

The question then became, since homogeneous samples from both *Charles XII* and *Joseph Andrews* had been obtained, what would happen when these were analysed together?

The two 25-sentence samples were therefore analysed in a combined sample, this being the crucial test of whether the translated material was consistent with the control test from Fielding's *Joseph Andrews*. The resulting chart is shown as Figure MH-4. This would seem a most heartening result to the scholar wishing to prove that Fielding was indeed the translator of the French text. In a combined analysis, the two samples cannot be distinguished: they must be homogeneous.

However, it is one thing to show that an anonymous translated sample is indistinguishable from the supposed translator, in this case an eighteenth-century writer. Can the same sample also be shown to separate significantly in a combined sample using utterance by other eighteenth-century writers?

In an attempt to establish the link with Fielding even more closely, four other eighteenth-century writers were chosen for analysing with the sample from *Charles XII* – Amhurst, Smollett, Swift and Steele. Further tests would bring the added advantage of introducing other prose genres into the project. The Smollett sample would, like the Fielding sample, be taken from a novel (*Roderick Random*), but samples from the other writers would be from various kinds of essay.

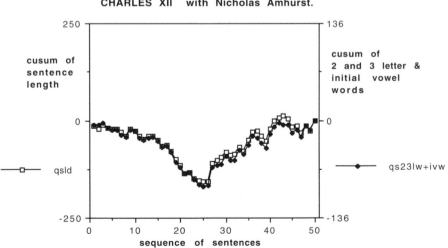

Fig.MH-5: Combined sample of CHARLES XII with Nicholas Amhurst.

Figure MH-5: A combined analysis of two samples: the twenty-five sentences from *Charles XII* followed by twenty-five sentences written by Amhurst, taken from *The Craftsman* (2 February 1733–4) starting 'There is such an agreeable Mixture of Horatian Salt . . .' to '. . . does not come within the Due Bound of Liberty.'

The first combined test was with a sample of the writing of Nicholas Amhurst, taken from an essay in *The Craftsman*, of which he was the editor at the time when the pseudonymous essays were published. The resulting chart is Figure MH-5. The QSUM consistency for the first twenty-five sentences, the sample of *Charles XII*, is pronounced (thus confirming that the earlier 'blips' of MH-3 were indeed anomalies).

Thereafter there appears to be some loosening in the combined chart from the point where the Amhurst sample joins the *Charles XII* sample at sentence 26. It is pronounced enough to suggest mixed authorship; but it could be argued that the separation is not *very* pronounced compared, say, with others already encountered by the reader in earlier chapters (the correspondence of the lines even seeming to the inexperienced eye 'too close for comfort' – or, more scientifically, for statistical probability).

An experienced analyst would be satisfied, but critical doubt may persist for the novice, since from visual inspection alone, the separation may look insignificant.

What of the other combined samples? These now follow, and the next analysis combined the *Charles XII* sample with a sample of Smollett's writing, taken from his novel *Roderick Random*.

The resulting chart is shown as Figure MH-6. This result looks even closer.

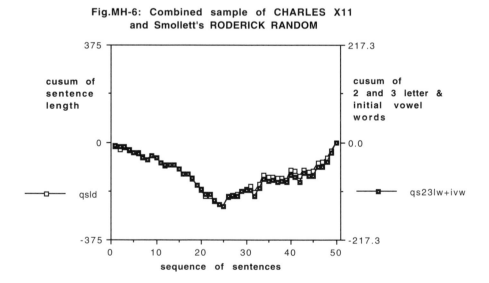

Fig.MH-6: Combined sample of CHARLES X11 and Smollett's RODERICK RANDOM

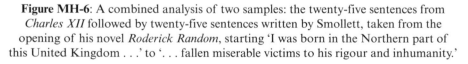

Figure MH-6: A combined analysis of two samples: the twenty-five sentences from *Charles XII* followed by twenty-five sentences written by Smollett, taken from the opening of his novel *Roderick Random*, starting 'I was born in the Northern part of this United Kingdom . . .' to '. . . fallen miserable victims to his rigour and inhumanity.'

There *is* a displacement, but here the slight separation after the first 25-sentence sample looks even more tentative than it was in the case of the Amhurst combined sample. From visual inspection alone, it must seem difficult to say with any certainty that these two samples could be distinguished. Despite the loosening in the correspondence of the two lines after sentence 25, where the *Charles XII* sample ends, the trained analyst would want to go back and look at the text in this case (which, of course, would show what we already know, that these are two samples from separate works). On the whole, the combined analysis appears to fail to show a significant separation. Given the certainty that Smollett had no connection with this translation, why was there not a positive break in the chart?

But first, would a sample from Jonathan Swift yield more positive results? The answer to that question lies in the next chart, Figure MH-7. The project now seemed as if it might be running into trouble: the results using authors other than Fielding were beginning to resemble life in Alice's *Wonderland* – 'curiouser and curiouser'. In this combined analysis, the result showed that the two samples were almost completely indistinguishable by visual inspection, with just a faint loosening at sentences 25–9.

It may be suggested that those new to the method, faced with such a result, would now be rather confused: indeed, might begin to question if there was

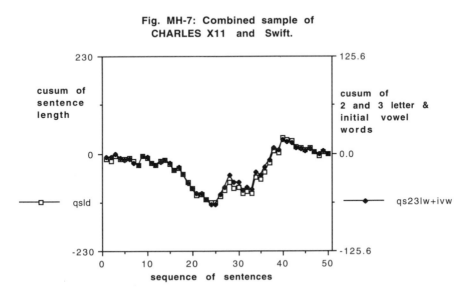

Fig. MH-7: Combined sample of CHARLES X11 and Swift.

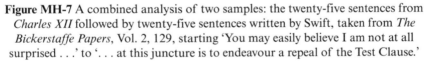

Figure MH-7 A combined analysis of two samples: the twenty-five sentences from *Charles XII* followed by twenty-five sentences written by Swift, taken from *The Bickerstaffe Papers*, Vol. 2, 129, starting 'You may easily believe I am not at all surprised ...' to '... at this juncture is to endeavour a repeal of the Test Clause.'

any eighteenth-century writer who, on the basis of QSUM-analysis, had not had a hand in translating *The Military History of Charles XII*.

Fortunately, the answer is in the affirmative, as the next combined analysis with essayist Richard Steele, the last of the four writers selected for comparison, shows in Figure MH-8. (Obtaining a sample of twenty-five sentences for Steele involved using *two* of his essays from *The Reader*.) The usual regularity for the *Charles XII* sample is easily observable; but thereafter, at sentence 25, there is a significant cross of the *qs23lw+ivw* line below the *qsld* line, and another cross above it at sentence 34, with a six-sentence separation at sentences 36 to 42.

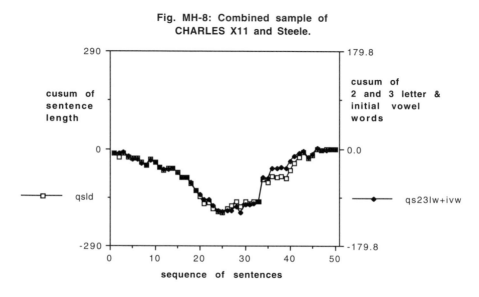

Fig. MH-8: Combined sample of CHARLES X11 and Steele.

Figure MH-8: A combined analysis of two samples: the twenty-five sentences from *Charles XII* followed by twenty-five sentences written by Steele, taken from two letters in *The Reader*: 30 April 1714, starting 'Though I have not the Honour to be acquainted with you . . .' to '. . . one of the newspapers of Yesterday has it thus', and 7 May 1714, starting 'The Love by which your Paper you seem to have . . .' to '. . . than to your own selves and your own families'.

Here, then, is an unequivocal separation: when the twenty-five sentences written by Steele follow the twenty-five sentences of *Charles XII* , the resulting analysis produces significant separation, as the reader can recognize.

To summarize the project at this stage: it now seemed that *Charles XII*, could have had, courtesy of QSUM-charts, four possible translators – Henry Fielding, Nicholas Amhurst, Tobias Smollett and Jonathan Swift: at the very least, strong visual separation expected from using these writers as a comparison did not *seem* to have been found for three of them. Only one writer had revealed clear distinction in the combined test, Richard Steele, in Figure MH-8.

Readers will realize that there has to be an explanation for these results, and that a happier ending than they suggest lies further down the road of understanding cusum analysis.

There are two reasons for the results just illustrated in Figures MH-5, MH-6 and MH-7, which apparently fail to show the normal unequivocal 'spring-apart'.

The first reason is that all the charts in question contained large amounts of cumulative sum information derived from exceptionally long texts containing very long sentences. As indicated earlier, too much information creates a tendency to lose sensitivity and to flatten out differences.

In the Amhurst text, for instance, ten of the selected sample of twenty-five sentences were over forty-five words long, making more than 450 words for just ten sentences. Compare that with an excerpt from a Muriel Spark novel under analysis, in which the number of words in a sequence of sentences analysed ran: 7, 8 6, 9, 4, 10, and the six sentences amounted to just forty-three words. The sentences by Amhurst are four to five times as long on average.

But there is a second and far more important reason for the failure of significant separation, which one would have expected from combining samples by authors already known to be different. Both the *Charles XII* translator and Henry Fielding proved to be homogeneous by two tests: two- and three-letter words on their own (*23lw*), and also two- and three-letter and initial vowel words (*23lw+ivw*).

When the *Charles XII* sample was tested with the other eighteenth-century writers in the charts above, the test used was the *23lw+ivw test*, and by this test the disputed sample could not be strongly distinguished from the selected samples of three out of the four writers selected for comparison.

So, when trying to establish whether a particular writer has written an anonymous piece, the lesson is clear:

• **It is essential to use the discriminating test for the author who is the subject of the enquiry.**

Here the subject is Fielding – we are seeking to determine whether Henry Fielding had the consistency of language habit which would make him indistinguishable from the anonymous translator of *Charles XII* (whereas QSUM testing with other authors would decisively prove that consistency was not the same, so that they could *not* have been the author – as in the D. H. Lawrence example). For Fielding, as had been found in numerous other QSUM-tests where samples from Fielding have been combined with other eighteenth-century writers it is the *23lw* test which is the positive discriminator. No other writer tested uses that habit consistently in just the way that Fielding does. Therefore, that is the test which should be applied – and in fact was used for the *Joseph Andrews* and *Charles XII* combined-sample chart shown as Figure MH-4. It may be pertinent to advise the new chart-reader to remember always to check the habit being used in the charts under scrutiny. Some readers may have noticed already that the habit used for the combined samples in Figures MH-5, MH-6, MH-7 and MH-8 was different from the one used in the chart which had positively attributed Fielding as the translator in Figure MH-4.

It may be objected that a combined analysis of *Charles XII* and Richard Steele (Figure MH-8) *did* actually produce a satisfactory separation by the *23lw+ivw* test. True; there is no suggestion that any and every writer will produce an indistinguishable combined chart by the 'wrong' test, in this case the *23lw+ivw* test. Steele is clearly distinguishable by it, Swift close enough to be indistinguishable, and the other two unsatisfactory in combined analysis. The point to be grasped at this stage is that if a non-positive result is obtained where a positive separation is expected, the first thing to do is to check is whether the decisive test has been used.

Finding this not to be the case in the present project, then, the right course of action became:

(a) to use the correct discriminating test – the Fielding discriminator, the *23lw* test and;

(b) to reduce the over-long samples to a more sensitive size.

One very useful method of doing the latter is by breaking up long combined samples into a series of *alternating* shorter samples. This can be done by following a small number of sentences (between four to eight) of one author with a similar number of the second author, until your sample is completely used up. What is actually being done is to run a series of mini-tests one after another – as was the process carried out as the final chart in the D. H. Lawrence test case.[9]

The next four charts, Figures MH-9 to MH-12, show the resulting charts of 'alternating combined tests' for the four comparison authors. The breaking up of the original combined analyses was deliberately varied, so as to provide as great a number of examples as possible. The alternating samples are given below:

Sentences of	**/ Sentences of**	**Sentences of**	**/ Sentences of**
Charles XII	/ Amhurst	*Charles XII*	/ Smollett
4	5	8	8
4	4	8	8
4	4	9	9
(Total: 25 sentences)		(Total: 50 sentences)	

Sentences of / Sentences of		Sentences of / Sentences of	
Charles XII / Swift		*Charles XII* / Steele	
5	5	5	5
5	5	6	4
5	5	5	5
(Total: 30 sentences)		5	
		(Total: 35 sentences)	

First, then, the combined alternating sequences of *Charles XII* and Amhurst, in Figure MH-9. The lack of homogeneity here is obvious. There is now marked separation along the whole chart until the very last few sentences. This can clearly be seen to be what it is, a text of mixed authorship.

Fig. MH-9: Six alternate samples of Amhurst and CHARLES XII.

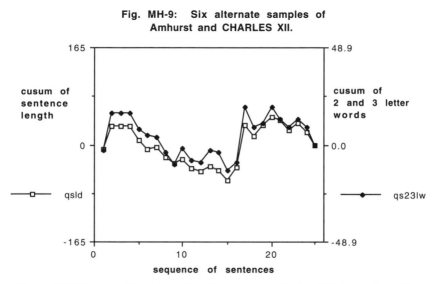
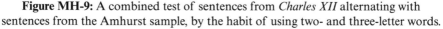

Figure MH-9: A combined test of sentences from *Charles XII* alternating with sentences from the Amhurst sample, by the habit of using two- and three-letter words.

Next we move on, in Figure MH-10, to an alternating test using sentences from the Smollett sample of *Roderick Random*. The nature of the combined sample has been randomly altered, so as to give a variety of examples. Here the sequence of sentences chosen as alternates has been increased in number to virtually double the number of sentences in the previous Amhurst 'alternates' test. Starting off at a sequence of eight sentences of *Charles XII*, there is brief homogeneity at the start because there are enough sentences to produce some correspondence; but soon the lines diverge and remain separated until the last sequence of nine sentences by Smollett finally brings them together again.

Once again, this is visibly a text of mixed authorship. Whoever translated this sample of *Charles XII* , it was not Smollett.

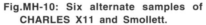

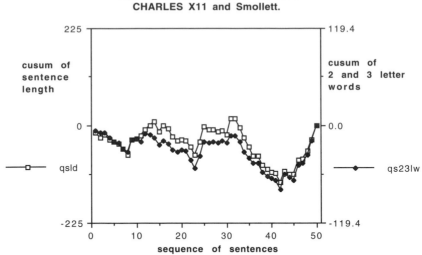

Figure MH-10: The same habit in a combined test of sentences from *Charles XII* alternating with sentences from the Smollett sample from *Roderick Random.*

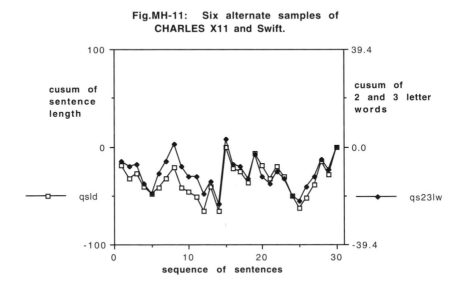

Figure MH-11: A combined test of sentences from *Charles XII* alternating with sentences from the sample from Swift, analysed by the same habit.

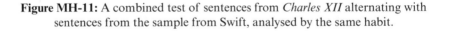

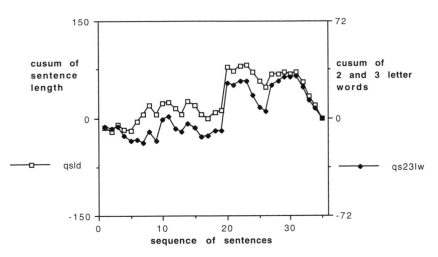

Fig. MH-12: Seven alternating samples of CHARLES XII and Steele.

Figure MH-12: A combined test of sentences from *Charles XII* alternating with sentences from the sample of Steele.

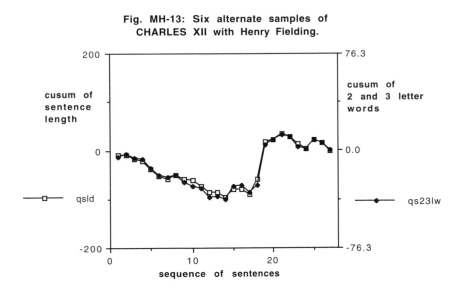

Fig. MH-13: Six alternate samples of CHARLES XII with Henry Fielding.

Figure MH-13: A combined test totalling twenty-seven sentences from *Charles XII* alternating with Henry Fielding's *Joseph Andrews* (*23lw* test).

The next test of alternate passages was compiled from the sample of Swift given above, and resulted in Figure MH-11. Yet another form of selected small sequences, this time all of equal size, was used. The discontinuity is obvious. This is a sample of mixed utterance by two authors, as we indeed know it to be.

Finally, although the original analysis with Steele has already shown a satisfactory separation, a test of alternating passages was included for the sake of completeness in Figure MH-12. Apart from the closing sequence of the five-sentence sequence from *Charles XII*, the separation is massive throughout. The combined sample has been shown to be of mixed authorship.

The crucial question now becomes, what happens when you make a similar sequence of alternating small sequences of sentences from *Joseph Andrews* and *Charles XII*? Two such combined analyses were made, one of twenty-seven sentences, Figure MH-13, and one of fifty sentences, Figure MH-14.

A sequence as low as four to five sentences is almost as low as the analyst would want to go in doing a test of this kind. (A slight 'blip' of four to five sentences due to anomalies could be quite satisfactorily absorbed in a long sample of 50–100 sentences.) Yet here we are asking that a very short sequence of five sentences from a translated sample of a military history, with the attendant constraints we have examined, should remain consistent with similar short sequences of five – or even four – sentences from a work of fiction. Indeed, the whole sequence of sentences in the combined sample is only twenty-seven, close to the recommended size of sample for testing.

Despite all this, the chart in Figure MH-13 shows evidence of a consistent habit. There is some loosening in the middle section (always the most sensitive part of a chart), but well within the parameters of statistical significance. If the reader will look back at Figures MH-9 to MH-12, the difference will be immediately apparent. This is a homogeneous chart.

When a longer analysis of ten samples comprising fifty sentences was made, again of very short sentence-sequences, and chosen in a very random manner, the result is shown in Figure MH-14. Here the much larger amount of textual material has been able to show even more positive consistency than in Figure MH-13. This is a chart where a consistent habit of using two- and three-letter words has been demonstrated making the two samples indistinguishable.

All the 'alternate' tests by the other four eighteenth-century writers have shown clear evidence of non-homogeneity except for the last two, where the interwoven sentences-samples are clearly from a homogeneous source, namely Henry Fielding.

It is worth showing here the actual combined text(s) used for the Fielding and *Charles XII* alternating combined sample, simply as a reading exercise. An attempt to read what follows (where the *Joseph Andrews* text is from the twenty-five-sentence sample which comprises the same two separated segments

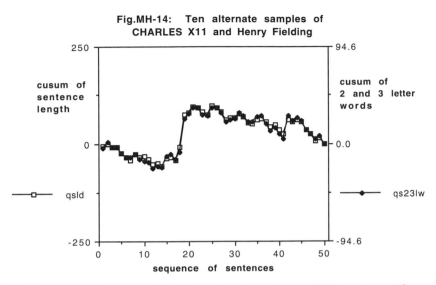

Figure MH-14: A longer combined test of sentences (total of fifty sentences) from *Charles XII* alternating with sentences from *Joseph Andrews*, by the same habit.

of text used in Figure HF-2) as if it were one sequential text only shows that the difference between the two varieties of writing could not be more clear.

Combined Alternating Text of Samples from Fielding's *Joseph Andrews* and from *The Military History of Charles XII* Comprising Figure MH-13

The poor Wretch, who lay motionless a long time, just began to recover his Senses as a Stage-Coach came by. The Postillion hearing a Man's Groans, stopt his Horses, and told the Coachman 'he was certain there was a dead Man lying in the Ditch, for he heard him groan.' 'Go on, Sirrah,' says the Coachman, 'we are confounded late, and have no time to look after dead Men.' A Lady, who heard what the Postillion said, and likewise heard the Groan, called eagerly to the Coachman, 'to stop and see what was the matter.' Upon which he bid the Postillion 'alight, and look into the Ditch.' /// The 15th, in the morning we saw there three ladders, which the enemy had abandoned. We gave one sol a day more to every man, on account of their being obliged to work night and day. The enemy forbore firing; but took possession of the side of the WARTA, both with foot and horse, and drew a line of eighty paces round about the bridge, among the ruins of the suburb, which had been burned down. This line they furnished with gabions, and we observed they had begun a battery against the great gate intermission, from their small arms on that gate, and the MUHLENSCHANTZ; notwithstanding which, we had but one dragoon wounded. /// He did so, and returned, 'that there was a Man sitting upright as naked as ever he was born. 'O Jesus,' cryd the Lady, 'A naked Man – Dear Coachman, drive on and leave him.' Upon this the Gentleman got out of the Coach; and Joseph begged them, 'to have Mercy upon him: For that he had been robbed, and almost beaten to death.' 'Robbed,' cries an old Gentleman; 'Let us make all the haste imaginable, or we shall be robbed too.' A young Man, who belonged to the Law answered, 'he wished they had past by without taking any Notice: But that now they might be proved to have been last in his Company; if he should die, they might be called to some account for his Murther. /// The Governor gave orders, the same day, to all the citizens who had their houses most exposed to the fire of that battery, to cover them with dung and earth. At night I was informed that a great noise of workmen was heard behind the stable, near the castle. Upon which I ordered immediately pots of flaming pitch to be thrown, in order to discover what they were about; when I perceived they had placed a great quantity of gabions all along the ditch, in order to raise a battery; and thereupon ordered a Lieutenant and forty men to reinforce that quarter, and fire upon the labourers all night. As it came into my head, that the enemy, after having taken possession of the other side of the Warta, had entirely cut off our communication with the country, and that, after they had, by the help of their batteries, beat down the great gate, and rased the parapet of Muhlenschantz, which they might accomplish in one day, they would not fail to seize upon the bridge, and extend their whole line close to the water, not to mention that they would ruin the only mill we had remaining, and prevent our very horses from being led to water, I proposed to Meyerfield to burn down the bridge. /// Joseph Andrews , the Hero of our ensuing History, was esteemed to be the only Son of Gaffar and Gammer Andrews, and Brother to the illustrious Pamela, whose Virtue is at present so famous. As to his Ancestors, we have searched with great Diligence, but little Success: being unable to trace them farther than his Great Grandfather, who, as an elderly Person in the Parish remembers to have heard his Father say, was an excellent Cudgel-player. Whether he had any Ancestors before this, we must leave to the Opinion of our curious Reader, finding nothing of sufficient Certainty to relie on. However, we cannot omit inserting an Epitaph which an ingenious Friend of ours hath communicated. /// To which he replied, that, as it was an affair of consequence, I should do well to consult the colonels. Accordingly, having sent for them to my apartment, and given them my reasons for this proposal, they received it with applause; and even added, that, when the enemy had battered down the tower of the great gate, it would be impossible to burn the bridge if we would. In consequence of which resolution, Captain Palman had orders that very night to set fire to it, which was immediately put in execution. The enemy placed certain cannon that day on the battery, near the convent of Carmelites. /// [end of Figure MH-13]

To the ordinary reader, this is obviously a text of meaningless utterance. It does not, as we would say, 'make sense' as a single communication from one human being to another. Yet by cusum analysis it can be shown to be homogeneous.

Clearly, Henry Fielding is the only writer to have survived the test of alternating samples with the text of *The Military History of Charles XII*, which supports the suggestion that he is its translator.

APPENDIX

Analysing and cross-checking texts in order to produce QSUM-charts is a time-consuming procedure. No single researcher can do more than take samples of a three-volume work. However, in the interests of presenting further evidence, to add to the results of the initial tests a single sample was taken from each of Volumes 1 and 3 of *Charles XII*. These were chosen completely at random, by opening each volume somewhere in the middle.

The sample from Volume 1 (103–5) comprised twenty-two sentences beginning 'The King was not at first content with this capitulation . . .' to '. . . faithful and exact relation written in High Dutch.'

The sample from Volume 3 (99–102) comprised twenty-two sentences beginning 'The thirteenth, the army proceeded two lengths to Cologne . . .', to '. . . having passed over, returned to join his Majesty.'

The two charts resulting from analysing these in further tests are shown below (coded 'App-' for 'Appendix').

First, the result, in Figure App-1, of a combined analysis of the sample from Volume 1 followed by a sample from Fielding's *Joseph Andrews* – the **final** twenty-two sentences of the forty-two-sentence sample shown in Figure HF-1 above.

Second, the result of adding to this combined analysis a third sample, from *Charles XII*, Volume 3, thus effectively making a 'sandwich' comprising the two samples from Volumes 1 and 3 with the Fielding sample of twenty-two sentences in the middle – this is shown in Figure App-2.

Figure App-1 is a significantly consistent chart for the use of two- and three-letter words, with a very slight loosening in the middle, and indicates that the combined sample is homogeneous.

Once again, this is a satisfactory QSUM-chart, well within the parameters of statistical probability, showing evidence of single authorship. There is little doubt that, if combined with the samples of the other four eighteenth-century writers chosen for purposes of comparison, there would be significant separations.

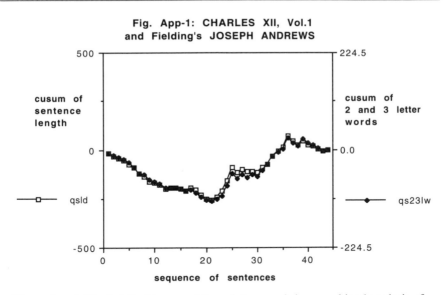

Figure App-1: The habit of two- and three-letter words in a combined analysis of twenty-two sentences from the *Military History of Charles XII*, Volume 1, followed by twenty-two sentences from Fielding's *Joseph Andrews*.

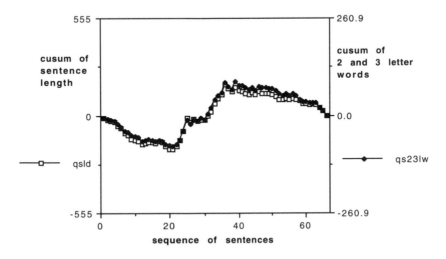

Figure App-2: The same habit in a 'sandwich' analysis of two samples from Vols. 1 and 3 of *Charles XII*, with twenty-two sentences from *Joseph Andrews* inserted.

Chapter 6

QSUM AND YOUNG LANGUAGE:
THE UTTERANCE OF CHILDREN
– and Helen Keller as Plagiarist?

Once convinced – by the very wide range of testing carried out in its development – of the validity of statistical analysis of language by the cusum technique, any researcher might consider the proposition that all individuals will use language in a personally consistent way to be a reasonable one (no exceptions having been found to date).[1]

If it is true that every individual's utterance can be recognized by cusum analysis, one important question this raises is the age by which such identification becomes possible. How soon after learning language does a child's speech and writing become personally consistent?

The Analysis of Children's Utterance

A critic who examined the technique in a forensic setting focused on the nature of the stability claimed for the habits shown in QSUM-charts, and commented: 'If no developmental process is implied this leads to the challenging suggestion that a young child would reveal the same "habits" when grown to adulthood.'[2] As it happened, I had myself been investigating children's written language for some time prior to the publication of the report which included this comment.

Results from the work so far undertaken do indeed suggest that children's personal utterance can be identified by cusum analysis from a very early age. The propositions arising from research into this area are three: by means of cusum analysis of sentences

(a) Children can be shown to have consistent language habits.
(b) Children can be shown to differ recognizably from each other in their writing.
(c) In the limited research undertaken, QSUM consistency is an early development and does seem to remain stable into adulthood.

There is one uniquely useful example of a child both learning language and communicating via the written word – moreover in published text – through which we can confidently explore linguistic development, and this is the case of Helen Keller.

The Case of Helen Keller

The story of Helen Keller's acquisition of language is well-known and expressed in her own words in the book comprising her autobiographical essay, a selection of her letters from the age of 7+ when she started to 'talk', and a further commentary by her teacher, Miss Annie Sullivan.[3] (Helen Keller became deaf-mute from the age of eighteen months, after an illness.)

After Miss Sullivan undertook to teach her, she first learnt language first like any *sign*-using organism, using words in the classic behaviourist way of stimulus-response.

It was in May, 1887, that she made the breakthrough to the *symbolic* use of words: she received both a tactile stimulus (the sense-impression of water flowing from a well near her home in Tuscumbia, Alabama), and, simultaneously, the symbol for the word 'water', finger-spelt into her hand by her teacher, Annie Sullivan. The novelist and writer on language, Walker Percy, has argued that from these two stimuli received simultaneously, Helen made that triadic 'coupling' (as he has called it) between a concrete apprehension and an abstract symbol which is the characteristic mark of human language.[4] Leaving aside speculation about what exactly had occurred that day, it is undeniable that Helen had learnt that everything had a *name*, and at once wanted to know what the name for everything was.

Being blind and deaf, Helen's only mode of communication at first was by the hand-language taught her by Annie Sullivan, which was her substitute for the acquisition of spoken language familiar to us in every ordinary child's development. Helen used hand-language; or else, for communicating with anyone other than her beloved 'Teacher' (as she called her), she wrote letters. She was taught to write by 'Teacher' very quickly, and three and a half months after acquiring language, in July, 1887, she started to write simple letters.

In Helen Keller's book, there are seven letters to correspondents printed for 1887. These early letters are simple, very short, and unpunctuated.

It is easy to discern, in these letters, the new fascination with naming which is characteristic of the child who has just acquired language; indeed, the letters are full of typical 'naming' observations about her family and her home. In the sixth letter, Helen is defining her discoveries about the world, and enjoying the new knowledge – the heuristic push – provided by the linguistic tool: 'photographer does make pictures, carpenter does build new houses, gardener does dig and hoe ground', and so on. All children begin their language use (after the babbling stage) by using naming or defining sentences. Even single-word utterances are virtual 'naming' sentences, the accompanying 'pointing-at-in-context' being a substitute for the connectives (i.e. the function words) of syntax.

Saying something *about* what the child has learnt to name, i.e. making an assertion or asking a question, comes as a secondary feature. It is this secondary development that calls for verbs, prepositions, pronouns, conjunctions, and connectives of all kinds: it calls, in other words, for structure (or syntax). It is tempting to speculate how far QSUM draws on syntactic form for its success, since it is consistency in the use of these function words that proves so useful as an attributive measure.

Analysing Helen Keller's Writing

Since the first stage of language acquisition is the *naming* stage, then the preponderance of nouns in the 1887 letters seemed to offer scope for cusum analysis by the use of two- and three-letter words and nouns. However, the average sentence lengths of the letters was so small (six to nine words), and the dominance of the *23lw*+nouns so large (60 to 80 per cent), that the results, though promising, were statistically predictable, and thus this aspect of early analysis was abandoned as unsuitable.

By the time six months had elapsed since her first brief letter to her mother in July 1887 – that is, by January 1888 when she was aged seven and a half – we find Helen Keller able to write longer and more fluent letters. Analysis of her letters for the year 1888 shows a fully consistent use of the two most common tests: that of using words of two and three letters, *23lw*, and that of two- and three-letter words and words starting with a vowel, *23lw+ivw*.

Illustrations will be shown of letters written throughout that year, starting with Figure HK-1. This shows the results of analysing the full texts of a letter written to Miss Sarah Tomlinson (2 January 1888, from 'I am happy to write to you this morning' to 'I do love good girls'), and one written to Dr Edward Everett Hale (15 February 1888, from 'I am happy to write you a letter this morning' to 'I am tired') in a combined analysis.[5] This is a reasonably consistent result, with a few small 'blips' here and there (since her language use was so new, one must bear in mind the possibility of occasional help with a word or phrase); but there can be little doubt that this is *substantially* a homogeneous chart.

Next, the combined analysis, Figure HK-2, of two letters from later in the year, one to Mr Michael Anagnos, Director of the Perkins Institute for the Blind (3 May 1888, from 'I am glad to write to you this morning' to 'I send many kisses and hugs with this letter'), and one to Mr Morrison Heady, Helen's uncle (1 October 1888, from 'I think you will be very glad to receive a letter from your dear little friend Helen' to 'Now I am tired and I will rest').[6] This will be at once seen to be a very satisfactory chart, with a consistent habit which confirms homogeneity.

The next combined chart, however, for the same October letter combined with one written to Mrs Sophia Hopkins (on 11 December 1888, from 'I have just fed my dear little pigeon' to 'I hope you will come to see me soon and stay a

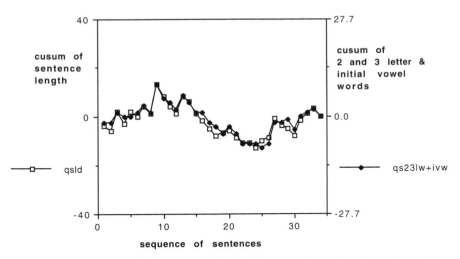

Figure HK-1: The habit of using two- and three-letter words and words starting with a vowel in a combined sample of two letters written by Helen Keller on 2 January 1888 (twenty-three sentences) and 15 February 1888 (eleven sentences).

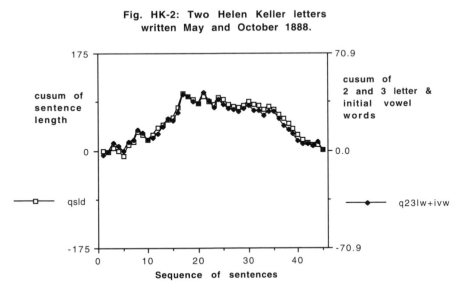

Figure HK-2: The same habit in a combined sample of two letters written by Helen Keller on 3 May 1888 (nineteen sentences) and 1 October 1888 (twenty-six sentences).

long time') produced an unsatisfactory result, in Figure HK-3.[7] Something in this combined chart has disturbed the former consistency of the October letter, and caused a separation. The problem must lie with the December letter. Figure HK-4 shows the result of analysing the single sample of the December letter. Something goes very evidently wrong with the middle of this letter. Notice the cross-over at about sentence thirteen. The visible separation suggests that there must be extraneous material between sentences 8 and either 15 or 16.

This is a useful demonstration calling for application of the rule stressed throughout this book: when there is apparent non-homogeneity

• **it is always necessary to go back to the text**.

On examining the text of the letter, a disparity was found. Count the sentences which track each other – these comprise the first eight, which read as follows:

> I have just fed my dear little pigeon. My brother Simpson gave it to me last Sunday. I named it Annie, for my teacher. My puppy has had his supper and gone to bed. My rabbits are sleeping, too; and very soon I shall go to bed. Teacher is writing letters to her friends. Mother and father and their friends have gone to see a huge furnace. The furnace is to make iron.

But what is 'a furnace' to a blind and deaf child not yet eight years old? The next seven sentences which follow (sentences 9–15) read:

> The iron ore is found in the ground; but it cannot be used until it has been brought to the furnace and melted, and all the dirt taken out, and just the pure iron left. Then it is all ready to be manufactured into engines, stoves, kettles and many other things. Coal is found in the ground too. Many years ago before people came to live on the earth, great trees and tall grasses and huge ferns and all the beautiful flowers covered the earth. When the leaves and the trees fell, the water and the soil covered them; and then more trees grew and fell also, and were buried under water and soil. After they had all been pressed together for many thousands of years the wood grew very hard, like rock, and then it was ready for people to burn. Can you see leaves and ferns and bark on the coal?

There is no need to be a psycho-linguist, or even a trained primary schoolteacher, to see that what Helen has 'written' strongly indicates that she has been surely been consulting a children's information book with the help of 'Teacher'. The increase in sentence length is obvious, and the sentence reading 'Can you see the pattern of the leaf on the coal?' suggests that the source of this factual material was written for sighted children, with an accompanying illustration. As far as 'Teacher' was concerned, she rightly used every opportunity possible to extend both Helen's knowledge and her skill as a correspondent, and in this case, the two aims must have fused.

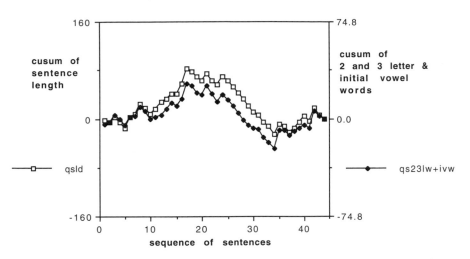

Fig. HK-3: Two Keller letters, written October and December, 1888.

Figure HK-3: The same habit in a combined sample of two letters written by Helen Keller on 1 October 1888 (twenty-six sentences) and on 11 December 1888 (eighteen sentences).

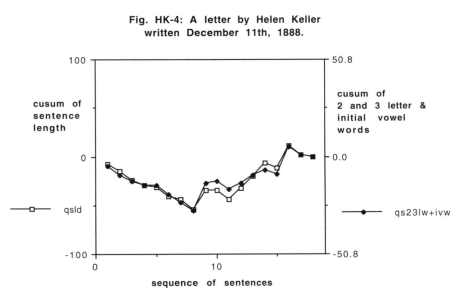

Fig. HK-4: A letter by Helen Keller written December 11th, 1888.

Figure HK-4: The same habit in a sample of the letter written by Helen Keller on 11 December 1888 (eighteen sentences).

The sixteenth sentence of the letter seems a possible composite: 'Men go down into the ground and dig out the coal, and steam-cars take it to the large cities and sell it to people to burn, to make them warm and happy when it is cold out of doors.' As far as 'to burn', the content seems like information provided for Helen; but the last sentiment has much in common with her child's 'effusive' style of writing (it is always possible that she took her stylistic cue from the children's reading material current in her day, which was often rather 'gushing', rather than developing it from inclination).

The last two sentences (17 and 18), which are consistent with the eight sentences which open the letter, are Helen's own. 'Are you very lonely and sad now? I hope you will come to see me soon, and stay a long time.' Removing the interpolation – including the doubtful sentence 16 – leaves us with pure 'Helen Keller utterance'. Thus edited, with the extraneous eight sentences removed, the 11 December letter combines consistently with the letter of 3 May 1888, in Figure HK-5 and the letter of 11 October, 1888, in Figure HK-6.

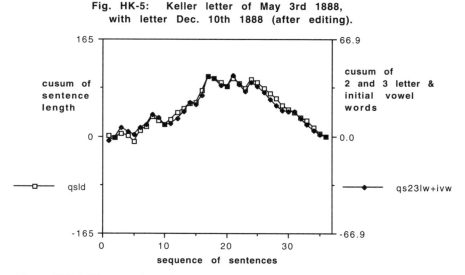

Fig. HK-5: Keller letter of May 3rd 1888, with letter Dec. 10th 1888 (after editing).

sequence of sentences

Figure HK-5: The same habit in a combined sample of the letter of 1 May 1888 and 11 December letter edited to ten sentences.

Figure HK-5 is a satisfactory QSUM-chart. The next chart should be compared with its earlier version in Figure HK-3 which revealed the non-homogeneity of the December letter. Again, this result is now satisfactory.

Before leaving the letters of 1888, it seemed useful to ask whether Helen Keller's utterance remained consistent by cusum analysis throughout the year from January to December 1888. Accordingly, samples were selected from each of the January, May, and October letters (the first fifteen sentences of

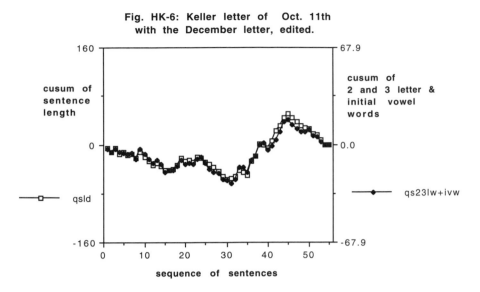

Figure HK-6: The same habit in the combined sample first shown in Figure HK-3, but with the December letter edited to ten sentences.

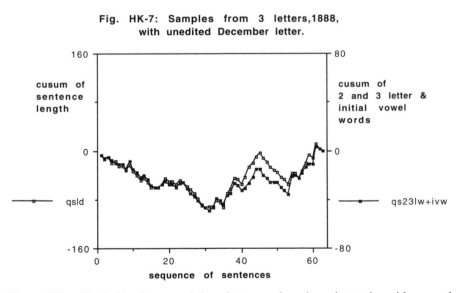

Figure HK-7: The habit of two- and three-letter words and words starting with a vowel in a combined sample of four Keller letters, 2 January, 3 May, 1 October and 11 December (unedited): total of sixty-three sentences.

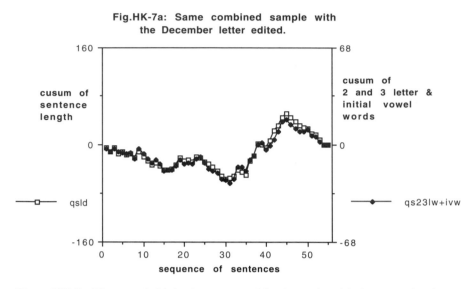

Figure HK-7a: The same habit in the same combined sample, with the December letter edited: total of fifty-five sentences.

each); and the December letter was added first in its unedited form, in Figure HK-7, and then in its edited form, in Figure HK-7a.

Figure HK-7 shows a large separation. The pure Keller utterance continues until sentence 45, but it is noticeable that the extraneous material in the December letter causes a disturbance as early as sentence 40, showing once again that separation does not always occur at the exact point of insertion.

Figure HK-7a next shows the same combined sample with the December letter having been edited. This is now a homogeneous combined sample showing consistency by Helen Keller in the *23lw+ivw* habit for the year 1888.

It is important to be clear about what these particular tests of the December 1888 letter have demonstrated. They have shown that cusum analysis is able to identify precisely the exact 'foreign' material in a letter written by a blind, deaf girl of eight and a half, who has acquired language about eighteen months previously. This seems to me a remarkable achievement for the method, and a great co-incidence if QSUM merely demonstrates a random, arithmetical property of language – as postulated by the critic quoted at the start – rather than truly individual utterance.

It may be objected, by those who are more familiar with judging language in a literary critical way, that one would not expect material from an information book to be consistent with the simple utterance of a child. This would, of course, be a familiar misunderstanding of the way QSUM works by ignoring 'content words' and independent of genre, as we have seen in earlier chapters.

Nevertheless, to address such a misgiving, it remains to ask:

i. whether Helen Keller's utterance can be shown to separate from the writing of another child of a similar age;

ii. whether the eight-year-old Helen remains consistent with the writing of Helen as a mature adult;

iii. whether she clearly separates from another adult – say, her teacher, Annie Sullivan.

i. Helen Keller's Writing Tested Against Another Child's Writing

The first question may be answered by combining thirty-three sentences taken from homogeneous Keller charts (in effect, homogeneous extracts from two letters from the combined sample, those written in October and December, 1888), and analysing them in combination with thirty-two sentences of writing by another child when aged 7+, 'Katherine' (whose own homogenous chart will appear later). In this chart, Figure HK-8, Helen Keller's text comes first and Katherine's second. This chart is clearly one of mixed utterance. Separation occurs in the Keller sample shortly before the new utterance starts, that of the second girl, Katherine – a (non-handicapped) child, who was between seven and eight years of age when she wrote the sample used. When the combined sample is re-arranged to make a sandwich – that is, inserting Helen Keller's thirty-three sentences into the middle of two halves of Katherine's text (seventeen and fourteen sentences) – the result is shown in Figure HK-9. The separation is again obvious, though it has a different

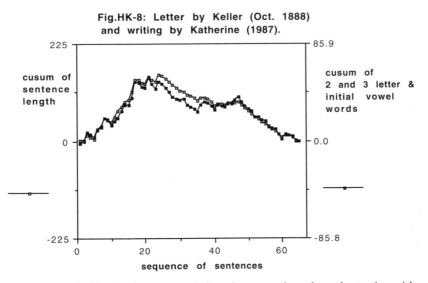

Fig.HK-8: Letter by Keller (Oct. 1888) and writing by Katherine (1987).

Figure HK-8: The habit of using two- and three-letter words and words starting with a vowel in a combined sample of thirty-three sentences written by Helen Keller in 1888 followed by thirty-two sentences written by 'Katherine' in 1987

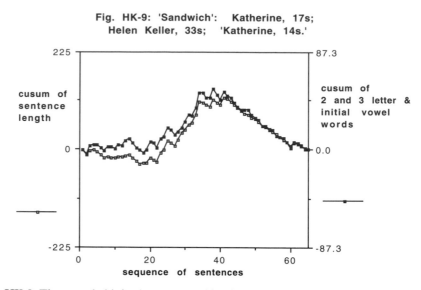

Figure HK-9: 'Sandwich': Katherine, 17s; Helen Keller, 33s; 'Katherine, 14s.'

Figure HK-9: The same habit in the same combined sample arranged as a 'sandwich'.

appearance in this 'sandwich' analysis: this chart reveals mixed utterance. The writing of Helen Keller, then, *can* be shown to separate from another child of a similar age.

ii. Helen Keller's Utterance: Stability Over Time
The answer to the second question – does early Keller match her mature utterance? – may be seen from the next charts.

To examine Helen Keller's mature utterance for internal homogeneity first, Figure HK-10 shows an analysis of a letter written when she was aged twenty-one (to Dr Edward Everett Hale, 10 November 1901, from 'My teacher and I expect to be present . . .' to 'With kind greetings in which my teacher joins me.').[8] Despite the small number of sentences, this is a homogeneous chart for the utterance of the mature Helen Keller and suitable for combining with her homogeneous utterance at eight years old. The 'blip' at sentence three is due to the 'list' structure of alternative phrases it contains (cf. the Lawrence essay on Thomas Mann in Chapter 3): '*Sitting here in my study, surrounded by my books, enjoying the sweet and intimate companionship of the great and the wise*, I am trying to realise what my life might have been if Doctor Howe had failed in the great task God had given him to perform'.

The October letter, twenty-six sentences written at the age of eight, was chosen for a combined analysis. The resulting chart is shown in Figure HK-11. Visual inspection indicates that there is apparently some inconsistency: a small blip appears at sentences 15–20, and a much larger one at sentences 25–31, though neither are statistically significant.

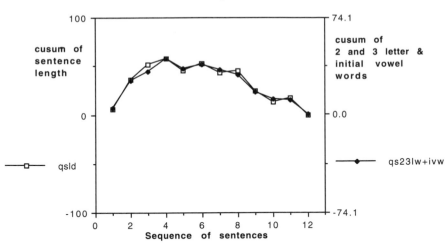

Fig. HK-10: Letter by Keller, aged 21, November,1901.

Figure HK-10: The habit of using two- and three-letter words and words starting with a vowel in a sample of twelve sentences written by Helen Keller, aged twenty-one, in a letter to Dr Hale, 10 November 1901.

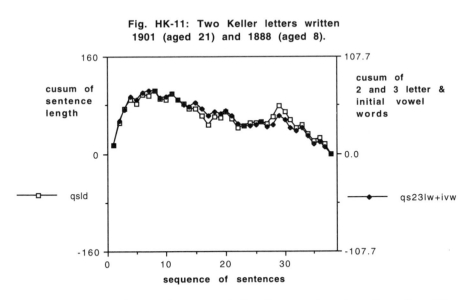

Fig. HK-11: Two Keller letters written 1901 (aged 21) and 1888 (aged 8).

Figure HK-11: The habit of using two- and three-letter words and words starting with a vowel in a combined sample of twelve sentences written by Helen Keller, aged twenty-one, followed by twenty-six sentences written by her, aged eight, in a letter to Mr Morrison Heady, 1 October 1888.

It is the latter sequence of sentences in the combined sequence where the actual problem is located, at sentences 27–9, reading

Poor people were not happy for their hearts were full of sad thoughts because they did not know much about America. I think little children must have been afraid of a great ocean for it is very strong and it makes a large boat rock and then the little children would fall down and hurt their heads. After they had been many weeks on the deep ocean where they could not see trees or flowers or grass but just water and the beautiful sky, for ships could not sail quickly then because men did not know about engines and steam.

Sentence 27 has a very low habit occurrence, but it is the last sentence (29) which has caused the disturbance: it is the second longest in the sample, of an abnormal construction, and contains a list.

In this exercise of testing for homogeneity over time, it seems useful to show another chart of the same combined sample by a combined analysis of the second habit by which Helen Keller is homogeneous, the habit of using two- and three-letter words. The result of such an analysis is shown in this second Figure HK-11a. This analysis confirms the overall consistency apart from the 'blip' already described (it would be tedious to show that removal of the sentences responsible removed the 'blip'). This is a statistically indistinguishable combined sample, demonstrating stability in the utterance of Helen Keller from the age of eight to twenty-one.

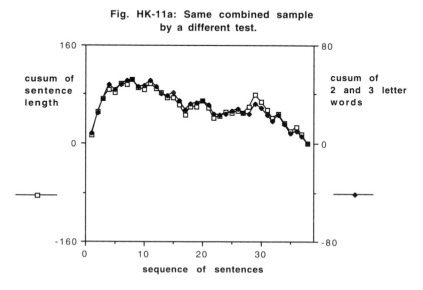

Fig. HK-11a: Same combined sample by a different test.

Figure HK-11a: The same combined sample by the habit of using two- and three- letter words.

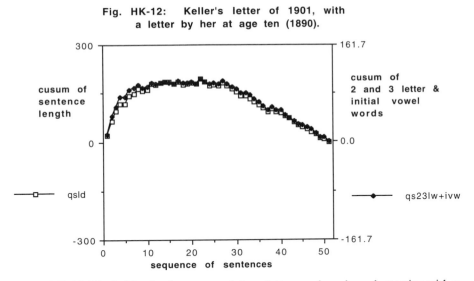

Fig. HK-12:   Keller's letter of 1901, with a letter by her at age ten (1890).

Figure HK-12: The habit of using two- and three letter words and words starting with a vowel, in a combined sample of twelve sentences written by Helen Keller, aged twenty-one, followed by thirty-nine sentences written by her, aged ten, in a letter to Mrs Kate Adams Keller, 10 November 1890.

Since this particular question of stability over time seemed to be one of special importance, further tests were carried out. Another letter by Helen Keller, written when she aged ten, was chosen for a combined test. This was written to her mother on 10 November 1890, starting 'My heart has been full of thoughts of you and my beautiful home ever since we parted so sadly on Wednesday night' to 'Now, sweet mother, your little girl must say good-bye.' The result of combining this with the mature November 1901 letter is shown in Figure HK-12.[9] This is a homogeneous chart by the *23lw+ivw* habit (an equally good result was also obtained from the *23lw* habit analysis).

These analyses offer evidence that Helen Keller's utterance as a child and a mature woman exhibits consistent language habits, allowing combined samples to be seen to be homogeneous.

iii. Helen Keller Analysed with Another Adult Writer

The charts just shown should be compared with the next Figure HK-13, where the utterance of Helen Keller as a child is combined with the utterance of another adult – her teacher, Annie Sullivan (seventeen sentences of Miss Annie Sullivan's diary 10 April 1887, from 'Everything must have a name now' to '. . . and already understands a great deal').[10] There is a brief regularity at the start of the chart (the opening Keller sentences), but at the point of insertion of Miss Sullivan's utterance, sentence 11, there is a cross-over and a wide

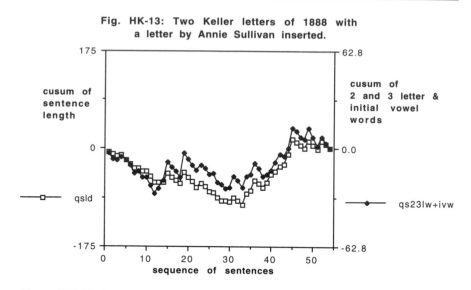

Figure **HK-13**: Combined 'sandwich' sample of eleven sentences of Keller's letter 3 May 1888, followed by seventeen sentences of Miss Sullivan's diary 10 April 1887, and another twenty-six sentences of Keller's letter 1 October 1888, analysed by the habit of using two- and three-letter and initial vowel words.

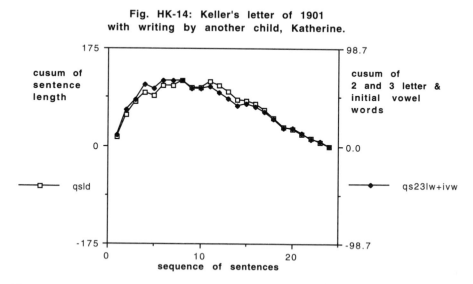

Figure **HK-14**: The habit of using two- and three-letter words and words starting with a vowel in a combined sample of twelve sentences written by Helen Keller, aged twenty-one, followed by twelve sentences written by 'Katherine', aged nine.

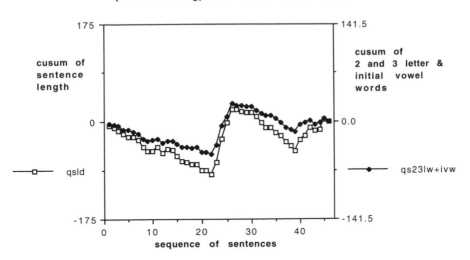

Fig. HK-14a: Alternate samples of R.P. (child's writing) and Keller letter, 1901.

Figure HK-14a: The habit of using two- and three-letter words and words starting with a vowel in a combined sample of twenty-two sentences written by R. P., aged eleven, followed by the first five sentences of the HK letter, aged twenty-one; twelve more sentences by R. P, and the final seven sentences of the Keller letter.

separation right through to the end of the chart, showing that the combined sample is of mixed utterance. Helen Keller's letter-writing as a child, then, is consistent with her own mature writing but not with the mature writing of another adult.

Further combined analysis took the analysis in the opposite direction, by combining the letter of the mature Helen Keller with the utterance of two modern children: 'Katherine', at age nine, and an eleven-year-old girl, R. P. (both of whose personal charts, YL-1 and YL-2 appears in the next section). Helen Keller has been shown to remain consistent with herself over time. But does her mature utterance match any other child? Figures HK-14 and HK-14a shows the combined analyses just described. Figure HK-14 is a clearly inconsistent chart, with the *qsld* and *qs23lw+ivw* lines crossing over in the centre. The different samples are distinguishable.

Next, in Figure HK-14a, a similar test with the writing of a second girl, but here the two samples have been split into four alternate sections. This a widely divergent chart, with no consistency between the separated alternate samples, and this is the sign of mixed utterance it is known to be.

Helen Keller has, then, been shown to remain consistent in her own utterance, by two habits, from the age of eight and of ten to the age of twenty-one. Her juvenile utterance separates from the utterance of 'Teacher' and also separates from another child, 'Katherine'; while her mature utterance can be distinguished from the juvenile utterance of two different children, R. P. and 'Katherine'.

Analysis of Helen Keller's letters – only a fraction of which has been shown here – provides an indication of how soon language consistency begins after language has been acquired, and would appear to offer significant support for the importance of the cusum technique in identifying authentic utterance.

The Analysis of Other Young Writers: Some Contemporary Children's Utterance 1980–1990

Since speech is primary utterance, and writing is just a form of speech, the teaching of writing to young children is quite a difficult task. Anyone who has taught writing to children will be familiar with the classroom question 'Do I have to write about it?' Writing is a tiresome and arduous chore to the child. It is secondary linguistic behaviour, and heavily influenced, for all but the brightest children, by all sorts of outside sources.

Tests carried out on children's writing, where the integrity of the text could be safely ascertained, have provided the following interesting results, the charts being designated **YL**, for 'Young Language'.

The first chart, Figure YL-1, shows the cusum analysis of a short story of forty-two sentences – in themselves homogeneous – written by a girl of eleven when combined with that girl's later utterance, aged eighteen, in a written piece of literary criticism. There is a slight movement between sentences 20–40,

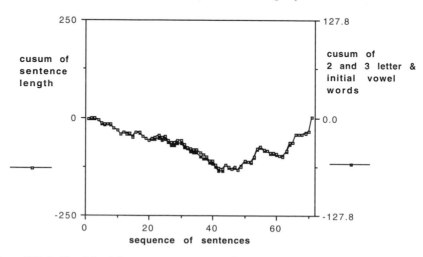

Fig. YL-1: Two samples of writing by R.P.

Figure YL-1: Combined forty-two sentences written by R. P. aged eleven, followed by twenty-nine sentences of her mature writing aged nineteen, analysed by the habit of using two- and three-letter words and words starting with a vowel.

Fig. YL-2: Sample of Katherine, (7+).

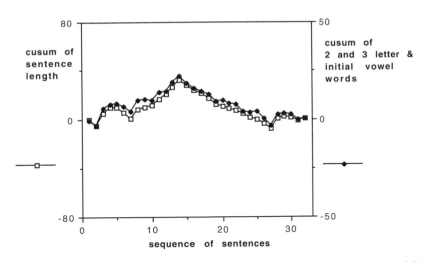

Figure YL-2: Sample of thirty-two sentences of writing by 'Katherine' when aged 7+, analysed by the habit of using two- and three-letter words and words starting with a vowel.

perhaps due to the difference in sentence length between the early and the mature utterance, but the solid consistency is undeniable. This consistency confirms the Keller result – that language habits can remain consistent from childhood to maturity, or at least, from age eleven to eighteen.

The utterance of children younger than eleven has also been analysed. Figure YL-2 is a successful QSUM-chart of writing by a child when aged 7+, 'Katherine'. This sample of text has already been used earlier to show separation from writing by Helen Keller, and is here shown in a single analysis.

As well as having been shown to separate from the writing of Helen Keller, Katherine's thirty-two sentences produce in themselves a satisfactory homogeneous chart. Note that it is slightly loose, a feature often noted on the charts of very young writers and on those of immature adult speakers and writers: this has to do, in the main, with sentence length.

This result confirms that cusum analysis, from this example, would seem successful for the utterance of children as young as seven. (It should be borne in mind that the seven-year-old Katherine acquired language in the ordinary way, and was, by this age, more fluent than Helen Keller).

With another child, Nerys, written material from the age of 4–5 up to age 9–10 was provided by her parents.

Figure YL-3, a chart of ninety-three sentences, is an encouraging example of what the cusum technique can do. In it, the texts were analysed in a sequence of samples, starting with the text for age 4–5 up to age 9+. This is a

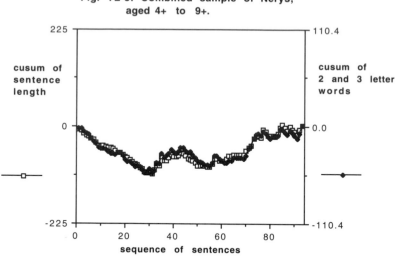

Fig. YL-3: Combined sample of Nerys, aged 4+ to 9+.

Figure YL-3: Combined sample of ninety-three sentences of writing by 'Nerys' when aged 4+ to 9+, analysed by the habit of using two- and three-letter words.

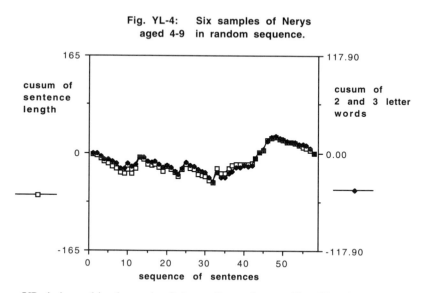

Fig. YL-4: Six samples of Nerys aged 4-9 in random sequence.

Figure YL-4: A combined sample of six small samples, totalling fifty-eight sentences of writing by Nerys aged 4+ to 9+, analysed by the habit of using two- and three-letter words.

very long combined sample, of ninety-three sentences spanning about five years. As the early material was written so young, when the sentences were considerably shorter than the later samples, the analysis was by the *23lw* habit – which was, in any case, a good identifier for 'Nerys'. As can be seen, the consistency is reasonable, if slightly wobbly. (Analysing this kind of material does, of course, call for a knowledge and experience of children's writing, taking care that *only the child's utterance* is used for the analysis, not work that has been 'helped' by a teacher.)

Does chronological order make any difference, or is it possible to make a chart at random, interposing texts from different ages between each other? This was done in Figure YL-4, where a selection of six samples spanning the years 4+ to 9+, were analysed together in random order, in a reduced total number of fifty-eight sentences (reducing the number of sentences gives greater detail). The result is quite successful. There is no separation in this chart, indicating that the utterance is homogeneous.

To confirm the Keller/Katherine result – i.e., that it is possible to differentiate between samples of two children by making a 'sandwich' – a sample of twenty-six sentences by Nerys, taken from the set of six mixed samples above, was divided into two parts of thirteen sentences each. Then, fifteen sentences from the Katherine text were inserted, and the combined sample analysed by the habit of using two- and three-letter words and words starting with a vowel. The resulting Figure YL-5 shows clear non-homogeneity. This is a disturbed chart showing mixed utterance. Notice that

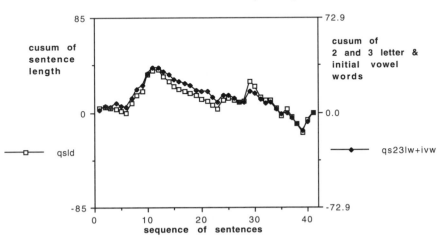

Fig. YL-5: 'Sandwich' of Katherine sample inserted between two Nerys samples.

Figure YL-5: Combined 'sandwich' sample of (a) thirteen sentences by Nerys (b) fifteen sentences by Katherine and (c) thirteen sentences by Nerys, analysed by the habit of using two- and three-letter words and words starting with a vowel.

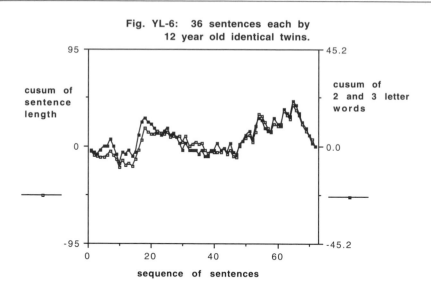

Fig. YL-6: 36 sentences each by 12 year old identical twins.

Figure YL-6: Combined sample of thirty-two sentences each written by identical twins, aged 12+ (describing the same incident) by the habit of using two- and three-letter words, total of sixty-four sentences.

the lines actually cross at about sentence 28, where the second 'Nerys text' joins the 'Katherine text'.

Finally, one last example demonstrates that this method is capable of differentiating between the written utterance of twelve-year-old identical twins – Jonathan and Jeffrey. Their samples of thirty-two sentences each were written as diary entries at the same time on the same day in September, 1988, and describe the same incident which had just happened.

In Figure YL-6, the writing of one twin separates from that of the other. This is a chart showing mixed utterance. The fact that a reasonable consistency shows up for the second twin, Jeffrey, by the *23lw* test reminds us that cusum charts are a shorthand method, compared to transparencies: every so often it will usefully show the internal consistency of one sample, but only transparencies would show the relative consistency of each on its own.

Investigation into children's acquisition of language by cusum analysis will eventually need to analyse the *spoken* language of children. It cannot be emphasized too strongly that the results shown in this chapter are few and limited in relation to the scope of the subject. They should be regarded as preliminary and encouraging.

In evaluating the cusum technique as a method of identifying utterance, the best approach seems to be to proceed, by the process of abduction: a scientific approach which starts from facts and seeks an explanatory theory.[11] In other words, let us start with the facts as presented in this research into using the technique on the utterance of children.

By examination of published data available in the public realm (Helen Keller's *The Story of My Life*), it is possible to observe that

• Helen Keller writes homogeneous sentences six months after acquiring language, January/February 1888.

• During 1888, it is possible to observe consistency sustained throughout her letters in that year, using the 23lw+ivw test, for four of her letters, written January to December.

• An exact interpolation from an unknown source can be identified within the letter written 11 December 1888.

• Helen Keller's written utterance at age eight can be shown
  i.   to separate from that of a child of similar age;
  ii. to be homogeneous with her utterance aged twenty-one, as is also her written utterance aged ten (a consistency confirmed by weighted cusum tests, i.e. the more sophisticated statistical method later outlined in Chapter 10);
  iii. to separate from the writing of another adult.

• The writing of other children can be seen
  (a) to produce personally consistent charts;
  (b) to separate from that of other children (and from the mature Helen Keller);
  (c) to be consistent (in the single case analysed) from childhood to maturity;
  (d) to differ in identical twins.

Given these results, is it possible at this stage to offer an explanatory theory? It is scarcely likely that the facts are due to natural chance. The statistical odds against it must be overwhelming. In the realms of pure (and tentative) speculation, it may be said that perhaps these results demonstrate *personal separateness through language* i.e. the active development of what the American philosopher, Charles Peirce, called *interpretant, interpreter, judge,* and Walker Percy calls *coupler* – that is, whatever/whoever in a child acquiring language *couples* name and thing, subject and predicate (should one wish to adopt the triadic model of language earlier postulated).

The Helen Keller results may, of course, be replicated by anyone who wishes to do so, using her autobiography. Further investigation into children's utterance should reward the interested researcher.

Helen Keller and Plagiarism: 'The Frost King' and the 'Rose Fairies'

In the modern world of single-authored works, where readers expect and assume a text published under one author's name to be solely the work of that author, the accusation of plagiarism is surely a distressing experience – provided it is an accusation known to be unfounded by the person so accused.

A case of *unwitting* plagiarism must be profoundly rare – if indeed such an occurrence could be thought to be possible; at least, such a case has rarely, if ever, been documented. Unconscious plagiarism would certainly be a most painful experience for the innocent perpetrator. This is obvious from the publication of a story entitled 'The Frost King', supposedly an original by Helen Keller, which was submitted in good faith by 'Teacher' to Mr Anagnos, the Director of the Perkins Institution for the Blind, as an example of the extraordinary language gifts of her young pupil, then aged ten years old (in 1890). It was immediately published in the Institution's journal *Mentor*.

The story was written in the autumn of 1889 over a period of about two weeks and originally called by Helen 'Autumn Leaves'. Miss Sullivan records that, when read aloud to the family, 'we could not understand how Helen could describe such pictures without the aid of sight.'[12] At Miss Sullivan's suggestion, the title was changed to 'The Frost King' as being 'more appropriate to the subject of which the story treated', and then sent as a birthday gift from Helen to Mr Anagnos.

After its publication in *Mentor*, it was reviewed in a newspaper, the *Goodson Gazette*, and its similarity to an already existing story 'The Frost Fairies' by a children's writer, Margaret Canby, was duly noted.[13] Helen Keller's own account of this episode is pertinent here:

> Mr Anagnos was delighted with 'The Frost King' and published it in one of the Perkins Institution Reports. This was the pinnacle of my happiness, from which I was in a little while dashed to earth. I had been in Boston only a short while when it was discovered that a story similar to 'The Frost King' called 'The Frost Fairies' by Miss Margaret T. Canby had appeared before I was born in a book called *Birdie and His Friends*. The two stories were so much alike in thought and language that it was evident Miss Canby's story had been read to me, and that mine was – a plagiarism. It was difficult to make me understand this, but when I did understand I was astonished and grieved.[14]

This incident raises several interesting questions from the point of view of the development of children's acquisition of language and its relation to cusum analysis. Helen Keller had, as we have already seen, acquired language from Miss Sullivan in May 1887, just before her seventh birthday. By the end of 1888, four letters written by her show a consistent cusum 'fingerprint'. Nine months later, in the autumn of 1889, she wrote her story 'Autumn Leaves', and, following its publication, was accused of plagiarism.

'Teacher' also was deeply upset by the whole episode, and set herself to find out how Helen could have encountered the story: it transpired that Margaret Canby's book of stories had been 'read' to Helen by a family friend when away on holiday in Brewston, Massachusetts.[15] If indeed Helen was not consciously aware of Margaret Canby's story, and had forgotten having had it read to her (read in, remember, by a laborious process of communication), then its retention in her linguistic memory is astonishing. As Margaret Canby herself notes in a letter to Miss Sullivan:

> What a wonderfully active and retentive mind that gifted child must have! If she had remembered and written down, accurately, a short story, and that soon after hearing it, it would have been a marvel; but to have heard the story once, three years ago, and in such a way that neither her parents nor teacher could ever allude to it or refresh her memory about it, and then to have been able to reproduce it so vividly, even adding some touches of her own in perfect keeping with the rest, which really improve the original, is something that very few girls of riper age, and with every advantage of sight, hearing, and even great talents for composition, could have done as well, if at all.
>
> Under the circumstances, I do not see how any one can be so unkind as to call it a plagiarism; it is a wonderful feat of memory; and stands *alone* . . .[16]

Miss Canby also noted of other writing by Helen 'I find traces, in the Report which you so kindly sent me, of little Helen having heard other stories than that of "Frost Fairies". On page 132, in a letter, there is a passage which must have been suggested by my story called "The Rose Fairies" . . .'[17]

The letter she refers to here was one written by Helen to Mr Anagnos (2 and 3 February 1890); and Helen's version of the 'Rose Fairies' story, which appears in it, is indeed very similar to Margaret Canby's original, in story-line and linguistic feature.[18]

When children acquiring language have stories told or read to them, we all know how determinedly they resist attempts to deviate from a single word of a previously heard text – of a fairy-story, say. Woe to the weary parent or baby-sitter who attempts to skip a passage or alter a word and who is firmly reminded of the 'real' text by the listening infant. Can it then be regarded as quite characteristic that the two children's stories read to Helen by the holiday friend remained firmly embedded in her mind, so firmly that they surfaced as her own three years later?

But that is the question. Are they her own or not? Or, how *much* are they her own? They are not identical word-for-word reproductions. They match in the narrative 'plot'; and some passages of description and incident are so close as to leave no doubt that the one has produced the other. It is interesting to compare both the similarities and differences. Where the original story describes the rosebuds, Canby writes:

> Some were red, some white, and others pale pink, and they were just peeping out of the green leaves, as rosy-faced children peep out from their warm beds in wintertime before they are quite willing to get up . . .

But Helen has written

> Some were red, some white, and others were delicate pink, and they were peeping out from between the green leaves like the beautiful little fairies.

The moralizing children's author, Canby, who wants to hint at the 'naughtiness' of children staying in their beds too long, has quite disappeared from the child's version in favour of the fantasy element – the fairies. It is interesting, too, to notice how firmly the colour-description has impressed itself on the mind of the blind girl who has only description and memory by which to know colour.

Can QSUM shed any light on the general question of the consistency of the sentence structure, and on what agrees with what here?

As will by now be abundantly clear, the cusum recognition system attributes authorship in a quantitative manner. It has nothing to do with style or literary quality. The stories in question are examples of a certain kind of nineteenth-century writing for children which was based on moralistic messages, often embedded in an unrealistic 'fey' context, and written in a style so artificial that it would be the utterance of no real living human being, adult or child. Miss Canby is quite right – Helen's version, even at ten years old, *is* an improvement on her own.

Even so, Margaret Canby's deliberately artificial style of writing stories for children was found to be consistent with her own natural utterance (in the two published letters written to Miss Sullivan in 1891).[19]

An extensive study of the two Canby stories, the letter by Helen containing her version of the 'Rose Fairies' story, and her 'Frost King' story was carried out, and cross-matched. It would be tedious to give the results here in minute detail: these can be summarized and only the most pertinent of the charts reproduced for scrutiny, for those interested in language acquisition or the subject of plagiarism.

Margaret Canby was found to be no exception to the technique, proving homogeneous in her letters and in both her stories by the *23lw+ivw* habit.

The most immediately interesting question, though, is whether Helen Keller's unconscious reproduction of the Canby material can be detected in analysis. Helen's letter, to which Miss Canby referred as containing part of her story 'The Rose Fairies' was written to Mr Anagnos on 2 and 3 February 1890. Can it be clearly seen to be of mixed utterance, her own normal utterance separating from the inserted (i.e., the unconsciously remembered) story?

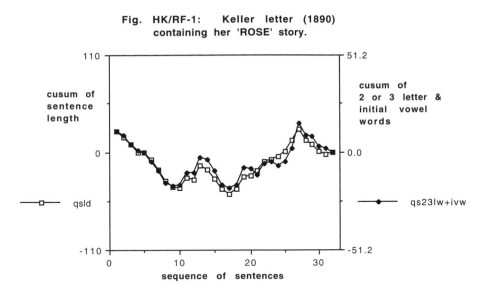

Figure HK/RF-1: The habit of two- and three-letter words and words starting with a vowel in the analysis of Helen Keller's letters to Mr Anagnos, 2 and 3 February 1890.

An analysis of the complete letter is given above in Figure HK/RF-1. This is a clear case of mixed utterance, and a similar case to the Helen Keller letter of 11 December 1888 which contained the inserted passage from the (presumed) children's information book. The first twelve sentences are her normal correspondence, and are a spot-on-spot fit, until separation begins shortly after sentence 10 on the chart. At this point, the letter reads 'I wonder if you would like to have me tell you a pretty dream which I had a long time ago when I was a little child? Teacher says it was a day-dream, and she thinks you would be delighted to hear it.'

Thereafter, the 'habit' line on the chart crosses over, from being on top to being underneath (at sentence 20), and then works its way on top again at the end of the chart, until the last five sentences, starting 'Do you like my day-dream?', which are Helen's own utterance. So seventeen of the sentences in this letter are Helen's normal utterance, the rest being derived from the Canby story.

This would be said to be a non-homogeneous chart indicating mixed utterance – except that we *know* it to have been 'written by' Helen Keller! Her version of the story – by no means a word-for-word re-telling – appears to be an example of a 'remembered language-impression' dominating the utterer's own 'habitual' expression. The stories are not identical, but at the same time the re-telling is *not habitual in terms of the natural utterance of Helen Keller*.

It may be asked whether those sentences shown to be consistent by Helen,

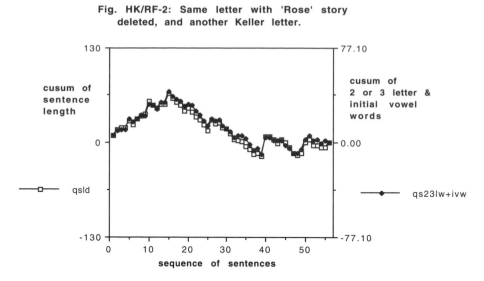

Figure HK/RF-2: The habit of two- and three-letters and words starting with a vowel in a combined analysis of two samples: a letter (nineteen sentences) by Helen Keller written to her mother on 10 November 1890, and her seventeen sentences in the letter to Mr Anagnos of 2 and 3 February 1890.

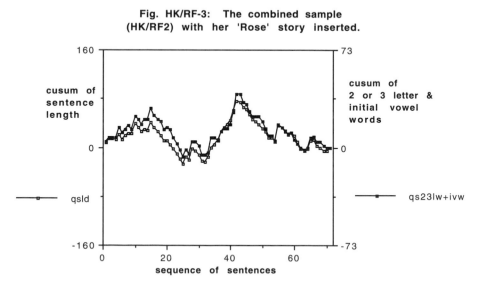

Figure HK/RF-3: The habit of two- and three-letters and words starting with a vowel in a 'sandwich' of the same combined sample (fifty-six sentences) with the Keller 'Rose' story (seventeen sentences) inserted at sentence 31.

her own sentences, will match her utterance in another letter of the period? To find out, another letter of 1890 was combined with her sentences in this letter and a combined analysis made, the result being given in HK/RF-2.[19] This is visibly a homogeneous combined sample, confirming the consistency of Helen Keller's use of this habit in the Anagnos letter and a later one written that year, 1890 (February and November).

To emphasize the separation of her 'Rose' version from her own utterance, observe the effect of placing that derived version in the middle of the combined sample of Helen's utterance just shown as Figure HK/RF-2.

The next chart, showing the inserted 'Rose' version into the combined letters sample, appears as Figure HK/RF-3. Inserting Helen Keller's version of the 'Rose Fairies' story has disturbed the previously homogeneous chart Figure HK/RF-2. Although the insertion does not start until sentence 30, the two lines begin to separate round about sentence 5, heralding the inserted alien material, and only the last section of authentic Keller utterance has any semblance of homogeneity.[20]

The re-told 'Rose' version can, then, be shown not to match Helen Keller when her utterance is analysed (and was also found to combine much closer, in analysis, with the original story by Margaret Canby).

But the published story which had actually occasioned the charge of plagiarism was the Keller re-telling of the Canby story 'The Frost Fairies', and it is that 'plagiarism' which forms the main part of this study.

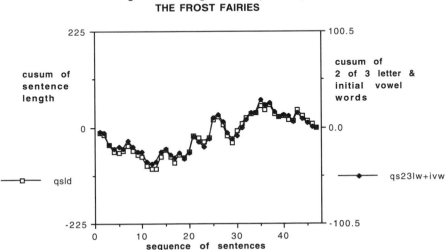

**Fig. MC-1: Margaret Canby's story
THE FROST FAIRIES**

Figure MC-1: The habit of two- and three-letters and words starting with a vowel in Margaret Canby's story 'The Frost Fairies'.

First, a QSUM-chart of the Canby story, 'The Frost Fairies'. Writing for an audience of children may seem to involve – and indeed generally *does* involve – a completely different style of writing. However, the analysis still reveals consistency and shows this story written for children to be homogeneous, be the writing ever so 'different' or 'artificial'. Figure MC-1 gives the result of the analysis. This is an extremely regular chart, pointing to what is already known, that the story had one author, and is homogeneous. (This is rather interesting given Miss Canby's account of its publication, and reference to alterations.)[21]

What of Helen Keller's story 'Autumn Leaves', which Annie Sullivan re-titled 'The Frost King' and sent off to the Perkins Institute as an illustration of her pupil's remarkable powers of invention? It is instructive to compare the two stories side by side, as they are indeed printed in Helen Keller's *The Story of My Life*.[22] The similarities are obvious, in story-line, incident, characters and language; but the differences are equally striking. Interested readers are referred to the book for a full comparison, but to look at even the first ten lines of each will give an impression of the differences:

First ten lines of Canby's 'The Frost Fairies'

King Frost, or Jack Frost as he is sometimes called, lives in a cold country far to the North. But every year he takes a journey over the world in a car of golden clouds drawn by a strong and rapid steed called North Wind. Wherever he goes he does many wonderful things. He builds bridges over every stream, clear as glass in appearance but often strong as iron. He puts the flowers and plants to sleep by one touch of his hand and they all bow down and sink into the warm earth until spring returns. Then lest we should grieve for the flowers, he places at our windows lovely wreaths and sprays of his white northern flowers, or delicate little forests of fairy pine-trees, pure white and very beautiful. But his most wonderful work is the painting of the trees, which looks, after his task is done, as if they were covered with the brightest layers of gold and rubies; and are beautiful enough to comfort us for the flight of summer.

I will tell you how King Frost first thought of this kind work, for it is a strange story. You must know that this king, like all other kings, has great treasures of gold and precious stones in his palace.

First ten lines of Keller's 'The Frost King'

King Frost lives in a beautiful palace far to the North, in the land of perpetual snow. The palace, which is magnificent beyond description, was built centuries ago, in the reign of King Glacier. At a little distance from the palace we might easily mistake it for a mountain whose peaks were mounting heavenward to receive the last kiss of the departing day. But on nearer approach we should discover our error. What we had supposed to be peaks were in reality a thousand glittering spires. Nothing could be more beautiful than the architecture of this ice-palace. The walls are curiously constructed of massive blocks of ice which terminate in cliff-like towers. The entrance to the palace is at the end of an arched recess, and it is guarded night and day by twelve soldierly-looking white Bears.

But, children, you must make King Frost a visit the very first opportunity you have, and see for yourselves this wonderful palace. The old King will welcome you kindly, for he loves children, and it is his chief delight to give them pleasure.

As the Keller version continues, it follows much more closely the narrative and language of the original, although it cannot be denied that, as a reading experience, the idiom of her story's opening is already in the 'children's author' mode – down to the use of the royal 'we' (*'we* might easily mistake . . .') and to her address to a listening audience (*'But, children . . .'*).

The Keller version totalled forty-nine sentences. Since it seemed proper to analyse it with Helen Keller's own utterance and with Canby, this large sample was halved in size in order to provide more detail. This gave two 'Frost King' (Keller) samples of twenty-four and twenty-five sentences for combined testing. Then each half was analysed both with Helen Keller's own utterance (in the two 1890 letters, shown to be homogeneous above, Figure HK-2), and with Margaret Canby's utterance in 'The Frost Fairies' (shown to be homogeneous in Figure MC-1). The result of analysing the first twenty-four sentences of 'The Frost King' with Helen Keller's own utterance is shown in Figure HK/FK-1. The effect of inserting twenty-four sentences of her version 'The Frost King' into the two Helen Keller letters has been to produce a clear separation. There is a brief consistency at the start for perhaps the first five sentences of her letters, and then the chart separates until sentences 53–80 provide consistency once again. This is a non-homogeneous chart.

The question is, if the twenty-four sentences do not match Helen Keller's *own* utterance, do they match Margaret Canby's?

The answer to this is shown in Figure HK/FF-1. The consistency this time is obvious: compare this combined chart with Figure HK/FK-1, and it seems that Helen Keller's story matches Margaret Canby's 'Frost Fairies', in the use of the *23lw+ivw* habit where it does not match her own letters. If this chart were produced independently for visual inspection, there would be little doubt that it would appear as indistinguishable.

Can we expect the same results from combining the second half of the Keller version with the same two samples? The result of a combined analysis of the second twenty-five sentences with the two letters is given in Figure HK/FK-2. The resulting chart from a 'sandwich' combination of the second half of 'The Frost King' is similar in its effects to the same analysis with the first half of her story: separation occurs here even before the tenth sentence. Then there is separation until consistency returns for sentences 53–81. Clearly,

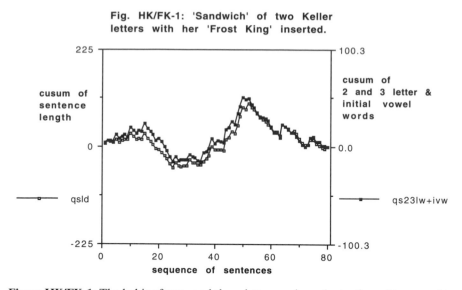

Fig. HK/FK-1: 'Sandwich' of two Keller letters with her 'Frost King' inserted.

Figure HK/FK-1: The habit of two- and three-letters and words starting with a vowel in a combined sample of fifty-six sentences of Helen Keller's two letters 1890, with twenty-four sentences of her 'The Frost King' inserted.

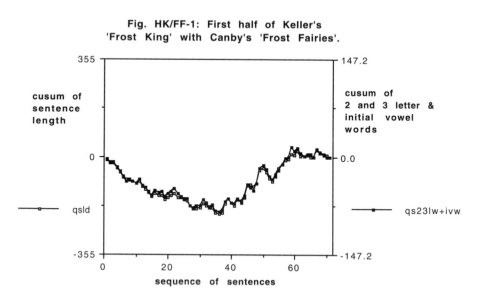

Fig. HK/FF-1: First half of Keller's 'Frost King' with Canby's 'Frost Fairies'.

Figure HK/FF-1: The habit of two- and three-letters and words starting with a vowel in a combined sample of twenty-four sentences of 'The Frost King' followed by forty-seven sentences of Canby's 'The Frost Fairies'.

**Fig. HK/FK-2: First half of Keller's
'Frost King' between two Keller letters.**

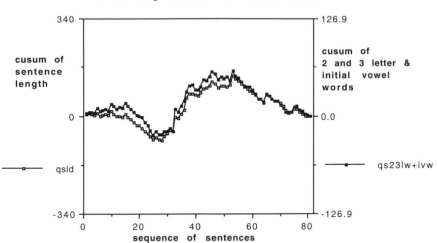

Figure HK/FK-2: The habit of two- and three-letters and words starting with a vowel in a combined sample of fifty-six sentences of Helen Keller's two letters (1890), with remaining twenty-five sentences of 'The Frost King' inserted.

this is mixed utterance: the QSUM analyst would say that these are samples from two different sources.

Since Helen Keller is homogeneous by two tests, the same combined sample was analysed by another habit in Figure HK/FK-3. The two samples are even more clearly distinguishable by this second test, which confirms the first result.

Lastly, the same twenty-five sentences were combined with Margaret Canby's 'Frost Fairies', and the resulting chart is Figure HK/MC-2. Once again, the contrast is obvious. There is a firm consistent habit running through the combined samples of the Keller and Canby stories. The samples are indistinguishable by cusum analysis.

The implications of this study are fascinating. Unless resort is made to conspiracy theories of deliberate deception by Annie Sullivan, who would have guided her pupil in this matter, Helen Keller is both the author and not the author of 'her' story. She acquired language very late in her childhood life, at the age of almost seven. At eight, she 'encountered' a book of stories by a children's author, Margaret Canby. Two of these stories impressed themselves in language structure, form, imagery, figure of speech, so strongly on her young mind that she was able to re-produce versions of them unconsciously, at the age of ten, as her 'own' stories.

A comparison of the two versions of these stories will show that in certain senses they *are* Helen Keller's own: she has altered, added to, and, it can hardly be denied, improved on the originals.

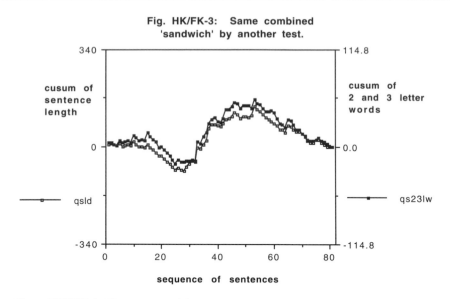

Figure HK/FK-3: The same combined sample by the habit of using two- and three-letter words.

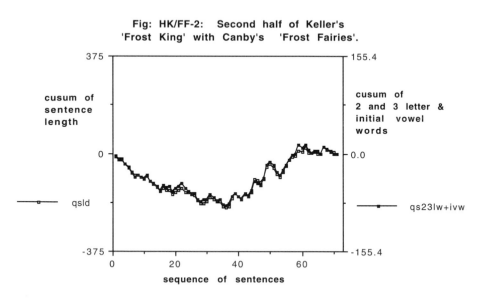

Figure HK/FF-2: The habit of two- and three-letters and words starting with a vowel in a combined analysis of half of Keller's 'The Frost King' (twenty-five sentences) with the forty-seven sentences of Canby's 'Frost Fairies'.

But in whatever it is that the cusum technique measures, they are not her own.

At a very early language-learning stage, then, it was in this one case possible for someone else's structural consistency and habitual language patterns to be laid down in the mind of the eight-year-old Helen and reproduced at a later date – but, surely, because the learning process was only just beginning for her. Canby's story, so packed with the visual/aural sense impressions Helen Keller had never experienced but would want to remember, must have made a deep impression on her young mind. Moreover, the extent to which the normal eye/ear stimuli (which bombard hearing/sighted children) could overwhelm and 'interfere' with this early memory would have been vastly reduced.

One may speculate that for children without hearing loss, such 'echoing' may occur at the age of two to four years, when children are so insistent about the exact wording of what the story 'says'. In cases of feral man – children nurtured by animals and later reclaimed by the human community – the latent capacity for acquiring language appears to remain: but the language-learning of Kamala 'the wolf-child' did not develop beyond a vocabulary of about fifty words and the use of simple three-word sentences, and the possibility of any 'story-imprinting' for her must have been totally lost.

As Margaret Canby describes it in her letter, quoted earlier, '. . . it is a wonderful feat of memory; and stands *alone*'. The only thing with which this unique case can be compared is the memory of a tune or rhythm, and its re-surfacing after an interval of time, despite being 'heard' only once.

Chapter 7

LITERARY ATTRIBUTIONS: VARIETIES AND FORMS

> Each mortal thing does one thing and the same:
> Deals out that being indoors each one dwells ;
> Selves – goes itself; *myself* it speaks and spells,
> Crying *What I do is me: for that I came.*
> (G. M. Hopkins's sonnet: 'As kingfishers catch fire')

Many questions will occur to the literary scholar newly acquainted with QSUM. There may well be curiosity as to how well it works for varieties of literary form and genre, for texts of early historical period, and about its reliability for solving questions long disputed. Earlier examples in the book will have partly provided an answer to such questions already – for Henry Fielding and other eighteenth-century writing, for children's utterance, and for different literary genres in the work of D. H. Lawrence and Muriel Spark, and attribution will be shown in Part IV for Greek prose.

This chapter will provide brief applications of QSUM relating to some frequent questions asked when the cusum technique is first introduced to the interested scholar: for example, can the technique attribute dialect, or inventive, experimental literary form?

Analysis of Dialect: Mark Twain's *Huckleberry Finn*

The first example is taken from American literature. When Mark Twain published his book *Huckleberry Finn*, it carried a foreword from the author:

> In this book a number of dialects are used, to wit: the Missouri Negro dialect; the extremest form of backwoods South Western dialect; the ordinary 'Pike-County' dialect; and four modified varieties of this last. The shadings have not been done in a hap-hazard fashion, or by guess-work; but painstakingly, and with the trustworthy guidance and support of personal familiarity of these several forms of speech.

It seems apposite, then, to begin with the representation of dialect in a literary context, thirty sentences of dialogue from this novel. These thirty sentences comprise a conversation between Huck and the escaped slave, Jim: in context,

**Fig.HF-1: 2 dialects from
HUCKLEBERRY FINN.**

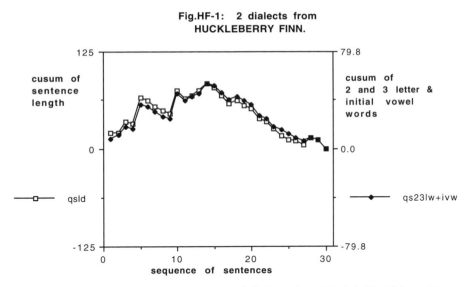

Figure HF-1: A sample of thirty sentences of dialogue from Twain's *Huckleberry Finn*, analysed by the habit of using two- and three-letter words and words starting with a vowel.

this is a conversation involving two distinct dialects, Huck's (a variation of ordinary Pike County) and Jim's (Missouri Negro), of which a sample is given below.[1]

[Huck] And you ain't had no meat nor bread to eat all this time? Why didn't you get mud-turkles?
[Jim] How you gwyne to git 'm? You can't slip up on um en grab um; en how's a body gwyne to hit um wid a rock? How could a body do it in de night? En I warn't gwyne to show myself on de bank in de daytime.
[Huck] Well, that's so. You've had to keep on the wood all the time, of course. Did you hear 'em shooting the cannon?

Figure HF-1 is the result of analysing the thirty sentences of dialogue, between Huck and Jim (starting 'Well, when it come dark, I took up out de river . . .' to 'He said it was death'). The tracking of the two lines may look slightly uneven, as if drawn by a shaky hand, but nevertheless there is a real and satisfactory correspondence between the two lines. The utterance is statistically indistinguishable and thus homogeneous, the work of one writer.

Next, these thirty sentences (i.e. two dialects) were combined with a further twenty-five sentences of dialogue between Huck and the woman whom he meets when he goes ashore dressed as a girl. This is the most 'normal' variety of which the following sentence is an example:

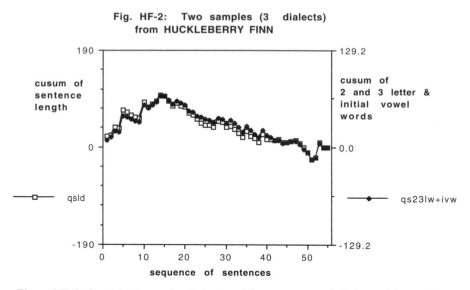

Fig. HF-2: Two samples (3 dialects) from HUCKLEBERRY FINN

Figure HF-2: Combined sample of the first thirty sentences of dialogue followed by a further twenty-five sentences (including a different dialect) analysed by the same habit.

Yes; and couldn't the nigger see better, too? After midnight he'll likely be asleep, and they can slip around through the woods and hunt up his camp fire all the better for the dark, if he's got one.

The sample starts 'I put down the needle and thread and let on to be interested . . .' to '. . . his nose out of a hole in the corner every little while'.

This brought the total number of dialects under analysis to three, and the result may be seen in Figure HF-2. The consistency is undeniable and there is no doubt that this is a homogeneous sample, demonstrating that three different dialects, recognizable to the reader, can be shown to be the utterance of a single source, Mark Twain.

Finally, the combined sample above was enlarged by the addition of a further twenty-two sentences of dialogue incorporating another dialect spoken by the character Buck Shepherdson, who uses another variety of Pike County dialect (starting 'Laws how do I know!' to . . . 'becuz they don't breed any of that kind'). This is an example of the dialect:

Bout three months ago my cousin Bud, fourteen year old, was riding through the woods on t'other side of the river, and didn't have no weapon with him, which was blame foolishness. And in a lonesome place he hears a horse a-coming behind him, and sees old Baldy Shepherdson a-linkin' after him with his gun in his hand and his white hair a-flying in the wind. And 'stead of jumping off and taking to the brush, Bud 'lowed he could outrun him. So

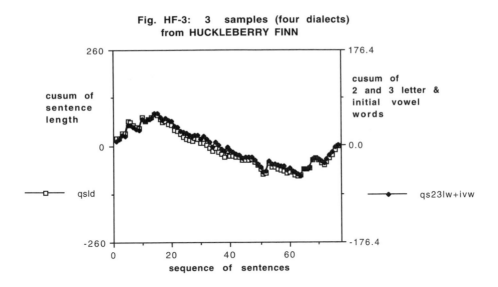

Fig. HF-3:   3   samples (four dialects) from HUCKLEBERRY FINN

Figure HF-3: Combined sample of the three examples of dialect (30, 25, and 22 sentences), analysed by the same test.

they had it, nip and tuck, for five mile or more, the old man a'aiming all the time.

Figure HF-3 thus shows the result of analysing a combined sample which now comprised four dialects in the book: the original three dialects in combined sample Figure HF-2 followed by another dialect from the later sample. This is a perfectly consistent QSUM-chart. Given the fact that the textual dialects under analysis present a genuine reading problem for the less sophisticated reader, the fact that the combined analysis is homogeneous shows that dialect, as such, will present no problem for cusum analysis.

• **This is often an important point for legal enquirers doubtful about the kind of utterance which they may need to have analysed.**

An Invented Language: Anthony Burgess, *A Clockwork Orange* and 'Nadsat'

In *A Clockwork Orange*, Anthony Burgess invented a whole new 'dialect', a demotic which included an invented vocabulary based on Russian, for his central character.[2] This celebrated example is a teenager's argot spoken by the young anti-hero, Alex, and his friends (or 'droogs'), called 'Nadsat'.

This is a sample of 'Nadsat', part of a monologue by Alex (the book is told in the first person):

I jumped, O my brothers, and I fell on the sidewalk hard, but I did not snuff it, oh no. If I had snuffed it I would not be here to write what I written have. It seems that the jump was not from a big enough heighth to kill . But I cracked my back and my wrosts and nogas and felt very bolshie pain before I passed out, brothers, with astonished and surprised litsos of chellovecks in the streets looking at me from above. And just before I passed out I viddied clear that not one chellovek in the whole horrid world was for me and that music through the wall had all been like arranged by those who were supposed to be my like new droogs and that it was some vetsch like this that they wanted for their horrible selfish and boastful politics.[3]

While the invented lexis is striking, with many new nouns and verbs, the formal arrangement is structurally (or syntactically) traditional. The sentences of Alex's narrative are unusually long: one sample of twenty-three sentences numbered 797 words (averaging 34.6 words per sentence). However, the retention of traditional formal syntax should mean that a combined analysis with the 'ordinary discourse' in the novel would yield a homogeneous QSUM-chart, since it was all written by Anthony Burgess.

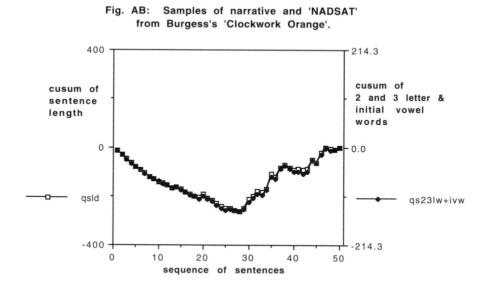

Fig. AB: Samples of narrative and 'NADSAT' from Burgess's 'Clockwork Orange'.

Figure AB: The habit of using two- and three-letter words and words starting with a vowel in a combined sample of twenty-five sentences of dialogue (pp. 85–6), starting 'Of course it was horrible' . . . to '. . . presence of the hateful with fear and nausea', and twenty-three sentences of 'Nadsat' (pp. 132–4), from 'I jumped, O my brothers . . .' to 'but the three from whose flat I had jumped out, namely DBdaSilvca and [names]'.

A sample from the twenty-five sentences (averaging 12.9 words per sentence) of normal discourse is given below, as a contrast.

'Of course it was horrible', smiled Doctor Branom. 'Violence is a very horrible thing. That's what you're learning now. Your body is learning it.'

'But,' I said 'I don't understand. I don't understand about feeling sick like I did. I never used to feel sick before. I used to feel the very opposite. I mean, doing it or watching it I used to feel real horrorshow. I just don't understand why or how or what – '.

'Life is a very wonderful thing', said Doctor Branom in a like very holy goloss [*sic*]. 'The processes of life, the make-up of the human organism, who can fully understand these miracles?'[4]

The result of making a combined analysis of the 'Nadsat' extract with the ordinary discourse is shown in Figure AB. This is a very good homogeneous result. Not only is the language of the invented 'Nadsat' shown to be consistent with the dialogue, but both samples were also found to match samples from Anthony Burgess's autobiography, although space does not allow the inclusion of these extra results: the important point here is the ability of QSUM to 'over-ride' any novelistic invention of this kind.

A Hostile Sceptic: Tom Stoppard and *Arcadia*

While in the process of writing this book, my attention was drawn to a new play by Tom Stoppard, *Arcadia*, first produced in London, April 1993. The play is based on the relation between past and present, between what we can humanly know as a matter of historical record, together with what can be deduced by scholarship, and the truth of what actually happened. It moves backward and forwards in time, between scenes in the same country house (or 'Stately Home', as it has now become), contrasting events and characters in the early nineteenth century and the present day.

The plot turns on an enthusiastic attempt by a contemporary university academic to attribute a newly discovered poem to Byron, a one-time guest at the house, on the basis of all sorts of circumstantial evidence ('Did it happen? Could it happen?').[6]

The real focus of the play is the futility, or perhaps the inconsequence, of all such attempts at 'knowing' the past; and the eternal recurrence – co-existence even – of time, this being mirrored in the static set, the continuing presence of objects in the 'now' and the 'then'. The play has all the brilliance and theatrical invention for which Stoppard is justly celebrated.

In Scene Two of the play, the following exchange occurs:

[Bernard]: Yes. One of my colleagues believed he had found an unattributed short story by D. H. Lawrence, and he backed up his claim with an analysis of the prose style, on his home computer, most interesting, perhaps you remember the paper?

[Valentine]: Not really. But I often sit with my eyes closed and it doesn't necessarily mean I'm awake.

[Bernard]: Well, by comparing sentence structures and so forth, this chap showed that there was a ninety per cent chance that the story had indeed been written by the same person as *Women in Love*. To my inexpressible joy, one of your maths mob was able to show that on the same statistical basis there was a ninety per cent chance that Lawrence also wrote the *Just William* books and much of the previous day's *Brighton and Hove Argus*.[7]

This fictional reference may be entirely co-incidental, of course; or it may conceivably be that Mr Stoppard had heard from some literary contact of the attribution exercise on the story attributed to Lawrence, carried out in 1992, which now forms the test case in Chapter 3 of the present book. Certainly the knowledge that there is now a scientific method of attribution might disconcert a writer embarked upon a play which turns upon authorship attribution.

What is interesting, however, is the *attitude* which the quoted dialogue embodies. Scepticism is a frequent reaction upon first encountering the technique. But beyond natural disbelief lies the derision proper to anyone aware that ours is a factual age in thrall to the quantitative and the mechanical, an age mesmerized with measurement and the claims of statistical 'proof' against which the humanist's world of value needs defending. The idea that there are lies, damned lies, and statistics has become a cliché of our time, not without cause, thus giving much ammunition to the satirist.

Hostility on the part of the literary academic, and even more the artist, is therefore predictable. It is recognizable in the exasperation and contempt with which Stoppard's contemporary character, Hannah, jeers 'Analysed it?'; and, later, 'Analysed it, my big toe!' in Act Two.[8]

The author has every sympathy with this gut reaction of the literary sensibility. What, after all, has 'analysis' to do with a living text, let alone a living human being?

The answer is, nothing. Wordsworth – and the Romantic Imagination – told us that 'we murder to dissect'; and a poem by Emily Dickinson condemns the literalist's requirement of 'proof':

> Split the Lark – and you'll find the Music –
> Bulb upon Bulb in Silver rolled –
> . . . Scarlet Experiment! Sceptic Thomas!
> Now, do you doubt your Bird was True?[9]

To take things apart to find out how they work is a procedure fitted to machines but not to living beings or to a living work of art – Dickinson's lark stands for the poetic imagination, the fount of song. Split the living source, and you'll find not the music of life but a dead and bloody body; 'Doubting Thomas', or the literalist, requires something for which there can be no objective proof – the living spirit.

'Analysis' can say nothing about what makes a work art or lifeless. It is a common but gross mistake to misunderstand in this kind of way that the limits of this attribution technique are fully acknowledged: to repeat what has been reiterated throughout this book, QSUM makes no claim to judgments of *quality*. The qualms of Tom Stoppard's character are groundless. If a scientific method of identifying utterance has been established, it is on the same level as any other science: the physical fingerprint, the discovery of penicillin, or a method of splitting the atom – all are limited and morally neutral – few of us, however, including the artist, would care to be without such benefits of the scientific method as penicillin.

QSUM as an attributor of utterance may be less widely beneficial than medical discoveries but it is as scientific. It therefore leaves art exactly where it was before, though perhaps with less room for the lively fun of speculation, and for the harmless games of academics that form the basis of *Arcadia*'s elegant enquiry into time and human curiosity.

An equivalent harmless game, fun for the QSUM analyst, would be to 'analyse' the very text in which Tom Stoppard's small diatribe against literary computing makes its appearance.

Two combined samples were chosen. First, two pages of text from Scene Two.[10] The first consists of stage directions, starting 'The lights come up on the same room . . .' to 'His tendency is to dress flamboyantly'. (The latter sentence, which in the text continues over the page, has been reduced to a simple sentence by putting a stop after 'flamboyantly' at the end of page 15.) The sample combined with this starts 'Oh, can't you use the toilet?' down to 'Well, I'll take Lightning for his run'.

The first combined sample analysis is shown in Figure TS-1. This chart looks like a gallant effort at spot-on-spot homogeneity which has not quite made it – after the first twenty-two sentences of the 'stage directions' extract, there is a slight but definite shift in the chart at sentence 22, when it meets the next extract (the thirty-four sentences of dialogue) but this is not a separation. Rather, it is due to the first extract having longer sentences of written composition than the short conversational sentences which follow between Bernard and Valentine, which has features common to human speech but anomalous in terms of the cusum technique's reliance on syntax.

For example, the average sentence length of the combined sample is 10.9 words, and this *includes* the lengthy stage directions. As is normal, the

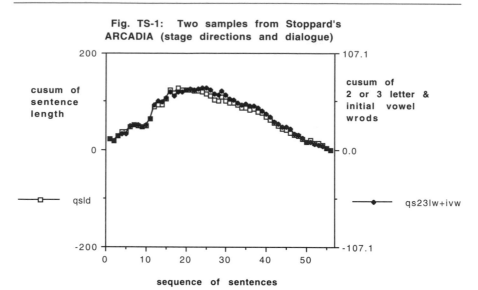

Figure TS-1: The habit of using two- and three-letter words and words starting with a vowel in a combined sample of fifty-six sentences on two pages of text from Tom Stoppard's *Arcadia*.

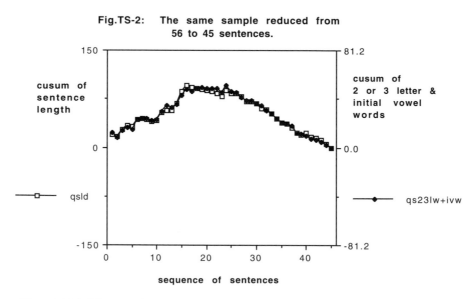

Figure TS-2: The same habit in the same sample when reduced to forty-five sentences.

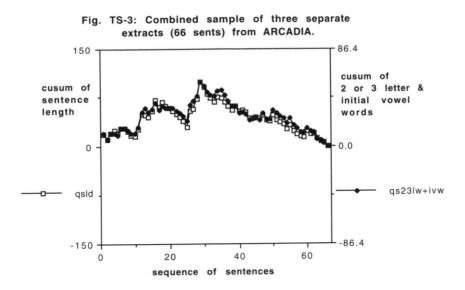

Figure **TS-3**: The same habit in a combined sample of sixty-six sentences from Tom Stoppard's *Arcadia*.

conversation is characterized by pauses, hesitations, repetition, self-correction, exclamations, unfinished sentences, and so on: for example, 'To me? Ah! Yes! Sorry!'. There is also the occasional anomaly, like 'My mother basically reads gardening books' (a sentence in which there is one two-letter function word and no initial vowel words).

Well might the playwright, and playgoer, exclaim 'Ah! Yes! Ha Ha! *Well* then!' at this point, since the features of spoken utterance in any everyday conversation – i.e. life – may seem to have caused a recognizable disturbance in the chart. However, it needs no close scrutiny to see that this chart is perfectly homogeneous statistically. It is, rather, how closely it remains so despite such different modes of writing – stage directions and simulated dialogue – which should give the sceptic pause.

If such anomalies and constraints are allowed for in terms of QSUM's usual procedure (by joining together very short sentences of four words or less, by excluding the exclamations which are not 'sentences', and so on), the same combined sample reduces from fifty-six to forty-five sentences. The result of analysing the new combined sample is given in Figure TS-2. This is very clearly a satisfactory example of homogeneity.

One final chart was made, this time making a combined analysis of three samples.[11] These consisted of Tom Stoppard's own utterance again, the same stage directions; a page of dialogue of the present-day characters, from

'Actually we've met before . . .' to '. . . the photograph doesn't do you justice'; and a page of dialogue of the nineteenth-century characters in Scene 3, from 'So much the better . . .' to 'I am tired of him'. In this latter sample, the average sentence length rises noticeably, in accordance with the characteristics of nineteenth-century literary conventions.

The result appears in Figure TS-3. The variation in sentence length makes this look rather like a ride on the roller-coaster; but the two lines of the *qsld* and the *qs23lw+ivw* analysis stay close together throughout the stylistic differences.

This is yet another demonstration of something we already know: the samples which have been analysed by QSUM are the homogeneous utterance of one person, playwright Tom Stoppard.

A Confederacy of Sceptics: Professor Martin Battestin and the Attribution of *New Essays by Fielding*

In 1989, a collection of forty-one essays, which had appeared pseudonymously during the period 1734–39 in *The Craftsman* – a journal edited by Nicholas Amhurst – was published as the writing of Henry Fielding: if true, then it would be 'one of the best kept, but one of the most important, secrets of eighteenth-century literature'.[12]

These *New Essays by Henry Fielding* had been discovered and attributed by the eminent Fielding scholar Martin Battestin, who had supported his belief that they were Fielding's essays by extensive and meticulously researched parallels from other work by Fielding. The book's claims were supported by a stylometric analysis by Michael Farringdon – using the earlier statistical methods then in use and referred to in Chapter 1: 85 per cent of the essays fell well within the statistical parameters enabling the analysis to stand as supportive evidence, while evidence for the remaining 15 per cent was inconclusive.

The methods used for the analysis included collocations, pairs of words, and preferred positions of words, and the results, however sound, appeared in tables of statistics which undoubtedly alienated some reviewers. In this respect, cusum analysis, with its clear visual display, is much easier for the statistical lay person to understand and grasp.

Many reviews were favourable and accepted the attributions: 'The volume makes an overwhelming case for the extension of the Fielding canon.'[13] Some reviewers, however, were not prepared to accept the essays as indisputably the work of Henry Fielding, as in the following comment: '. . . on the basis of the evidence put before us here, the verdict on the attributions must be "Not Proven" at best.' The same reviewer, a literary academic, displayed typical bafflement in the face of the statistical tests: 'I found the stylometry, reliant on

Joseph Andrews as a "control text", to be something of a rigmarole, and the evidence it produced seemed less weighty than the sheer unlikeliness of the attributions.'[14] Perhaps by the seventh chapter of this book, reactions like 'rigmarole' to quantitative analysis will seem over-hasty.

The use of the particular control text(s), as used again in Chapter 6, was a source of unease to other reviewers as well. One queried the choice of the comparison texts chosen by Michael Farringdon in the stylometric analysis:

> The choice of these comparison texts seems to have been determined by their being already available in machine-readable form: for it is hardly a surprise that an author born in 1707 would write in a different style from authors born in 1667, 1672, 1672 and 1697 respectively.
>
> A group of near-contemporaries and younger writers who had felt Fielding's influence would have been more satisfactory.[15]

This last quotation is a most useful demonstration of the confusion that can exist in the literary mind when quantitative approaches to literature are used. The procedures so crucial for literary comparison – comparing like with like, in genre and period – are carried over where they do not apply.

This reviewer was not the only one to scorn the comparison texts as being too unlike the essays to be of any use in the 'stylometric analysis'. However, as readers of this book will by now have learnt, such cavils are unwarranted; style in a literary sense is not the issue, and whether writers who are born fifty years before or fifty years later than the subject of the enquiry write 'in a different style' or not is not a fact that affects the analysis. The reader may care to recall here the 'Most Frequently Used' word-lists for Henry Fielding and Dylan Thomas respectively, in Chapter 2, to see how little a difference of 250 years affects the use of function words.

Attribution by traditional methods, like Martin Battestin's, allied to earlier methods of statistical support, may or may not convince academic colleagues. The advantage of cusum analysis is its great sensitivity and its visual display, which should satisfy even the most hostile sceptic, given the right degree of impartiality.

In due course, all forty-one of the *New Essays* will be analysed by QSUM, and the results published. Meanwhile, there follows the result for one of the essays.

Attribution of Craftsman *Essay 612, 'In Vindication of Laughter'*[16]
It will be recalled from Chapter 6 that, although two tests were able to prove homogeneity, the test which discriminates Henry Fielding was the habit of using words of two and three letters.

First, an analysis by that test was carried out on the complete essay, and the result appears in Figure CR-1. This will appear to the reader a most

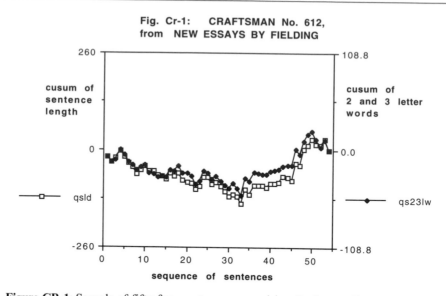

Figure CR-1: Sample of fifty-four sentences comprising Craftsman Essay No. 612, 'In Vindication of Laughter' analysed by the habit of using two- and three-letter words.

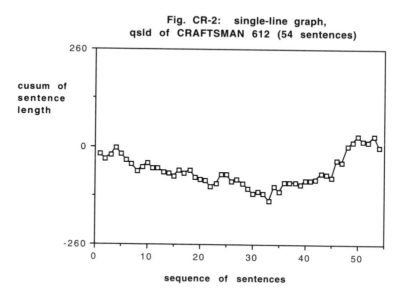

Figure CR-2: Single-line graph showing the *qsld* of the same sample.

Fig. CR-3:   qs23lw of the same sample

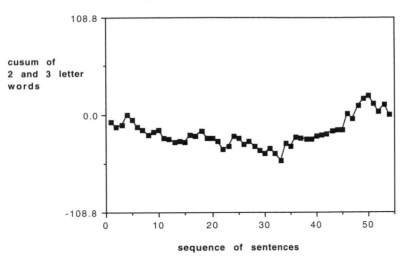

Figure CR-3: Single-line graph showing the *qs23lw* of the same sample.

unsatisfactory result, apparently showing separation and non-homogeneity. The two lines appear to separate at sentence 15 and to remain apart for the rest of the chart. But it is actually a very useful result for showing the necessity for using transparencies – *charts* are an inferior substitute for recognizing the source(s) of a linguistic disturbance, even though in many cases where perfect homogeneity is apparent, transparencies may seem superfluous. In this case of a sample of fifty-four sentences – totalling 1,823 words – separate graphs and the use of a transparency were obviously necessary. Figures CR-2 and CR-3 show the results of analysis.

With a transparency made of one of these graphs and then laid over the other, the problem sentences causing the apparent separation were identified as sentences 51 and 52, reading:

[Sentence 51] I could easily turn this Story into a very pretty Allegory; but That perhaps, might prove no laughing Matter for You.

[Sentence 52] I shall therefore only just hint, that this Dragon seem'd very fond of being worshipp'd and well-fed; whereas some of Them have been content with being cramm'd and pamper'd only.

The sample as a whole has an average sentence length of 33.5 words, of which 38.8 per cent (average, thirteen words) were 'habit' words, i.e. words of two and three letters. Sentence 51, at twenty-one words, is well below the average length and has only four 'habit' words (19 per cent); and at thirty words, sentence 52

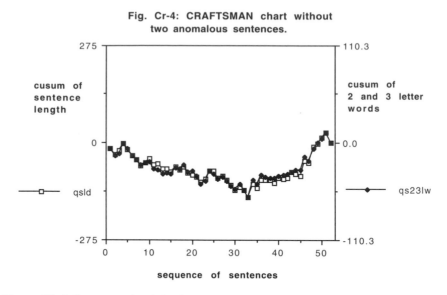

Fig. Cr-4: CRAFTSMAN chart without two anomalous sentences.

Figure CR-4: Same sample of *Craftsman* Essay No. 612, 'In Vindication of Laughter', with two anomalous sentences removed, analysed by the same habit.

is just below average length, and again has only four 'habit' words (13.3 per cent). The co-incidence of these two sentences following each other has created an anomalous effect and distorted the whole chart.

When these two sentences 51 and 52 are removed, the result is the chart in Figure CR-4. This can now be seen to be a homogeneous chart, indicating that *Craftsman 612* was written by a single author.

The next question becomes, is that author Henry Fielding?

The same problem occurs here as in comparing samples of Fielding with the sample of writing by the anonymous author of *The Military History of Charles XII*, namely the length of the samples to be combined. If the sample of forty-two sentences taken from *Joseph Andrews*, by Fielding, were to be combined and analysed with *Craftsman* 612, the combined sample of forty-two and fifty-two sentences, amounting to ninety-four sentences, would comprise a total of 3,187 words. At such a length, however homogeneous the result would appear, detail would have been lost; indeed, if the fifty-two sentences of *Craftsman* No. 612 were combined with twenty-five sentences by the *Craftsman*'s editor, Nicholas Amhurst, the total combined words under analysis would be 2,658, too large to show difference of authorship.

The following procedure was therefore adopted. *Craftsman* No. 612 was divided into three parts:

(a) Sentences 1–17 (17 sentences, 502 words)
(b) Sentences 18–34 (17 sentences, 540 words)

(c) Sentences 35–52 (18 sentences, 729 words)

Each of these was analysed in a combined sample with the last eighteen sentences (787 words) from the *Joseph Andrews* 42-sentence sample used in Chapter 6. This new sample started 'It was this Gentleman, who, having, as I have said, observed the singular Devotion of young Andrews . . .', and ended with the last sentence '. . . and at the same time received from the good Man many Admonitions concerning the Regulation of his future Conduct, and his Perseverance in Innocence and Industry.' These combined samples resulted in **Figures CR/JA-1, -2 and -3**.

Each of the three samples from *Craftsman* 612 was also combined with seventeen sentences (563 words) from an essay by Nicholas Amhurst – the same one used for comparison purposes in Chapter 5. The Amhurst sentences started 'Some of these Gentlemen are employed, at present, upon Business of a little more Importance than answering your Letters' and ended 'that the Discussion of such Points, whilst under Negotiation, does not come within the due Bounds of Liberty.' The combined analysis for these samples resulted in **Figures CR/AM-1, -2 and -3**. Note that by using an equal number of sentences from *Joseph Andrews* as the third extract of *Craftsman* 612, eighteen sentences, it was possible to do a sample of six equal-sized alternate sections for Figure CR/JA-3. All these results are now shown in illustration.

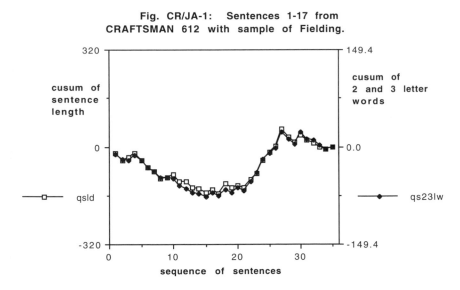

Fig. CR/JA-1: Sentences 1-17 from CRAFTSMAN 612 with sample of Fielding.

Figure CR/JA-1: Combined sample of sentences 1–17 of *Craftsman* 612 followed by eighteen sentences from Henry Fielding's *Joseph Andrews*, analysed by the habit of using two and three letters.

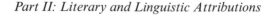

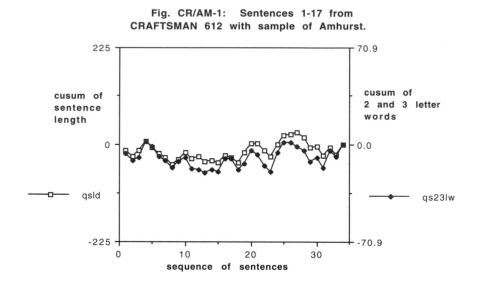

Figure CR/AM-1: Combined sample of sentences 1–17 of *Craftsman* 612 followed by seventeen sentences by Nicholas Amhurst, analysed by the habit of using two and three letters.

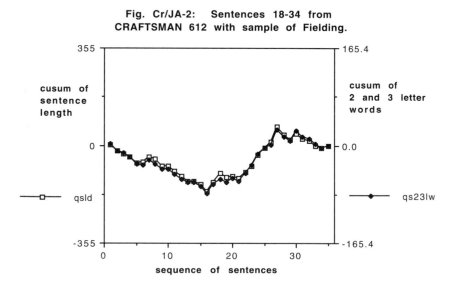

Figure CR/JA-2: Combined sample of sentences 18–34 of *Craftsman* 612 followed by eighteen sentences from Henry Fielding's *Joseph Andrews*, analysed by the habit of using two and three letters.

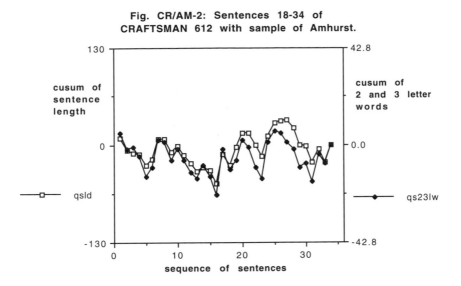

Fig. CR/AM-2: Sentences 18-34 of CRAFTSMAN 612 with sample of Amhurst.

Figure CR/AM-2: Combined sample of sentences 18–34 of *Craftsman* 612 followed by seventeen sentences by Nicholas Amhurst, analysed by the habit of using two and three letters.

Figure CR/JA-1 is a homogeneous chart. The two samples are indistinguishable, pointing to the conclusion of single authorship.

The next chart shows what happens when Amhurst's writing is substituted for Fielding's in the combined sample. Comparing this chart with the previous one, it is plain that this combined sample is of mixed authorship. The first reduced sample of *Craftsman* 612 separates from the writing of Amhurst as clearly as it is consistent with the writing of Fielding.

The second sample of *Craftsman* 612 shows a clear homogeneity with the sample from *Joseph Andrews*: It is consistent with the writing of Henry Fielding. Again, the analysis shown in Figure CR/AM-2 gives clear visual evidence of mixed authorship: the second sample of *Craftsman* 612 is not consistent with the utterance of Nicholas Amhurst. Even when split into six alternate samples from the two texts in the combination analysis (Figure CR/JA-3), the result is clear consistency. This is a homogeneous combined sample.

Once again in Figure CR/AM-3, there is a firm separation between the *Craftsman* sentences and the utterance of Amhurst – here, the split has come at the point of the joining of the two texts, where the *Craftsman* eighteen sentences can be clearly seen to follow a consistent path until the Amhurst sample starts at sentence 19.

These three demonstration comparisons have confirmed the attribution of

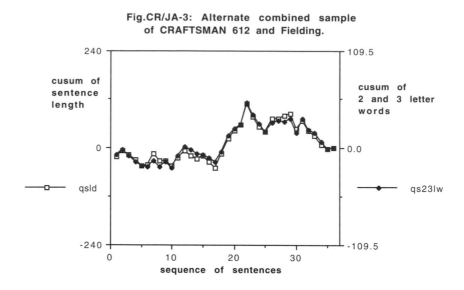

Figure CR/JA-3: Combined sample of sentences 35–52 of *Craftsman* 612 with eighteen sentences from Henry Fielding's *Joseph Andrews* analysed by the same habit, in six alternate sequences of six sentences each.

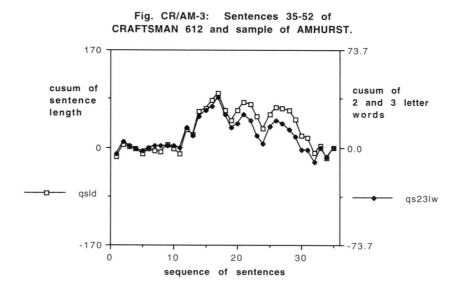

Figure CR/AM-3: Combined sample of sentences 18–34 of *Craftsman* 612 followed by seventeen sentences by Nicholas Amhurst, analysed by the habit of using two and three letters.

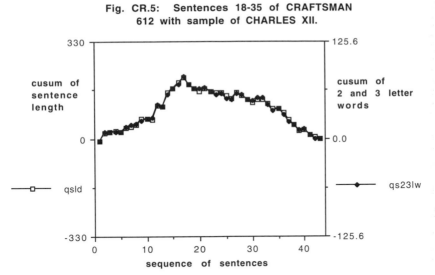

Figure CR-5: Combined sample of sentences 35–52 of *Craftsman* 612 followed by twenty-five sentences from *Charles XII*, analysed by the habit of using two and three letters.

Craftsman 612 to Henry Fielding, as claimed by Professor Battestin, while being plainly distinguishable from the editor of *The Craftsman*, Nicholas Amhurst.

But finally, there was one further test which gave a very interesting result. The last eighteen sentences of *Craftsman* 612 were analysed in a combined sample with the sample of twenty-five sentences (571 words, used in Chapter 5) of the *Military History of Charles XII*, and the result follows in Figure CR-5. This is a striking result, and demonstrably a homogeneous chart. Yet there is nothing whatsoever that connects the essay 'In Vindication of Laughter' with a sample from an anonymous translation of military history except the fact that both have been attributed to Henry Fielding.

Surely this is the strongest proof available both of the soundness of cusum analysis as a scientific attribution technique, and of the support it can give to attributions by a literary scholar, in this case, Martin Battestin.

The *Federalist* Problem Solved: Attribution of a Single Sentence

A question often asked by interested academics (or lawyers) seeking to attribute disputed utterance is about the size of the sample to be analysed. The greatest contrast imaginable is the attribution of a complete book and of a single disputed sentence. The caution with which the first of these two problems must be approached will be illustrated in the next section, which addresses the authorship of a full-length book (*Famine Diary*). Theoretically, every single sentence should be analysed to ascertain that there have been no insertions, plagiarism, or half-conscious 'borrowing' in a book which appears under a single author's name. For pre-Gutenberg texts, every sentence of what first appeared as a written manuscript *must* be analysed; but for modern texts, careful analysis of a number of samples from different parts of the text will give a high probability of authorship and is usually reliable.

Attribution of one single sentence is the opposite extreme. QSUM has been used on two occasions to try to resolve such an attribution. The first instance involved a criminal dispute, where conviction had been made on the basis of the utterance of one alleged sentence. The second involved a long-disputed historical attribution.

Mention has already been made in Chapter 1 of Mosteller and Wallace's study of the *Federalist* papers, and of the results of their investigations. The most doubtful of their attributions was of *Federalist* paper 19: their conclusion was that it was composite – the paper was jointly written by Madison and Hamilton.

This joint paper offered a good opportunity for a QSUM study, and reference was also in given in Chapter 1 (Note 11) to a study by Andrew Morton using the technique to attribute this paper. It was possible to identify the exact contributions of each author to this paper, an essay of sixty-six sentences.

To summarize Morton's conclusions, he found that thirty-four sentences – the first fifteen and the last nineteen – showed a good coincidence, and further tests established that they were homogeneous (attributed to Hamilton). Morton's analysis showed that 'the central section is quite different'.[17]

The central section, sentences 16–47, was homogeneous (and attributable to Madison) apart from one sentence, number 28, which was identified as one large paragraph. Morton may be quoted here:

> Inspection of sentence 28 shows it to be the whole of a short paragraph which resumes the subject of sentence 15 and anticipates the subject of sentence 48. An obvious hypothesis to explore is that this sentence belongs with the beginning and end of the paper.[18]

Further work by Morton supported his hypothesis, the project then having successfully attributed the single sentence 28 of the disputed paper. Morton pointed out that this evidence alone would need the backing of original textual analysis of the undeniable utterance of both Hamilton and Madison in order to provide absolute proof of the authorship of *Federalist* paper 19.

But the overwhelming experience of attribution by cusum analysis is that further comparative work supports the conclusions reached by the initial analysis. Morton's final point is worth repeating: 'The immediate relevance of this illustration is that the technique can show up quite small differences of authorship.'[19] Although the 'single sentence' in the case of the *Federalist* paper was actually the length of a paragraph, as was often the case in eighteenth-century writing, the single sentence in the legal case referred to earlier consisted of only twenty-nine words.

This is a significant demonstration of the technique's sensitivity, and it is good to know that it has successfully explained a long-standing conundrum.

The Diary of Gerald Keegan: The Irish Diary and the Canadian Publisher – Two Authors?

One of the clearest instances where QSUM would seem to be naturally useful is where doubtful authorship of texts is a matter of public dispute. One such study undertaken, first by Michael Farringdon and later continued by myself, concerns a contemporary dispute about a book published (apparently) as an authentic mid-nineteenth-century diary, *The Diary of Gerald Keegan*, but which some critics contend is the fictional work of its first publisher, Robert Sellar, not of its supposed author 'Gerald Keegan'. The contribution of QSUM to this dispute is now summarized.[20]

Initially, in 1992 a cusum analysis was requested in a letter to Dr Michael Farringdon from a representative of an Irish television company, concerning 'copies of two texts which we need to have analysed'.[21] These 'texts' came from *Gleaner Tales*, published in Huntingdon, Canada, in 1895, a collection of tales from Robert Sellar's newspaper: one was part of an introduction by Robert Sellar entitled 'How the Book Was Got', and the other comprised four samples from the *Diary of Gerald Keegan*. The diary purported to be a journal written by an Irish emigrant after the mid-nineteenth-century potato famine in Ireland, when he was aboard one of the emigrant 'coffin ships'.

The diary had since been reprinted in a collection of essays on the Irish, in 1987, as *Black '47: A Summer of Sorrow*.[22] This new publication had created some controversy in Canada, and doubts had been cast on the diary's authenticity.

The initial enquiry mentioned an even more recent printing in 1991, by an 'Irish publishing house'.[23] Entitled *Famine Diary,* the book had been widely read in Ireland ('a popular seller'). Some eighteen months later, it transpired that *Famine Diary* was not just another reprint of the original in Sellar's book. The fact is that, although the publication bore the title *Gerald Keegan's Famine Diary: Journey to a New World* , the book was actually a reprint of a fictional version of Sellar's original publication. This fictional narrative, called *The Voyage of the Naparima*, had been first published by a Canadian de la Salle Brother, James Mangan, in 1982.

As a derived version, it bore an introduction by Brother Mangan plainly stating that his story is 'a *fictionalised* account of Keegan's journal' (my italics), the source of which was claimed to be that very journal itself, '*Summer of Sorrows* [*sic*], written by a young Irish school-teacher, Gerald Keegan'. This fictionalized version contained a much more detailed pre-voyage section concerning the conditions of life in nineteenth-century Ireland that had occasioned the emigrant ships. Brother Mangan's reasons for his alterations concerned the type of language used in the original and the need for greater accessibility of Irish history to the modern reader. However, his introduction does not mention Robert Sellar or his *Gleaner Tales*. The name used for the diarist is 'Keegan', which was Sellar's heading (*The Diary of Gerald Keegan*), although the first mention of the diarist in *Gleaner Tales*, on page 360, is as 'Gerald O'Connor'. Occasional reference to 'Gerald O'Connor's Journal' by critics has been a somewhat confusing feature of this investigation.

It seems an even more unfortunate omission that when *The Voyage of the Naparima* was re-published as *Famine Diary*, it should have been printed without Mangan's introduction, appearing instead as a straightforward diary by the 'young Irish schoolteacher, Gerald Keegan'. When some degree of controversy ensued, this omission was rectified in the 1992 reprint of *Famine Diary*, now prefaced by a completely new introduction by Brother Mangan, ending:

> Following the very successful publication of *Famine Diary* by Wolfhound Press in 1991 widespread interest in the subject has led some historians to question the existence of Gerald Keegan and the authenticity of the original diary. However, I have no hesitation in standing over this fictionalised version as an accurate representation of the conditions and events of that period.

The nature of the dispute was, of course, that academic scholars had disputed the origin of the diary, maintaining that it was entirely a fictitious work by the Canadian publisher, Robert Sellar, instead of an eyewitness first-hand account, which had been sought, found, and then published by Sellar, of an emigrant's voyage in 1847 from Ireland to Canada.

Since the television company had completed four documentaries on the Great Famine of the 1840s in Ireland, and had included extracts from the diary in their work, it was natural that they should seek further information about the publication, an investigation of whether it was an authentic diary or a fiction. Even if it was the latter, their use of a vivid imaginative account based on historical facts would obviously be quite justifiable in itself, but curiosity about its origin was strong.

The example of the test case in Chapter 3 on the story attributed to D. H. Lawrence will have familiarized readers with the procedure for a professional testing of disputed authorship, and will give some idea of the intensive nature of the analyses necessary for a full and comprehensive conclusion to be made.

In the case of 'The Back Road', the complete story comprised a mere twenty-two sentences, so that its very brevity made possible the exhaustive testing, and made the finality of the conclusion certain.

In the case of *The Diary of Gerald Keegan*, however, the question raised concerned the authenticity of the origin of a piece of writing subsequently found to comprise some 87 pages long in its original printing (in 12mo), and some 37 quarto-sized pages long in its 1987 re-printing. Clearly, it was only going to be possible to analyse samples of the work. QSUM should be able to give a preliminary indication of whether such samples were consistent or not with undisputed writing by Robert Sellar.

Eventually, there were to be three investigations into the problem, as controversy multiplied. There were several difficulties which made necessary three separate projects, stretching over a period of time from March 1992 to November 1993, with misunderstandings on both sides. The analysts did not appreciate that more than one version of the 'Diary' was in circulation; the enquirers did not appreciate that initial sampling of a long text will not always provide a definitive answer – *a text is not necessarily all by one author*.

Robert Sellar was a journalist, a historian and the publisher of his own newspaper, *The Gleaner*. Both historians and journalists traffic in reportage, the re-presentation of source material. There was certainly enough writing published by Robert Sellar to undertake analysis of his utterance; but any work by him which had drawn heavily on historical documentation, and/or quotations, would naturally need careful scrutiny – for example, some sections of a book indisputably by him, *The Tragedy of Quebec*, fell into this category of historical reportage using source material.

The first project concluded that there was evidence of non-homogeneity between Sellar and some of the 'Diary' samples provided. This justified the conclusion that Robert Sellar had not, on the basis of QSUM analysis of these samples, been shown to be the unquestionable author of the diary. Mixed authorship, or at least editing, was a distinct probability.

However, the extent of the controversy surrounding the best-seller *Famine Diary* was much wider than this brief report on limited sampling could satisfy. A further analysis was requested by the Director of Action from Ireland, in Dublin, who had contributed a foreword to the 1991 publication of *Famine Diary*, and this request led to a second project, carried out by myself.[24] Apparently, a critical article entitled '*Famine Diary* – Fact or Fiction?' had appeared, stating 'categorically that *Famine Diary* was written by Robert Sellars [*sic*]'.[25]

A counter-argument was in prospect, to be carried out by an academic in Canada, who had understandably asked for a second check to be made on the diary using further textual material.[26] The new material consisted of four extracts of Robert Sellar's utterance from a book entitled *The Tragedy of*

Quebec , and a random selection of 'four extracts from *Summer of Sorrows* [*sic*] attributed to a young teacher by the name of either Gerald Keegan or Gerald O'Connor': again a variation in the name of the supposed diarist – was it 'O'Connor' or was it 'Keegan'? Certainly, the review by Dr Jim Jackson referred to the 'Journal of Gerald O'Connor'.

The extracts from Robert Sellar's *The Tragedy of Quebec* (coded here as TRGQ) were each four pages long. However, two of the samples contained unsuitable, long quotations of historical documentation of the kind referred to earlier as often occurring in works of historical journalism – for example, in the first, there were extracts from recorded conversation between a bishop and a Canadian premier named Mercier; and in the second, from legal patents issued to lands held in the townships. A combined sample of fifteen sentences each from Samples 1 and 2 from Robert Sellar's TRGQ resulted in a homogeneous QSUM 'fingerprint' suitable for testing with the diary extracts.[27] Figure TRGQ is a satisfactory homogeneous chart of Sellar's utterance from two samples in his *Tragedy of Quebec*.

It was at this point that pressure of time available, combined with an urgent need for the outcome of the new tests, resulted in the research moving in a less than desirable path. Four new samples from the diary in Sellar's original *The Summer of Sorrow* had been supplied, each of four pages. Analysing and

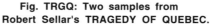

Fig. TRGQ: Two samples from Robert Sellar's TRAGEDY OF QUEBEC.

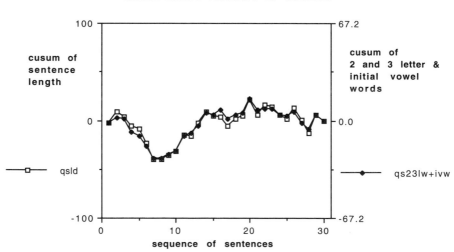

Figure TRGQ: A combined sample of fifteen sentences each from two extracts from Robert Sellar's *The Tragedy of Quebec* analysed by the habit of using two- and three-letter words and words starting with a vowel.[28]

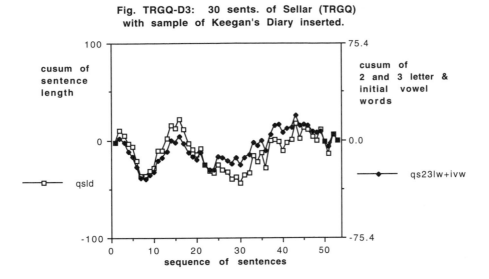

Fig. TRGQ-D3: 30 sents. of Sellar (TRGQ) with sample of Keegan's Diary inserted.

Figure TRGQ-D3: A 'sandwich' test of thirty homogeneous sentences of Robert Sellar (shown in Figure TRGQ) with **Diary Sample 3** inserted, analysed by the habit of using two- and three-letter words and words starting with a vowel.[29]

testing this new material would obviously have made the new project far too lengthy for the limited time available: the computer processing, the analyses, and the cross-matching of sixteen new pages of text would have been (as it *was* eventually to be) a careful research job of some weeks' duration.

The less desirable option was, therefore, the only one then open: that is, to make combined analyses using the new Sellar control text from TRGQ, which had at least proved for a second time that Sellar was no exception to cusum analysis, with the four diary samples already processed and in machine-readable form: that is, those extracts which had already been analysed with the *Gleaner Tales* samples from 'How The Book Was Got'.

This meant that, as there was not enough time available to make cusum analyses of the sixteen pages of new diary extracts, the text by Sellar would be analysed with the original diary extracts supplied by the television company, which had already been computer-processed. This confirmed the earlier conclusion. When the TRGQ sentences were combined with the Diary samples, at least two of the results showed mixed authorship or editing, one of which is shown in TRGQ-D3. As in the first project, a result of mixed utterance is demonstrated here.

In essence, this repeated the experimental analyses already carried out *although with a new Sellar 'fingerprint'*, so a duplication had occurred. The similar results and conclusions inevitably obtained, based on the kind of non-homogeneity seen above, only served to increase the controversy already existing.

The director of Action from Ireland was aware that the second report had not satisfied critics of the work, and wrote to express his anxiety that the mystery of authorship had not been satisfactorily settled. In particular, academic debate had continued.[30]

Only in November 1993 did we, as analysts, receive a copy of *Famine Diary*, which was by this time carrying a Publisher's Note and a quotation from Dr Farringdon's first report, apparently endorsing the diary's authenticity.[31] The report supplied had referred to the analysis of '*samples* [my italics] from *The Diary of Gerald Keegan*'. However, the Publisher's Note states that Dr Farringdon '. . . studied the *text* of Keegan's Diary' (my italics). This could well have given the non-professional reader the unfortunate impression that the full text had been analysed – a task enough to keep an army of researchers occupied for six months.

It is no part of the impartial analyst's brief to become involved in controversy. What matters here is clarification of the facts, and what now seemed urgently called for was a more thorough investigation into the original text of the diary in *Gleaner Tales*. This led to the third project. The extra samples randomly chosen by the academic in Montreal were each about four pages of the original document – between fifty-six and sixty-three sentences each. The full length of each sample was QSUM-analysed and

- **all four of these longer samples proved to be homogeneous.**

Only one chart of the very many individual and combined tests made (and which appear in a 46-page report) will be shown. Figure DGK (*Diary of Gerald Keegan*) is an analysis which combines twenty-five sentences from each of the four new diary samples to make a total of 100 sentences.[32] These four 25-sentence samples from different parts of the diary cannot be distinguished.

When Robert Sellar's utterance (in the thirty sentences of TRGQ) was combined with this combined sample of 100 sentences from the diary, the result is shown in Figure TRGQ/DGK. This chart shows the result of inserting the thirty sentences from Sellar's historical study into the combined 100 sentences from all four diary samples shown to be homogeneous above. Here, the diary by the supposed shipboard emigrant cannot be distinguished from a sample of writing by Robert Sellar. It is clear that the two sets of utterance are indistinguishable, pointing to single authorship.

What are the final conclusions to be drawn from a consideration of the earlier and the later analyses?

- Certainly Robert Sellar is not an exception to the QSUM technique.
- Occasionally, he has been observed to use historical material – as, for example, in the unsuitable passages forming part of the random samples supplied by Dr O'Laighin from Sellar's historical work, *The Tragedy of*

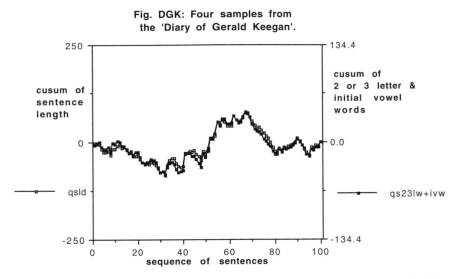

Fig. DGK: Four samples from the 'Diary of Gerald Keegan'.

Figure DGK: A combined sample totalling 100 sentences from *The Diary of Gerald Keegan*, (twenty-five sentences each) analysed by the habit of using two- and three-letter words, and words starting with a vowel.

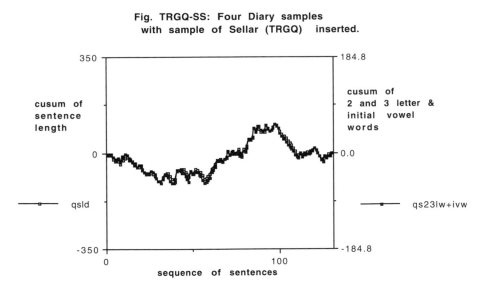

Fig. TRGQ-SS: Four Diary samples with sample of Sellar (TRGQ) inserted.

Figure TRGQ/DGK: 'Sandwich' of thirty sentences of *The Tragedy of Quebec* inserted (at sentence 51) into 100 sentences from *The Diary of Gerald Keegan*, analysed by the same habit.

Quebec. Such material would naturally not have been homogeneous with his own language habits.

- The second set of diary samples sent from Montreal *all* showed consistency with the utterance of Robert Sellar, and the conclusion is obvious.
- But some of the diary material supplied and tested in the first project was non-homogeneous, as shown above. Why? That inconsistent material could well have originated in an unknown specific source used by Robert Sellar: this may have been fragments of an actual diary – but, equally, it may have been due to his use of some other unknown historical data.

It is important to grasp that cusum analysis has only been applied to samples of the diary. Samples are supplied by chance, at random, but it must never be assumed that any single text is necessarily wholly the work of one writer. To make such an analysis of *The Diary of Gerald Keegan* would require painstaking lengthy comparison by the use of very many transparencies for cross-checking, in order to isolate either a single sentence or sequences of sentences from another source.

It must be remembered that QSUM-charts, as shown throughout this book, are a 'shorthand' method of conveniently illustrating, for the reader, what has been found by the researcher using transparencies, which is by far the most reliable method for detailed analysis. Where consistency is obvious to visual inspection, the QSUM-chart has proved satisfactory for illustrative purposes; but where there is inconsistency, and definitive answers are required, long-term work will ensue. Therefore, conclusive proof of the total authorship of any long work would require each and every sentence to be analysed, as it is for documents presented in a court of law.

Although analysis of a text in its totality is the only way of providing proof of authorship of every sentence, enough random sampling will provide a good idea of who wrote a single-authored book; that is, in the case of modern published books. In this particular case, one may estimate probabilities. What seems probable from the thorough testing of the third project is that Robert Sellar is likely to be the author of the majority of *The Diary of Gerald Keegan*. The early conclusion (first and second reports) was correct, but premature in the light of the exhaustive testing of the third project. It provides a salutary warning to both an enquirer and to the analyst.

In such a case, the reader may care to weigh the QSUM evidence together with the literary approach which addresses the *form* of this work, as it is comprehensively understood by literary criticism. Together with a common-sense grasp of the impracticability of writing such a work in conditions on board a 'coffin-ship', the literary form must weigh heavily in judging the complete work, especially given the support from the results of the third project.

Five Cautionary Tales from Andrew Morton

Every technique has its limitations and is subject to misunderstandings, misrepresentations and abuse, sometimes in circumstances where it is not easy to decide which description applies.

From a range of examples five have been chosen.

The Edinburgh Example

In the first of a series of lectures Morton offered to analyse a sample prepared by the audience. It could be Greek or English and, in view of the time available, should be no more than fifty sentences. It could contain the utterance of as many people as the setters decided but no insertion should be smaller than five sentences.

At the second lecture the sample was handed over: it was fifty sentences of English prose. The following week Morton described his results. The first fourteen sentences were one person, the rest was another person, but in the second half of the sample was a puzzling anomaly of two sentences. At this point Professor O'Neill, who had compiled the sample, rose and apologized: he had forgotten the restriction of insertions not to be fewer than five sentences and the sample was fifteen sentences of X, twenty-two sentences of Y, two sentences of X and eleven of Y.

O'Neill described the result as 'brilliant'.

The Crook

Morton was supplied, from an Australian prison, with a sample which purported to be a record of interview in which a confession to a crime had been made. It was not the utterance of the convicted man but matched the utterance of a police officer. The result aroused so much interest that a more detailed examination was commissioned. It then emerged that the sample was not a record of the *ipsissima verba* of the accused but had been taken from the police officer's record of interview prepared for his superiors and gave his version of what was said in his own words.

It is essential that the origin of all samples be precisely described.

The Anonymous Letter

A London solicitor sent Morton three short samples, a dozen sentences of each, and asked which of three men matched an anonymous letter which was not much longer. Testing revealed that samples 1 and 2 differed from the letter, but sample 3 was indistinguishable from the letter. Given the choice, the report was that the writer of sample three had written the letter.

The solicitor then revealed that sample three was from a former partner in his office – a man who had been dead for many years. In his eyes the technique was discredited.

The truth was that, as only differences are proof, the letter was not written by the writers of samples 1 or 2, and the sole conclusion was limited to that. The statement that one of the three people was the writer of the letter was a falsehood introduced by the solicitor and led inevitably to the further false conclusion. Anyone planning to set a test for a technique must grasp the fundamental principles of the technique and of statistical inference. Common sense is not a safe guide.

The Tabloid TV Test

A TV company sent Morton two short samples and asked if these could be accepted as the utterance of the same person. Analysis showed that one sample was homogeneous but the other was in two parts. The first part of the second sample was indistinguishable from the first sample.

Morton then stated his two conclusions. The first sample was the utterance of one person. The second sample was in two parts, of eight sentences and five sentences; only the first eight sentences were indistinguishable from the first sample.[33] The part of sample 2 which was similar to sample 1 could be accepted as from the same person.

This conclusion was so interesting that a film crew arrived and conducted an interview. Some way into the interview, they revealed it had been a concealed test and claimed it discredited cusum analysis, as both samples were recorded speeches by two different persons. But the second sample was a speech delivered by a company chairman and in the speech was incorporated a forecast of beer production overseas for years to come. When it was pointed out that this was likely to be the work of the marketing department which the chairman would quote, they were unaware that any speech might contain the utterance of a number of people. A minister of religion conducting a marriage will cite the Bible, the liturgy of his church, and some biographical detail suited to the particular situation. He will speak every word, but all are not his composition.

Once again this emphasizes the need for the origin of samples to be known with some precision before any hypothesis is framed. In this instance, one sample was homogeneous, the other was not. With so few sentences, the first part of the sample would match a number of people and no safe conclusion about its origin could be drawn. But the way in which the question which was put begged the question.

The Dutch Policewoman

A sample was shown which had a major insertion in it according to the analysis. The woman who had drawn the charts was disturbed; she was sure the sample was the work of her friend. On being questioned, it emerged that the sample was a magazine article and when it was suggested she ask her friend if the offending paragraph was an editorial insertion, she explained that the writer was dead – but she was certain she would never have allowed anyone to alter a word she wrote.

Samples of uncertain origin can only lead to uncertain interpretations.

QSUM can be, and has been, tested many times by blind trials, but experience has shown that many people who set trials use samples about which they have a made large assumption. The only safe samples are those produced for the purpose under control conditions.

It is also very desirable that the student have some background in the texts which are to be examined. The text of Shakespeare, for example, is a record of plays. Knowing what actors and producers do to plays, it is natural to expect that while the texts should display an overall homogeneity there is likely to be a large number of small emendations.

PART III

Forensic applications:
Preparing a legal report; attributing non-standard
English; the critics answered

Chapter 8

LEGAL APPLICATIONS

Michael Farringdon

Statistical techniques for the attribution of authorship had been accepted in evidence in several law courts in England, the USA and Australia for a number of years before cusum analysis was developed. In 1975 both A. Q. Morton and Bryan Niblett gave evidence for the defence of Steven Raymond at the Central Criminal Court, London. Raymond was charged with twelve counts; he was alleged to have made verbal confessions in four statements to the police officer who interrogated him, the officer claiming that he had taken down these statements verbatim. Raymond rejected having made these confessions. From a previous case, in which he had been found not guilty of murder, there were seven statements that Raymond admitted were genuinely by him.

Morton's evidence was based on a technique that he and his colleague Sidney Michaelson had developed in the early 1970s which they called 'positional stylometry'.[1] In positional stylometry three groups of words are considered: words which appear in preferred positions in sentences, for example, occurrences of A, BUT, THAT as the first word of a sentence, and words such as IT, OF, THAT as the last word of a sentence; the use of frequent proportional pairs of words, for example, ALL/ANY, AND/ALSO, THAT/THIS; and the use of frequent collocations, for example, FROM THE, AS A, THE *followed by an adjective*. A battery of suitable tests from these three groups is found, from an analysis of the undisputed, or control, texts, and used on the disputed texts. The statistical probability that chance would create differences between the control texts and the disputed texts can be calculated using the chi-squared test. Morton, using positional stylometry, found eleven consistent habits in the admitted statements. Using these eleven habits, Morton found that they differed by a significant amount in the rejected statements.[2]

In 1974 Niblett had just completed a developed a suite of computer programs to classify the text of documents, specifically for classifying the full text of the *Conventions and Agreements of the Council of Europe* using the statistical technique of cluster analysis. Niblett's analysis started by comparing the words and their frequencies in each pair of documents and obtaining a coefficient of similarity between the documents in each pair. The programs used the similarity coefficients to form clusters of documents with similar word content. With statutes and treaties the interest was in forming clusters of documents based on their content. Thus Niblett and his collaborator would exclude the common high frequency 'filler' words, which contained little information on the document content, from their analysis. However, when asked to analyse the statements in the Raymond case for authorship, Niblett knew that from work by Morton, and Mosteller and Wallace, it was generally agreed that it was the use of these common words that needed to be examined rather than the content words. Niblett reprogrammed his computer to include the eighty most frequent words in the English language and exclude all other words in the analysis of the statements. In court Niblett demonstrated that the four disputed documents were grouped in one cluster separately and distinguishable from the seven undisputed documents.[3]

Morton used positional stylometry to examine a will, in Pennsylvania, USA, in 1978, which was suspected of being partially fabricated, and records of interview, also suspected of being fabricated, in two cases in Australia in 1984 and 1985.[4]

QSUM evidence was first given and accepted in 1991 when Morton presented the technique and then his evidence, in the Court of Appeal in London, concerning a statement alleged to have been made by Tommy McCrossen.[5] Subsequently, Morton has given QSUM evidence, to the date of writing, in a further three cases.[6] Michael Farringdon presented the technique and gave evidence in the Central Criminal Court, Dublin in 1991 concerning a number of statements alleged to have been made by Vincent Connell, and has given QSUM evidence in a further five cases.[7] In 1993, M. D. Baker presented the technique and gave evidence twice in 'Diplock' courts in Northern Ireland.[8]

In all the cases in which QSUM evidence has been given in court, so far, it has been given for the defence. The defence lawyers are looking for evidence which will provide 'reasonable doubt'. To this end they appear to be hoping for an expert opinion to the effect that a disputed statement is not the utterance of the defendant, or that a disputed statement is the mixed utterance of two or more people. Either of these findings would question the prosecution assertion that the statements were taken down verbatim. In the case of mixed utterance the instructing solicitor is unlikely to request further analysis to identify the authorship of homogeneous sections of such a statement, interesting though this may be to the investigator. Whatever the findings, be they favourable or not to the defendant, they only speak of the origin of the utterance; analysis is not a way of testing whether the utterance is truthful or not. Prosecution lawyers would seem to have the harder task in providing evidence in which there is very little doubt. We are now getting close to the realm of probability and confidence levels, which is considered more fully in the next chapter. Suffice it to say that QSUM evidence is probably likely to be of most use to a defence case in court. Outside the court, during an investigation, QSUM evidence may well be of help in narrowing down a group of suspects. For example, an investigation into who wrote some anonymous letters may have produced a small pool of suspects. Use of QSUM to analyse samples of utterance from each of the suspects and compare these samples with the anonymous letters should help to reduce the number of the suspects by eliminating those whose utterance is distinguishable from the letters.

Types of Cases

In this chapter I shall concentrate on cases where the client is a defendant or an appellant; there are obviously similar types of cases where the approach is more investigative. The types of attribution in legal cases which we have so far been asked to investigate with QSUM have been concerned with:

- *statements* made under caution and disputed in whole or in part by the defendant;
- *witness statements*, usually of prosecution witnesses, which are thought by the defence to have been partially or wholly written by a person or persons other than the witness;
- *suicide letters*, usually in the dead person's own handwriting but where there is a question as to whether the composition of the letter(s) is entirely the unaided work of the dead person or was dictated by someone else – was it suicide or murder?;
- *anonymous telephone calls*, where a defendant denies having made the calls;
- *telephone and recorded conversations* alleged to have been spoken by a person who denies having made them;
- *plagiarism*, if there are suspected to be sections of text copied from someone else's work – obviously QSUM cannot help if the allegation is that (only) ideas have been plagiarized;
- *forgery*, where the authorship of the whole or part of a document, for example, a will, is in question.

In some of these investigations we have found nothing untoward and cannot sustain the contention of our client; in others, pleas have been changed, prosecutions have been dropped, or plea bargaining has taken place. (In a recent case concerning the source of some anonymous letters, after a report on their authorship had been handed to the instructing solicitor the anonymous letters stopped.) In only a fraction of cases are we asked to give our evidence in court. (In a very few instances we have been approached in the mistaken belief that QSUM can be used to help a defendant who denies saying anything in an interview statement where the transcript gives the defendant replying with the single word 'Yes' (or 'No') to, say, five questions, and making no reply to the other questions. In such cases we suggest an approach be made to forensic experts who use more appropriate methods.)

In the normal course of events, the initial approach for an investigation comes from solicitors on behalf of their client, though it is not unknown to us for barristers to approach us directly, usually when a case is just about to start – or has even started. Initial approaches from defendants, their families, friends and supporters are referred back to the solicitor handling the case. If, from a preliminary discussion or sight of the disputed utterance, it appears that it may be worthwhile making a QSUM investigation, then the question of control texts for comparison purposes arises.

Types of Control Utterance

The control texts are used to check that the client's utterance is not an exception to QSUM and to find which test or tests give homogeneity and can be used as discriminators when comparing with the disputed utterance. The main sources of utterance found useful for controls are:

- *letters* by a defendant which often provide good samples of written utterance, usually having been written, and sometimes over a period of several years, to family or friends or solicitor ;
- *recorded conversations* between, say, the defendant and a solicitor or the QSUM investigator, usually specially made for the investigation, should provide a good sample of spoken utterance, (the investigator should avoid asking questions of a form which allows the defendant to answer by repeating a phrase from the question, i.e. the defendant's utterance would then be mixed with the investigator's);
- *'essays'* specially written by a defendant in a solicitor's presence may provide a useful substitute for a lack of letters;
- *court transcripts* where the defendant or appellant has given evidence in court on a previous occasion may give a suitable sample of spoken utterance.

If the investigation was of the form of an academic research project (where time is not usually of the essence), the 'ideal', shall we say, then one would like to have a number of samples of spoken and written utterance both made over a period of years. However, with real legal cases the time scale for making the complete investigation, including writing and submitting a report, is often short, being of the order of one, two, or three weeks, including obtaining suitable and sufficient controls: in other words the practical situation is far from the academic ideal.

It should also be noted that there may be difficulties, often insuperable, in obtaining certain types of controls. A defendant may not be a letter writer, possibly being illiterate or semi-literate, or family and friends simply may not keep letters. A tape-recorded conversation may be difficult to obtain if the defendant is detained in prison and the prison authorities object to a tape recorder being introduced, even by a solicitor, to the prison. Obviously an illiterate person would not be able to write an essay. Transcripts of a previous court case involving a defendant may not exist or may not be readily available; a transcript is virtually impossible to obtain if the original shorthand writer(s) have retired or are otherwise unavailable. Also, the making of transcripts takes time, time which is usually in short supply for the QSUM investigation. If the QSUM investigator has been instructed by the defence it is usually very difficult, if not impossible in reality, to obtain controls for prosecution witnesses, including police officers. In the case where there is a suspicion of murder dressed up to look like suicide, there is unlikely to be any recorded spoken utterance of the dead person, and one has to hope for letters or other writings being found.

Integrity of the Controls

What is required of controls is that their content be accepted as authentic. As has been stated forcibly in earlier chapters, and cannot be reiterated too often, the integrity of the controls is most important – in other words, are the controls wholly the unaided natural utterance, written or spoken, of the defendant? A defendant's letters from prison, especially if written to a solicitor, may well contain legal, or pseudo-legal jargon, utterance which is unlikely to be natural and may have been aided by fellow prisoners who, over time, may have picked up some law. This leads us to the question as to whether a letter from prison is the defendant's whole and unaided work, or if other prisoners have given helpful suggestions, especially if the writer is semi-literate or unused to expressing himself in writing. On the whole, ordinary letters to family and friends, whether written inside or outside prison, seem to have the least likelihood of having been adulterated and thus make useful controls.

Recorded conversations between a defendant and a solicitor or a QSUM investigator, being made in a controlled manner especially for the investigation, should be free of integrity problems, apart possibly from those introduced by the necessary transcription; possible problems introduced by transcription are discussed below. Likewise, essays written in a controlled environment in the presence of a solicitor or the QSUM investigator, should be free of integrity problems. Court transcripts potentially suffer from the same transcription problems as recorded conversations.

Transcription and its Problems

Transcription is used frequently to produce documents for the court. When police officers, in the UK, interview a suspect after a caution they are expected to write down verbatim, by hand, the exact words used in the whole of the interview, with nothing added or subtracted and the words in the order in which they are spoken. Alternatively, and becoming a more frequent occurrence, the whole of the interview will be tape recorded. The officers will then produce a typewritten version of the handwritten notes or of the tape recording. Thus there will be two transcriptions in the former case from speech to handwritten form and from handwritten to typewritten form. In the latter case there will be only one transcription, from tape-recorded to typewritten form. Similarly with court transcripts: what is said in court is taken down by a court stenographer in shorthand and later, possibly, transcribed to typewritten form. (It is also quite normal to have a tape-recorded version of the court proceedings to which the stenographer can refer, if necessary.) Recorded telephone conversations and other recorded material will need to be transcribed to typewritten form. Handwritten letters and handwritten statements, which are likely to be produced in court in evidence, are transcribed to typewritten form. The list of examples could go on.

The question that needs to be asked, in a forensic setting, is just how accurate are these transcriptions? Transcribers are human and thus fallible and can make mistakes. Where possible, photocopies of original handwritten letters and statements should be compared with the typewritten versions; copies of the original tape recordings of interviews and telephone calls should be compared to the transcribed versions. I say 'where possible' since originals have a habit of being 'not available', of getting mislaid or of being destroyed after a period of time; tape recordings of the actual court proceedings, for checking against court transcripts, are unlikely to be made available.

Typical of the 'errors' to be found in transcripts are:

- *normalization of spelling*, for example, WON'T transcribed as WILL NOT, YOUS or YOUSE (colloquial Irish) transcribed as YOU;
- *punctuation*: this can be a difficult when transcribing from (recorded) speech: for example, there may be difficulty determining where sentences end, especially as in speech people often speak in incomplete sentences; examples of changes in punctuation have also been noticed in transcriptions from hand-written letters and statements;
- tape recording of an indistinct voice, or a voice in an unfamiliar accent or dialect, or when more than one person is speaking at the same time, or simply because the recording is of poor quality;
- *portions of utterance missing*, usually due to the transcriber having returned to the wrong position on a tape recording or the wrong line on a sheet of handwritten text.

Transcription, especially of recordings, is time consuming and can be tedious, and tedium may lead to mistakes being made. Those involved professionally in the transcribing of recorded speech consider a time ratio of 1:10 for transcription, in other words, for one hour of recorded speech they allow ten hours for transcribing it.

In QSUM investigations it is normal for a solicitor to supply photocopies of typewritten transcriptions of recorded speech and of handwritten matter. Furthermore, and remember we are talking about the real world, the photocopies are likely to be poorly reproduced (seemingly copies of copies of copies . . .), and pages slightly skewed so that portions of words are missing or cropped from the sides of the page. The QSUM investigator has to not only read this unpromising material but also to transcribe it onto a computer. If the photocopy is very good, then a typescript may be scanned into computer-readable form; if the copy is not so clear then it must by typed by hand into the computer.[9] Either way lends itself open to the introduction of errors in transcription. Thus, there must be careful checking of all transcribed utterance, checking as far back to the original source as practicable.

Editing

With the utterance in textual form on a computer and having been checked for accuracy of transcription, there may still be some editing necessary. Where alterations, such as changing the punctuation or deleting portions of answers, suggested below are made to the transcriptions, these changes should be clearly noted as such in the final report.

As suggested earlier in this book, we have found it sensible to run together the words in names and addresses, for example, 'John Z. Doe, 1445 W. Deloite Ave., Pine Ridge' would be more suitably edited to the two 'words' 'JohnZDoe, 1445WDeloiteAvePineRidge', which also has the advantage of having rid us of three full-stops used for abbreviation purposes rather than indicating the end of sentences. Any further full-stops used for abbreviations only should also be removed – these may have crept into the transcription if the text had been entered through a scanner.

Very occasionally, it may be useful to slightly modify the punctuation. From experiments I carried out in 1992 where an unpunctuated text was punctuated by about twenty separate participants, it appears that so long as the re-punctuation is *sensible*, even though not identical, homogeneity is not affected. Occasions when re-punctuation may be considered advisable are, for example, joining a very short sentence of three or four words to an adjacent sentence, or splitting a very long sentence into two or more shorter ones.

When the utterance being examined consists of the answers extracted from a question-and-answer interview one needs to be careful that the text of the answers does not contain substantial portions of the questions. Some people begin their answers by repeating the last part of the preceding question, thus mixing their own utterance with that of the questioner. It seems sensible, then, to delete the repeated question portion of their answer.

Tests for Discrimination

All the utterance to be examined should now be in a word-processor file on a computer, suitable for processing by the CusumChart program.[10] Samples from the control texts are examined for QSUM homogeneity under all the various tests, i.e. two- and three-letter words test, two- and three-letter and initial vowel words test, three- and four-letter words test, etc. Unless the author of these undisputed control texts is an exception to QSUM (to date we have found no exceptions), one or more of the tests will show homogeneity on a cusum chart. When tests have been found which are appropriate for our client, the disputed texts are compared with samples of the undisputed texts. If the comparisons show that the disputed texts are indistinguishable from the control texts then we are unable to sustain our client's contention that the disputed texts are fabricated. It should be noted here that we are *not* saying that our client is the author of the disputed texts, only that *we cannot distinguish* between the controls and the disputed texts using the technique, which would be the case, of course, if our client was indeed the author.[11]

On the other hand, if the comparisons between the disputed texts and the controls show non-homogeneity on the cusum charts then we can give an opinion that the disputed texts are not by the author of the control texts. Further examination of the disputed texts may well show large homogeneous sections, indicating that two or more people had a hand in their production. At this point, if not before, most QSUM investigations will stop, since this is probably as far as the solicitor's instructions go. The solicitor usually only wants an opinion as to whether the disputed texts are distinguishable or not from the defendant's utterance.

To pursue the investigation further, having satisfied oneself that the disputed texts have been fabricated or tampered with, usually involves a very great deal of extra testing. Even if the instructing solicitor wishes for further investigations to be made, time and cost limitations are likely to militate against this. The main reason for investigating further is in trying to find the author or authors of fabricated or altered texts. In most of the cases one is likely to investigate the number of potential authors of the disputed text(s) is doubtless small; probably only four or five people at the most will have had the opportunity in terms of place, time and access to have tampered with or concocted a disputed text. If the disputed texts contain substantial homogeneous portions and if one can obtain authentic utterance from each of the potential authors from this small pool, then comparisons can be made between each person's utterance and each of the homogeneous portions. With such a small pool of potential authors it is usually possible to eliminate from the investigation those whose utterance is distinguishable from homogeneous portions if the disputed texts. If the utterance of any in the pool of potential authors is indistinguishable from the homogeneous portions of the disputed texts then one might suggest that further investigations be made of these people.

It can be very useful if one finds two or more tests show homogeneity in the control samples. Say that a defendant is homogeneous on two different tests: then, even though a disputed text is indistinguishable from the defendant's controls when using one of the tests but is distinguishable using the other test, then we can give the opinion that the disputed text is not wholly the utterance of the defendant.

There are times when it appears that other forms of linguistic analysis or psychological analysis may be fruitfully employed in addition to cusum analysis, or when it is evident that QSUM is not going to be of use in the case. For example, one may have the feeling that there is an excessive use of 'police-speak' which seems unnatural, or possibly the statement seems too long to have been made within the times stated, or maybe in a witness interview there is the feeling that ideas may have been planted in a defendant's mind. At this point one recommends, to the instructing solicitor, experts in one of these other areas.

The Report and Presenting the Evidence

Since evidence using statistical techniques for the attribution of authorship is relatively new to courts, it has been considered judicious to preface the report, which is given to the instructing solicitor, with an introduction to cusum analysis and how to interpret the QSUM-charts. The core of the report shows the cusum analysis of the controls and the comparisons with the disputed text(s), complete with QSUM-charts, and is followed by the conclusions, being the opinions of the expert. When giving evidence, the charts in the report are re-drawn on overhead projector slides. This is particularly useful when one wishes to show that a statement, say, is composed of several distinct homogeneous sections. This can be well illustrated using separate charts and moving one on top of the other on an overhead projector.

It is quite likely that in cross-examination one will be asked if any part of a disputed statement is, 'in your opinion', by the defendant. However, remembering that one has usually been given specific instructions by the solicitor to give an opinion as to whether the disputed statement is defendant's utterance or not, it is highly unlikely that the considerable extra work involved is attributing sections of a statement has been done. One has not been asked to carry the investigation further, and the cost involved by the large amount of extra time likely to be taken would not necessarily be met by the solicitor's client, or more likely the Legal Aid Board. Again, one must remember that legal cases are not like open-ended research projects where one can often follow what look to be interesting byways; specific instructions, and time and cost constraints deny us this indulgence.

It is worth noting at this point the experience of those who have written QSUM-based reports for defence solicitors. In the majority of cases the reports have not sustained the contention of the appellants that they have been 'verballed', for example. In at least two cases the presentation of reports to the court have resulted in police officers changing their evidence such that it concurred with the opinions in the reports. There have also been a small number of cases where the appellant has changed his/her plea soon after the defence solicitor has received the report. In all such cases the QSUM evidence has not been called.

When giving evidence as an expert, one must always be prepared for the other 'side' producing their own expert to counter one's opinions. Detailed comment on this aspect is given in Chapter 10 when consideration is given to the critics of the technique.

The British legal system is an adversarial system. An expert witness is called by one of the two parties to give an expert opinion, presumably favourable, for the calling party. The other party appears to see its purpose, particularly in cross-examination, as primarily to destroy or discredit the expert's evidence (and maybe the expert as well). Most of the experts I have spoken with know this and admit to being unbiased and objective and they see themselves as 'friends of the court', realizing that this is the way the courts work. And, of course, expert witnesses need to remember that they only see part of the evidence in a case, often a very small part, and that it is the members of the jury who have to form an opinion after having heard all the admissible evidence that has been presented.

What is the definition of an 'expert'? Webster's dictionary defines an expert as 'one with special skill or knowledge representing mastery of a particular subject'. How do courts define an expert? *Stroud's Judicial Dictionary* says, 'An expert witness is one who has made the subject upon which he speaks a matter of particular study, practice, or observation; and he must have a particular and special knowledge of the subject', to which *Jowitt's Dictionary* adds, 'The expert need not be an authority in his profession or occupation, providing he has the necessary experience or qualifications.'[12]

Chapter 9

NON-STANDARD ENGLISH AND THE COURTS: LINGUISTIC/SOCIAL BACKGROUND

Two common questions asked by members of an audience at lectures on QSUM concern the linguistic and social background of the individual who is subject to cusum analysis. One query asks whether the technique will work on speakers or writers who habitually use non-standard English; and the second query asks whether the intelligence and the educational and/or social background of the individual will influence the results – can individuals of very similar background be successfully differentiated? Both questions are addressed in this chapter: M. David Baker, a consultant expert witness on the use of QSUM, will deal with the second question from his experience as an analyst of the language of four defendants in one case.

Firstly, though, some answers to the first question, also from legal experience of analysing the speech and writing of defendants or appellants.

Standard English and the EFL-speaker

For the reader who is not familiar with the terminology of linguistics, it is as well to define terms here.

Diversity of language usage and the existence of different of 'varieties' of language is usual in all languages. Whilst virtually everyone in the countries where English is the national language can speak English (as well as sometimes being bilingual, that is, fluent in another language), they do not all speak it in the same way. Variations will habitually occur according to country (say, the UK and the USA); to region (say, England's West Country and Northumbria); and to social situation (say, language used familiarly at home or formally in the law courts).

By 'Standard English' is meant that variety of English accepted as a norm throughout an English-speaking country, in our case, the UK. The fact that Standard English can itself be seen as a dialect, albeit the 'official' one, is well argued and exemplified in Trudgell's book on the implications for teachers of English.[1] For example, where (English)-Standard English usage would say 'We *go* there every week', a regional dialect form might say 'We *goes* there every week'. Neither dialect usage can be said to be 'correct'; one is Standard and a national form, and the other a local form (not a debased form of the Standard).

Most of the chapters in this book have dealt with textual examples of samples in Standard English, whether written or spoken. The samples of writing by D. H. Lawrence, Aldous Huxley, Muriel Spark, Henry Fielding, Helen Keller and the other children, Robert Sellar, and my own utterance, have all been written in Standard English (although local pronunciation would naturally vary).

Literary examples abound, of course, where the writer has presented a character who speaks the dialect of his region. We have already seen, in Chapter 7, the examples taken from *Huckleberry Finn*: the conventions of writing used to convey the speech of his character(s) were Mark Twain's invention, as the first American writer to use variations of American speech for the serious novel. As we saw, different dialects present no problem for QSUM.

Regional dialects in the UK should be carefully distinguished from accents. Most of the population can speak Standard English but with the accent of their region – Scottish, Welsh, Irish, West Country, Cockney, Liverpudlian, Mancunian and so on. But accent does not alter syntax, word-order or vocabulary, and the same standard English passage read in local accents by speakers from different parts of the country would obviously yield an identical cusum analysis. The passage would remain the same passage and homogeneous with its origin in whatever accent it was spoken.

Dialects do offer some differences of word-order, syntax, and even vocabulary, but are themselves consistent in their local morphological differences from the Standard version of a language. (Note that even Standard dialects themselves differ grammatically: compare 'She'd gotten home' – *American Standard English* – with 'She'd got home' – *English Standard English*.)

The question now addressed is, will cusum analysis work on samples of writing or speech which are clearly affected by differences in speech?

English as a Foreign Language

Many of the cases which police officers have to deal with today concern offenders who are speak English as a foreign language (EFL speakers), and whose grasp of the language is imperfect. Can QSUM successfully analyse their utterance for consistency?

There are two kinds of EFL speaker. One situation is where English is learnt, by an immigrant or the child of an immigrant, within an English-speaking country in a school of that country, and by teachers whose mother-tongue is English. Special training is usually needed for such teaching – TEFL (Teaching English as a Foreign Language).

Often, a child in this situation hears her/his mother tongue at home – Hindi, perhaps (or, within the UK, may it be suggested, Gaelic or Welsh?). This child will then learn English as a second language at school, and is further helped by hearing the language in all other social situations and also via radio or television. Such a child-speaker will certainly have been properly taught, but will lack the domestic support for extended practice in speaking English: some African, Asian, or West Indian immigrants into English-speaking countries would be in this category.

The second kind of EFL-speaker is the one who has learnt English abroad in her or his own country, often from teachers who are imperfect in English themselves, so that an imperfect Standard English is learnt by the school-children. As a former lecturer, I have encountered trained teachers from Brunei and Nigeria who were well aware that they fell into this category, and who wanted help in improving their methods of teaching English for the Malay or tribal language (Ibo or Yoruba, say) spoken by their pupils. An example of a country where American English is the Standard variety which is taught abroad would be in the Philippines.

It would seem useful to look at two legal examples involving EFL-speakers, one belonging to each of the kinds described above.

My first example concerns an EFL-speaker who had learnt English at school while he spoke one of the languages of the Indian subcontinent at home. The linguistic examples which follow are based on a real case history, but have all been slightly altered in content words to protect anonymity: the syntactic structure remains the same, the computation is the same, and the illustrative charts are thus identical. The nature of the invented sentences faithfully reproduces the number of words and relative simplicity or complexity.

First, in example (A), some typical utterance is shown.

A. Examples of spoken utterance of an EFL-speaker, when aged eighteen, taken from an Admission Statement (Average number of words per sentence in sample = 9.95)

I have already told the other two officers what I had seen.
Who's going to speak to me?
I turned and ran from there.
No, that is their story.
Yes, but I didn't want it brought down.

These sentences, recorded in a police officer's notebook, are perfectly good standard English. The only point to note is the short average sentence length, and that the sentences are either simple sentences or co-ordinate sentences joined by 'and' or 'but' – there is only one subordinate clause ('*what I had seen'*). This is more characteristic of a child's use of English than that of an eighteen-year-old.

After ten years in prison, the same man's spoken utterance had (perforce) improved, as the following example (B), will show.

These sentences have nearly doubled in length, and there is use of subordinate clauses. The greater sophistication in the later utterance will be obvious in these few sample sentences comparing those taken, in (A) from an officer's notebook, and, in (B), from a conversation with his solicitor.

B. Examples of spoken utterance of the same man, when aged twenty-eight (Average number of words per sentence in total sample = 19.867)

It was an establishment where all the convicts were lifers, or detained long term, and it was just a more acceptable community to live in than where you had short-termers or other sorts of prisoners.

I haven't been seeing TV all that much lately because my sight has been a bit weak, but, yes, I do get entertainment with the TV.

I was delayed, but I tried to get further explanation to find out what was going on and that became harder.

It is also useful to compare this subject's written utterance six years after his arrest with his official signed statement at the age of eighteen.

C. The same man's written utterance, aged eighteen, in a signed statement
For reasons of confidentiality, the statement itself will not be reproduced here, but its character may be summarized. The total number of sentences was ten, with an average word-length of 7.4 words per sentences. Two sentences will give an idea of its simplicity:

I did not go outside the station.
I went home then.

D. The same man's written utterance in a letter, aged twenty-four (Average wps of sample = 14.97)

I hated to embarrass you like that, especially as you had other ideas yourself.

Well, when I went down to the phone at the entrance today I quickly referred to my address and personal diary for the correct number and by mistake I dialled [J]'s (remember her?) phone number.

In terms of the subject's early spoken utterance in recorded spoken answers and in his official statement, the increase in fluency and general linguistic tone is notable.

The question is whether the simple use of English by a characteristic EFL-speaker may be successfully analysed by QSUM, and whether it remains consistent with the same subject's later, more sophisticated usage. This moves on to a consideration of learning and speaking two languages at the same time, of learning a new language as an adult, or of learning a language from a teacher who cannot use it as a mother tongue.

The first chart shown, Figure EFL-1, shows the result of combining a sample of early EFL-speech with the same speaker's later fluent utterance. This is a clearly homogeneous combined sample of utterance. The later longer and more sophisticated sentences share the same consistency in the use of the habit as the simple sentences of the written statement (example C above).

It is worth noting that there were three notebooks of officer's records of this man's utterance when he was aged eighteen, giving ample material for analysis.

The next result, Figure EFL-2, shows the result of combining the later sentences of conversation to the spoken answers given to one of those officers ten years before. The stability of the habit over ten years is obvious. Some sentences used in this combined sample of sentences analysed have been given in illustrative material in A and B above. Clearly, despite some very slight shifting of the graph lines, this is another homogeneous combined sample.

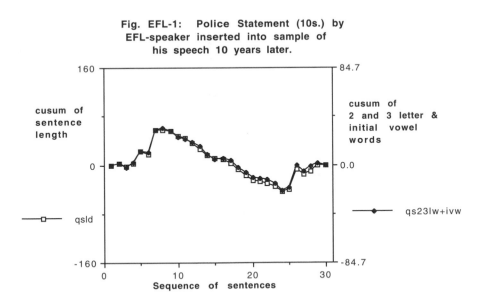

Fig. EFL-1: Police Statement (10s.) by EFL-speaker inserted into sample of his speech 10 years later.

cusum of sentence length

cusum of 2 and 3 letter & initial vowel words

qsld

qs23lw+ivw

Sequence of sentences

Figure EFL-1: Combined sample of twenty fluent sentences of an EFL-speaker with ten short sentences made by the same EFL-speaker ten years earlier being inserted, analysed by the habit of using two- and three-letter words and words starting with a vowel.

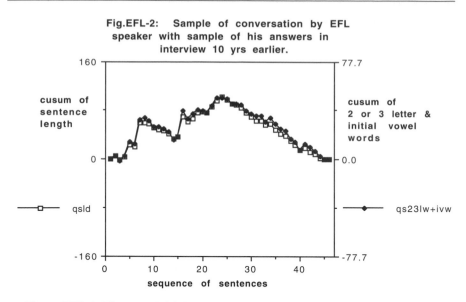

Fig.EFL-2: Sample of conversation by EFL speaker with sample of his answers in interview 10 yrs earlier.

Figure EFL-2: The same habit in a combined sample of twenty-four sentences of conversation by an EFL-speaker followed by twenty-two spoken sentences of interview answers made by the same EFL-speaker ten years before.

Similar results were obtained from analysing the answers to the replies in the notebooks of the other two officers: there was complete homogeneity for the EFL-speaker, proving that there had been very accurate recording by all three officers. This is a good demonstration of faithful note-taking by officers, and perhaps a reassurance that the technique may be used with confidence by the DPPS in cases where it may be necessary to attribute utterance, as well as by defence solicitors.

To summarize, there need be no doubt, then, about attribution of either dialect or very basic language-use by grown adults; indeed, the latter usage appears to merely recapitulate the language-learning development of young children already examined in Chapter 6.

However, the case of the EFL-speaker who has learnt a non-Standard use of English from a non-native speaker, as described above, is slightly different. What will have been learnt is a consistent but an imperfect use of English syntax.

The following is an example of such a speaker's utterance.

E. Samples of spoken utterance by a non-national EFL-speaker in conversation and police interview
(In the interests of anonymity, some of the content-words have been changed; italicized phrases point out non-Standard usage of English.)

I was just *stay at home* with my people.

No, she *is looking after* my children.

I was being waiter for almost ten years.

Yes, *I study English* in my country, I *was learn English in the school.*

I *was waiter* before I became a driver.

No *I never asked* to do that thing.

I *know nothing guns.*

She come to the shop.

If I tell truth now I spend the rest of my life in jail.

I *have address, I not know* where.

No I *not go out* on parade.

Could you say again, please sir.

I not out on street, I know nothing about this.

I *sign nothing*, sir, *I sorry.*

From the language usage italicized, this speaker has the EFL-speaker's characteristic difficulty with verb-forms; and the omission of the definite and indefinite articles is also a familiar sign of imperfect usage.

That the cusum technique works through syntax is clear from the fact that the most commonly successful *23lw* and *23lw+vw* tests were not successful in this case. There is, as indicated in Chapter 2, a whole range of further tests available to try, and, in a case like this, the whole range of analytic tests was

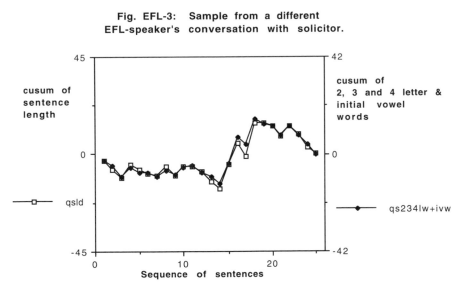

Fig. EFL-3: Sample from a different
EFL-speaker's conversation with solicitor.

Figure EFL-3: The habit of using two-, three- and four-letter words in twenty-five sentences of conversation with the non-national EFL-speaker's conversation with his solicitor.

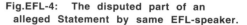

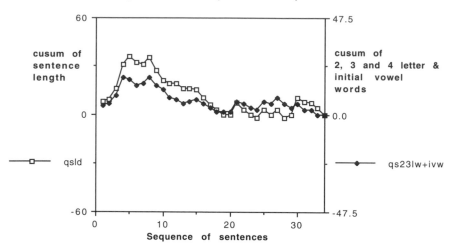

Figure EFL-4: The same habit in a sample of thirty-four sentences disputed by the EFL-speaker.

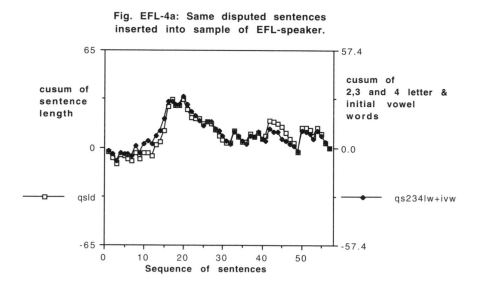

Figure EFL-4a: The same habit in a combined sample of thirty-four disputed sentences inserted into the twenty-five sentences of conversation by the EFL-speaker.

used to find the one applicable to the speaker: this was a non-national suspect, who had learned English abroad from a teacher who was not a native speaker.

The test which was the discriminator for this subject was that of two-, three- and four-letter words plus words starting with a vowel (*234lw+ivw*). This combination formed a high proportion of the man's sentences (but not so high as to render the test useless). By this test (shown in Figure EFL-3), the speaker's utterance is homogeneous, and provides a satisfactory control sample for matching against any disputed text.

The EFL-speaker was alleged to have made a statement. Half of this he agreed having made, and the other half he disputed.

When the thirty-four sentences comprising the disputed half were analysed by the test suitable for this subject, the result is shown as Figure EFL-4. This is very clearly a non-homogeneous chart by this test, indicating mixed utterance (and note the cross-over at sentence 20). It does not indicate a consistent use of the habit under analysis, *qs234w+ivw*. The utterance of the EFL-speaker shown to be consistent by this habit should therefore separate from the thirty-four sentences.

This proved to be the case. When the twenty-five sentences of conversation were combined with that portion of the alleged statement disputed by the EFL-speaker, Figure EFL-4a resulted. The visible separation occurring at

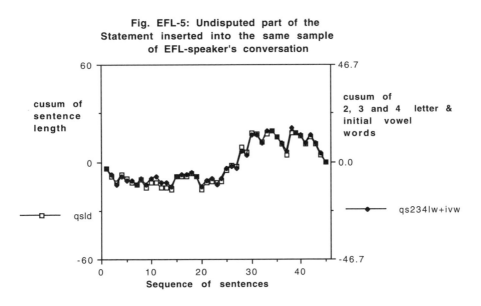

Fig. EFL-5: Undisputed part of the Statement inserted into the same sample of EFL-speaker's conversation

Figure EFL-5: The same habit in a combined sample of twenty-two undisputed sentences of the statement inserted into the twenty-five sentences of EFL-speaker's conversation.

sentences 5 through to 20 and from 40 to 50 indicated a clear case of mixed utterance. The sentences do not match those disputed by the EFL-speaker.

However, if the same twenty-five sentences of conversation are combined with that portion of the statement *undisputed* by the EFL-speaker, the chart in Figure EFL-5 emerges. This is a consistent and regular chart, indicating homogeneous utterance.

• **The EFL-speaker's own utterance cannot be distinguished from the utterance attributed to him in the alleged statement, and admitted by him**.

From these examples, we can see that QSUM works on the very short, simple sentences of a not very fluent EFL-speaker, sentences rather like those of young children. Further, the correct test for proving consistency of those simple sentences will then match any later, more sophisticated adult utterance.

We can see also that even where the use of English is imperfect, as in the second example, where an EFL-speaker has learnt English abroad and where the utterance seems very 'broken', there will still be consistency of syntactic habit from a wider range of tests. To ask if QSUM can deal with this sort of usage of the language is to ask an important question: when people are imperfect speakers, are their imperfections individually consistent? The answer from this single example is that they are.

There need be no problem, then, as regards dialect or EFL speech in using QSUM.

A CASE HISTORY
FOUR VOICES: THE INFLUENCE OF EDUCATION, INTELLIGENCE AND SOCIAL BACKGROUND

M. David Baker

The majority of my work with cusum analysis (or QSUM) as an expert witness has been, for the most part, in Northern Ireland, where criminal cases are heard without the benefit of a jury in the 'Diplock' Courts. Because of the necessity for evidence to be heard in this manner, it is obviously vital to ensure that the preparation of the evidence is undertaken with meticulous care and scrupulous attention to detail.

One of the facts drawn to my attention at an early stage of my work was that some solicitors would use a 'blunderbuss' approach and deluge me with mountains of paper. However, it was often the case that I was provided with the statements alleged to contain utterances of the accused but without any 'control' documents. When such 'control' utterance was requested, the sample(s) subsequently provided often proved unsuitable for a variety of reasons: a sample might contain mixed utterance, due to prompting by the solicitor, his clerk or even his cell mate or other third person, advising the accused as to the phraseology that should be used. This obviously rendered such documents useless for 'control' purposes and I soon learnt that the best source of authentic material was from letters sent to family or close friends, or else transcripts of tape-recorded interviews by the solicitor (or his clerk) which would comprise conversation on matters not normally forming any part of the case under consideration.

It was from such letters that I have drawn the material discussed in this chapter.

All four examples are from one case, where five youths who were all from the same locality, with similar upbringing (and, in all likelihood, having attended the same schools) were accused of a very serious crime. The solicitor instructing me represented four of these five men. In the final event, I was not called to present my evidence: one of the accused was acquitted after evidence was submitted concerning his mental age, which was described as 'that of a juvenile', and the others pleaded guilty to a far lesser crime allowing them to be freed after taking into account the amount of time that they had already spent in custody.

The examples shown below all come from letters sent to family members, and have been edited to conceal the originator's identity or other matters which might identify either them or the crime that they were alleged to have committed. Other editing for the purposes of cusum analysis is described separately for each individual. The examples show QSUM-charts of the prosecution's alleged statements/confessions, but the actual transcripts of these documents have not been provided, in the interests of privacy.

Voice 1

This youth was eighteen at the time of his arrest and spent two years in custody before the case came to trial. In this case the comparison document used as a control was a letter he wrote to his mother from prison. The letter required very little editing other than removal of superfluous exclamation marks and question marks which he tended to double for emphasis (!!). It could be argued that the usage of the exclamation 'Ha, Ha' should also be deleted; but this is an idiomatic form of language for the area, and on those grounds it was left intact.[2]

I received more than one letter from Voice 1's family and the opportunity was taken to compare documents. No difference was detected in the 'habit' and a clear homogeneity existed in both the separate and combined samples, i.e. sample 1 in the middle of sample 2, and/or vice versa. Since the letter shown below was of adequate length when compared to the alleged confession, this was used as the 'control'.

Voice 1's Utterance in a Letter to His Mother from Prison

I love and miss you all Millions!
Dear Mum,

Just the usual letter with the usual news to let you'se know that i'm keeping well and all that carryon. As per usual there isn't anything worthwhile writing about, things are quiet enough in here. I got the St Patricks day cards from you and our kid and I also seen the greetings in the [name] for me from you'se all, I'm glad they printed that one for [name] and the one from me for [name], it'll keep them happy and best of all it'll keep me in their good books!

I got the papers in as well tonight, I wasn't expecting them up seeing as I had no visit, you'se shouldn't of bothered coming all the way up with a few papers and a card, Ah well thanks anyway, I appreciate all you'se are doing for me! Well then how are you'se all doing out there? I hope that all is fine with you'se all and that you'se are all keeping the spirits up and putting on a brave face, don't let it get to you'se as that'll mean the [name] are succeeding in trying to demoralise the families, stay strong, you'se an do it, do it for me, it'll help me a lot! Well things are sound with me in here, they'll never break my spirit, I'm still training away, getting ready for when I get out (Ha Ha) I'm also still twanging away on the guitar, I've got to the hard bit now, learning to read the music but I'll stick at it and try to master it, it could pay of in the long run, Christy Moore eat your heart out (Ha Ha). Here it was good to see you, Dad, and our kid on Friday last, I'd a good visit with you and Gran on Wednesday, Gran was looking well, shes bearing all this rightly, tell her she is always in my thoughts and prayers, the same goes for everybody else in the family. Did you get that drawing on Wednesday? Hope so and I hope you like it, I think I'll do Gran a holly one for her house, I'm sure she would like it alright!

Right, the visit passes are out with this letter, I didn't do too bad with them, Wednesday PM, Friday AM and Saturday AM. You know what to do with them, the Saturday one can go to [name] or [name], I don't really care but maybe [name] will be looking up and if he is coming up tell him to bring [name] with him so that I can tell her a bit of sceal about him and also find out when the big day is (Ha Ha). I hope that all goes well for you'se in Scotland this weekend, well by the time you get this it'll be, I hope everything went well for you'se! Oh aye [name] said wait till he gets you for giving him a reddener on Wednesdays visit, he loves it all, he was in good spirits about it but he'll probably try to get his own bang on you, I hope he does and I might just help him. Watch the [name] News (Ha Ha Ha).

I'm away on here, I think I'll write [name] a wee letter tonight, but then again I mightn't, I don't know what I'm doing, I don't know if I'm coming or going. (Ha Ha) gets to you after a while, this place. (Ha Ha) well that's me for another week, tune in again next week for the rest of the rubbish. (Ha Ha) I'll see you'se all soon, tell all that I was asking, good night and god bless,

Lots of Love your loving son & brother [name].

The Chart of Voice 1's letter to his Mother from Prison after Cusum Analysis
The letter containing twenty consecutive sentences of Voice 1's utterance was used to establish whether or not he was an exception to the cusum technique. Figure

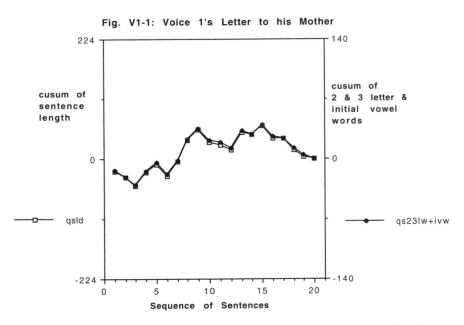

Figure V1-1: The occurrence of the habit of using words that have two or three letters or words that commence with an initial vowel in the sentences from the letter.

V1-1 shows a very clear consistent habit running through this sample of utterance. It demonstrates that Voice 1's utterance is not an exception to the technique.

The Chart of the Statement/Confession Purporting to be the Utterance of Voice 1 After Cusum Analysis

The next QSUM-chart (Figure V1-2) is taken from the statement or confession submitted as being by Voice 1. As always for work of this nature, it is essential to analyse the document with the same 'habit' as the one found to exhibit the subject's normal homogeneity.

Figure V1-2 very clearly shows that the habit is not consistent in this sample of utterance and is the utterance of another person or persons. It certainly bears no comparison to the consistency shown in the previous chart.

For completeness, below is shown the chart of the statement inserted within the letter, Figure V1-3

One point that should be emphasized is that it is not *normally* possible to state that any document does not contain a single utterance by the subject without a great deal of extra work, especially since it is unlikely that a control document could be obtained from the prosecution witnesses. However, one could contend that it is unlikely to contain a sequence of say five sentences by the subject. Furthermore in cases of this nature it is the sworn evidence of the

Fig. V1-2: Voice 1 Statement/Confession

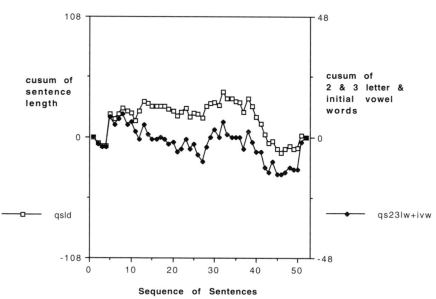

Figure V1-2: The occurrence of words with two- or three-letters or words that commence with an initial vowel in the statement/confession described above. It consists of fifty-two consecutive sentences.

officer taking the statement that these were the words of the accused, and normally reasonable doubt is the test applied by the court.

The Chart of the Statement/Confession Inserted in Middle of the Letter from Voice 1 to his Mother
Figure V1-3 clearly shows an insertion of the utterance of a person other than that of Voice 1. It is conceivable that here may be some utterance of Voice 1 at the beginning and possibly toward the end of the insertion. However, without further sub-division and significant extensive and costly testing, it is not possible to accurately determine if any of the sentences in this insertion are the utterance of Voice 1.

Conclusions Reached for Voice 1
My opinion reached for the purposes of my report to my instructing solicitor read: 'In my opinion the sentences in the alleged and disputed Statement, or Confession, purporting to be the utterance of Voice 1 cannot be accepted as the utterance of Voice 1.'

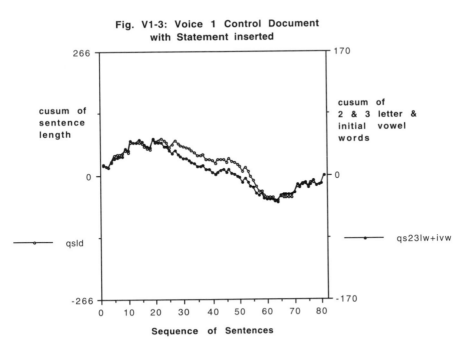

Fig. V1-3: Voice 1 Control Document with Statement inserted

Figure V1-3: The occurrence of words with two or three letters or words that commence with an initial vowel in the combined document described above, consisting of seventy-two sentences.

Voice 2

This youth was nineteen at the time of his arrest and also spent two years in custody before the case came to trial. In a similar way to the Voice 1 case, the comparison document used as a control was a combination of two short letters written to his mother from prison. The letters required very little editing other than removal of final salutations and some normal QSUM editing. These letters also contained some usage of 'Ha Ha', and again these exclamations were included as idiomatic expressions.

Voice 2's Utterance in Letters to his Mother

Hello MUM, How are YA? Well I am doing fine Just missing you's all and the drink. l hope you's all enjoyed your-selve's over Christmas as we all made the best of what we had. Well there's not much happening in here at the minute. They have started letting us out again at night from 5 to 7 it's not bad here in A/Wing aleast there is a pool table over here and it's a wee bit cleaner than C/Wing. Did YA get any photo's of the child on Christ-Mas morning? Well Christ-Mas day in here was [expletive] all it was Just another day. I got the radio [name] got for me on Christmas morning. I hear [name] is getting engaged again on Monday. [name] was telling me about the French people that was down seeing you's all. It goes to show how much surport we have it is know half way across the world. I am hoping we can give these [expletive] a red face in Court, and then the people well know them what there for. Well [name]s granny died there during the week she got out of hospital for Christmas she died of cancer. They only found out she had it about three months ago. Well Ma I am going to go on here so keep the head up high.

Hello MA, ANd how are you's all keeping. I am doing great. It was great seeing the child last week as I hadn't see him in ages. I am looking forward to seeing [name] on thursday tell her I will have crisps and sweets for her. How is [name] arm now. Scum bags hate to see any-one enjoying them-Selve's. Tell [name] I'll sent her out a visit next week as I think she has only be up to see me once or twice From I have came in. I have done anther poster you should get it before you get the letter as I am sending it out tomorrow morning (tuesday). Well I have not got my specks yet as It take's about a week for them to be made. I hope you'll like the Poster as I think it is a cracker. Well [name] was saying he sent [name] anther letter did she get it yet. ALL the lad's are doing well, enjoying there holiday HA HA. Tell [name] and big [name] and the rest of them thanks for them other things. Wee [name] said there was a good crowed at the last one. Well MA I will go for now nothing more to report from this side I am away to stuff my face HA HA Well whats new HA HA.

It is interesting to note the poor spelling and grammar. The sentence which is underlined occurred at the end of one page and ran over on to the next; it has not been modified at all, and its effect will be seen in the graph shown below.

The Chart of The Combined Letters of Voice 2 to his Mother After Cusum Analysis
The letters, containing thirty consecutive sentences of Voice 2's utterance, were used to establish whether or not Voice 2 was an exception to the technique. Figure V2-1 shows a reasonably consistent habit running through this sample of utterance. The apparent widening of the gap between the two graph lines in the middle of the graph is due to sentence 12, which is of poor and confused construction: the sentence runs over the end of one page to the next and is not coherent. This has affected the direction of both sentence 12 and possibly 13. When a transparency is used (as was done for visual demonstration in court, using an overhead projector), the consistency of the rest of the chart becomes apparent. The utterance taken as a whole reasonably demonstrates that Voice 2 is not an exception to the cusum technique.

The next graph (Figure V2-2 on p. 226) shows the statement that Voice 2 was alleged to have uttered. It contains what purported to be a confession and other incriminating evidence.

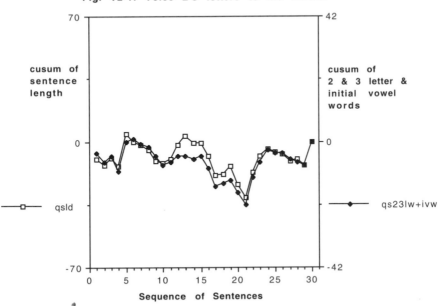

Fig. V2-1: Voice 2's letters to his mother

Figure V2-1: The occurrence of the habit of using words that have two or three letters or words beginning with an initial vowel in the sentences in the combined letters to his mother, the utterance of Voice 2.

The Chart of the Statement/Confession Purporting to be the Utterance of Voice 2 After Cusum Analysis

Figure V2-2 seems to begin quite well, until the two graph lines become disturbed, crossing and re-crossing, and in parts the lines move in different directions. Experience in reading QSUM-charts shows that the habit is not entirely homogeneous in this sample of utterance and may contain insertions of the utterance of more than one person.

The question that now has to be asked is, 'Is any of the statement/confession the utterance of Voice 2?' This can obviously be determined by combining the statement with the known utterance of Voice 2. The resulting chart is shown below.

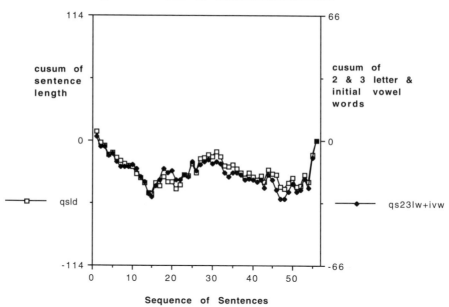

Fig. V2-2: Voice 2, Statement/Confession

Figure V2-2: The occurrence of words with two or three letters or words beginning with an initial vowel in the statement/confession described above, consisting of fifty-six sentences purporting to be the utterance of Voice 2.

The Chart of the Statement/Confession Inserted in Middle of the Letters from Voice 2 to his Mother.

Figure V2-3 clearly shows insertions of the utterance of persons other than that of Voice 2.

Since there are elements of the chart where the lines converge in the area covered by the statement it could be argued that some of these might contain sentences by Voice 2 and indeed it is conceivable that the officer taking down the statement did use some of Voice 2's actual words. However, once a statement can be shown to contain utterances that are not those of the accused person, especially when the officer concerned has sworn that they were uttered by the accused, the statement would normally be ruled inadmissible or would cast doubt on the reliance that can be placed on the document.

Conclusions Reached for Voice 2

My opinion reached for the purposes of my report to my instructing solicitor read: 'In my opinion the sentences in the alleged and disputed Statement, or Confession, purporting to be the utterance of Voice 2 cannot be accepted as the utterance of Voice 2 but contain the utterances of other persons.'

Fig. V2-3: Voice 2's Statement inserted into his letters

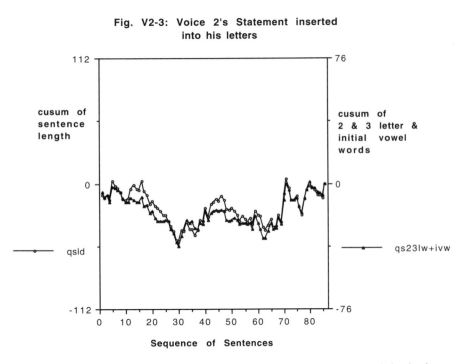

Figure V2-3: The occurrence of words with two or three letters or words beginning with a vowel in the combined document described above, containing eighty-six sentences.

Voice 3

This youth was also nineteen at the time of his arrest and also spent two years in custody before the case came to trial. Yet again the source of the control document was a combination of two letters to Voice 3's mother. Due to some initial difficulties with the first letter and because of the fact that a very infrequent 'habit' was detected, a second letter was requested via my instructing solicitor, in whose presence this letter was written at my request.

The first letter required some editing due to the presence of two sentences which in all essential respects were 'laundry lists' and as such would have caused the familiar 'list' anomaly. These sentences together with some extraneous sentence delimiters are all shown as / marks in the transcript below. The first letter also contained one occurrence of 'Ha Ha' and, as before, this was not altered or excluded.

Voice 3's Utterance in Letters to his Mother

To the one and only MuM in the world who i Love and Miss Lots and Lots and It will be good to see you to-morrow as i can't wait. I got your Letter on tueday also the parcel, everything was in it, thanks mum. How are you mum? i hope you are doing fine and Looking after yourself? as for me, i am doing fine in here and Looking after myself also keeping my chin up for you mum. Im very sorry to hear about [name] dad dying. Im sure your head was away with it when you were minding [name] and wee [name] HA HA. I feel sorry for [name], tell him i was asking about him also [name] and [name]. all the Lads were asking about you and said keep your chin up. [DELETION] Well mum i have nothing more to say on till i see you to-morrow on til then all my Love and kisses your Innocent son [name].

Dear Mum Just a few lines to let you know i Love and miss you millions and i hope you are doing well and looking after yourself for me as i am doing well in here and looking after myself for you and keeping my chin up for you. How is everyone / I hope fine, tell them all i was asking and i hope to see them soon. Everything in here is fine except i would like to be with you. There is no more football for me as the yard in B-wing is very small. I got your parcel on Monday, thanks. How is [name] also [name] tell her i was asking. I can't wait to see you again, it was good to see you last week you were looking well as always, i enjoyed the visit with you. Uncle [name] was looking well. The cell is very warm, you can hardly get a sleep in here. Well mum im sorry i couldn't write any more but as you know i love and miss you millions and can't wait to see you again so until i see you lots of love your innocent son [name].

Yet again the quality of the language usage is unsophisticated, but the nature of the work means that analysis will inevitably be applied to a wide range of levels of utterance, involving verbatim utterance. The charts resulting from analysis are shown below.

The Chart of the Combined Letters of Voice 3 to his Mother After Cusum Analysis

The combined letters containing twenty consecutive sentences of Voice 3's known utterance were used to establish whether or not Voice 3 was an exception to the technique.

As we know, only the most frequent habits can be expected to show a positive result, and in Voice 3's case the most frequent habit was that of using words of two, three or four letters and words that begin with an initial vowel.[4] This is a less common habit and for that reason very extensive testing had to be performed including obtaining the second letter so as to confirm its authenticity beyond any doubt. Figure V3-1 shows a very consistent habit running through this sample of utterance, demonstrating that Voice 3 is not an exception to the cusum technique.

The *234lw+ivw* habit was next tested on the statement alleged to be the utterance of Voice 3.

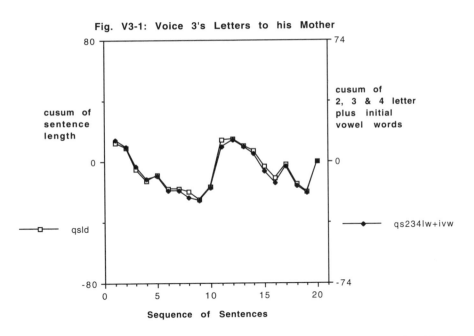

Fig. V3-1: Voice 3's Letters to his Mother

Figure V3-1: Combined sample of twenty sentences from letters by V3 analysed by the habit of using two-, three- or four-letter words and words starting with a vowel.

The Chart of the Statement/Confession Purporting to be the Utterance of Voice 3 After Cusum Analysis

Figure V3-2 apparently shows that the habit is consistent in this sample of utterance and could be homogeneous; however, one very important question

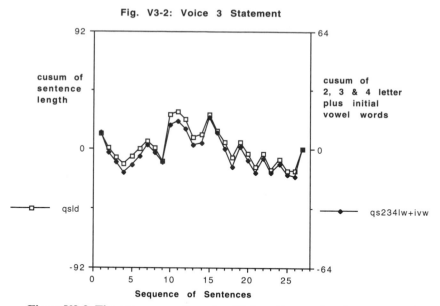

Figure V3-2: The occurrence of words with two, three or four letters or words beginning with an initial vowel in the statement/confession described above, which consists of twenty-seven sentences.

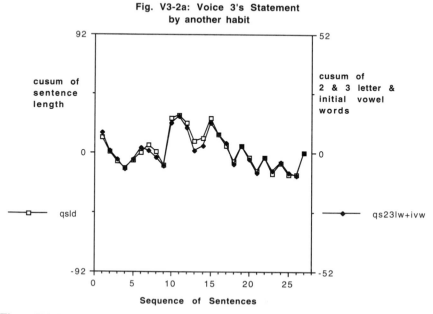

Figure V3-2a: The occurrence of words with two or three letters or words beginning with an initial vowel in the statement/confession already described (twenty-seven sentences).

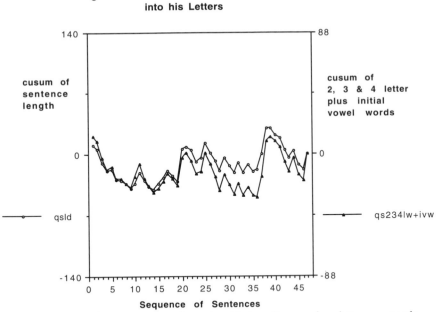

Figure V3-3: The same insertion by another habit.

Figure V3-3: The occurrence of words with two, three or four letters or words beginning with an initial vowel in the combined document described above.

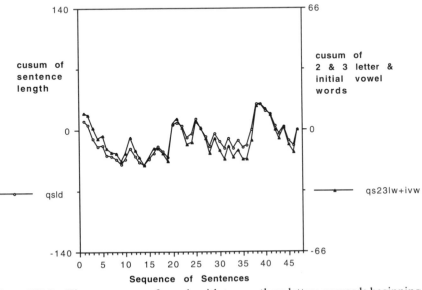

Figure V3-3a: The occurrence of words with two or three letters or words beginning with an initial vowel in the combined document described previously.

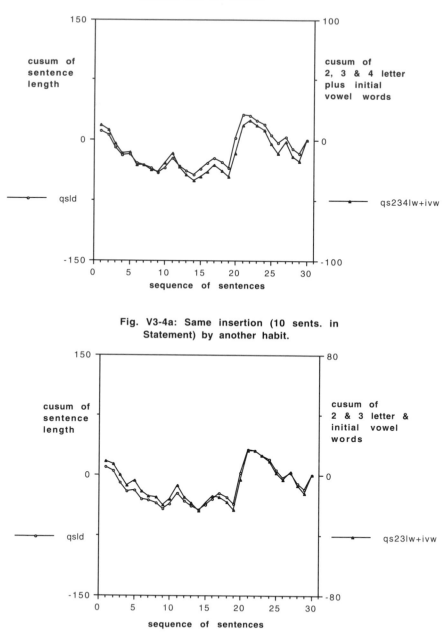

Fig. V3-4: First ten sentences of Statement inserted into the letters.

Fig. V3-4a: Same insertion (10 sents. in Statement) by another habit.

Figures V3-4 and V3-4a: Combined sample of the first ten sentences of the statement inserted in the middle of the letters, analysed by first, the *234lw+ivw* 'habit' and then the *23lw+ivw* 'habit'.

that needs to be addressed is '*Is this the discriminating habit?*' This can be determined by testing the statement for other habits, and the result of this testing is shown in Figure V3-2a (p. 230). Figure V3-2a clearly shows that the habit is consistent in this sample of utterance and is reasonably homogeneous, with the exception of a very small number of sentences – one or two at about sentence 6 to sentence 8.

Is this the utterance of Voice 3? The fact that the 'habit' (*23lw+ivw*) is not the one able to discriminate Voice 3 is probably indicative on its own that the statement/confession is not the utterance of Voice 3.

Confirmation of this may be obtained by combining the statement with the known utterance of Voice 3. This was carried out using both 'habits' and further extended as shown below.

The Chart of the Statement/Confession Inserted in Middle of the Letters from Voice 2 to his Mother

Figure V3-3 (p. 231) clearly shows an insertion of the utterance of a person other than that of Voice 3: it has affected those areas known to be the utterance of Voice 3, and disturbed the former homogeneity.

Further confirmation can be obtained by using the 'habit' previously shown to be valid for the statement/confession alone. This is shown in Figure V3-3a (p. 231). Figure V3-3a clearly shows an insertion of utterance by a person other than that of Voice 3, in a similar position to that shown in Figure V3-3.

Since, in both the above charts, the two graph lines at the first part of the statement appear to coincide, from sentence 11 to about sentence 19, further tests were carried out on the first ten sentences of the statement. The resulting charts (Figures V3-4 and V3-4a, on p. 232) using both 'habits' showed clear divergences indicating that it was highly unlikely that the insertion, i.e. the statement, was the utterance of Voice 3. The two samples are distinguishable by QSUM.

Further testing would have been impractical, and it was my belief that we had in fact proved beyond any reasonable doubt that Voice 3 could not have uttered the words attributed to him in the statement.

Conclusions Reached for Voice 3

My opinion reached for the purposes of my report to my instructing solicitor read: 'In my opinion the sentences in the alleged and disputed Statement, or Confession, purporting to be the utterance of Voice 3 cannot be accepted as the utterance of Voice 3 but is the utterance of another person.'

Voice 4

This youth was also nineteen at the time of his arrest and had also spent two years in custody before the case came to trial. The source of the control document was a letter to Voice 4's brother. This document was chosen after much careful work and extensive editing. The editing was necessary since the original letter had barely any sentence delimiters. It was necessary to visualize thought processes going on – almost treating this as if it were a play reading: only in that way was I able to place delimiters in what appeared to be the most sensible positions. No attempt was made to alter the sense or to improve the obvious grammatical or spelling errors. As in the previous voices the use of 'Ha Ha' has been left alone.

Voice 4's Utterance in a Letter to His Brother

Well [name]
How's things With you Big Bro? Good I hope as for myself I am not too Bad considering the Surroundings. But hopefully Not for Much longer As I have been here Nearly 2 years And Nothing yet. But at least the Ball is staring to Roll Now since Wee have the first Date. Anyway [name] I Was Sweating at the United and Wednesday Match. But You me I Brought them Good luk that Day. Bruce took them 2 Goals he Scored Good leaders. I'm Messing all the Lads about the one's who supported wednesday And they Were Cracking up HA HA. And as you say [name] I think they all the luck this season. hopefully Everything Workes Well for them. Well [name] you May try and Keep the darts Down a bit or the Girl Will Be telling you to Get on your Bike. and you Would not want that HA HA. And you Could be free and Single like myself No-Body loves Me except for the family HA HA. You can tell the Girl Your young Bro Was asking And maybe I Will Get to Meet her One Day. And what you at Getting Dropped from the Dart team you letting My Down Big lad. its Not like you so get the finger out. I've started Playing again We Were playing Cricket To-day With the Darts and I Will Give you clue who else But me HA HA. I'm Not Being Big headed about it HA! Here [name] I thought You were off the Drink HA! Its Bad for you Just Wait for me Getting out And Mind you We Will Be Doing Some Drinking. Well [name] So you had hard luck on your Bet its a Pity it Never Was. ah Well Sure you Got Your money Back Plus an Extra few Pound. Are you Giving any of it Away Since you have Plenty of it you Wish you had. Here [name] I Was Watching part of Snooker today for a while But it Wasn't Much. But It would have been Better if Wee Joe Swail Had of Win. But he Got a Bad start Playing Against Jimmy white. But Give it Another while and he Will be Well up in the Ranking Points hope he Does. Here [name] I'm Sure you were Glad lent Was Over to Get Doing a Wee Bit to try And touch for A few Pound. And give me half of it ha! Well [name] I am still on the Diet But I am Going to tell Mum to stop the Biscuits Because they Dont do Any Good. Well [name] United Will Be A Good Birthday Present for them to Win the title. Well [name] Not a lot Much to Say. So Ill Probaly See you Next week. here what about [name] Getting the New United top he

said he it Was a Brilliant top Id love to Get it. But you Would Not get it in here. Well Big Bro ill Go for Now TAKE CARE YOUR WEE BRO [name].

Since cusum analysis works on sentences, a form of alteration of the type undertaken above becomes necessary to split up what otherwise would have been exceptionally long 'sentences'. This enables an appropriate 'habit' to be determined.

The Chart of Letter from Voice 4 to his Brother after Cusum Analysis
The letter containing thirty-six consecutive sentences Voice 4's utterance, was used to establish whether or not Voice 4 was or was not an exception to the technique. Figure V4-1 shows a reasonably consistent 'habit' running through this sample of utterance. Even though the lines appear to diverge it can be seen that all segments follow approximately the same direction. It can be demonstrated by the use of transparencies of the separate elements in the chart that the lines do overlay when vertically adjusted.

• **This pattern of line divergence has been shown to be typical of people who have a less articulate command of the language, or are of a retarded mental age.**[5]
The latter was shown to be the case in evidence given by medical experts,

Fig. V4-1: Voice 4's Letter to his Brother.

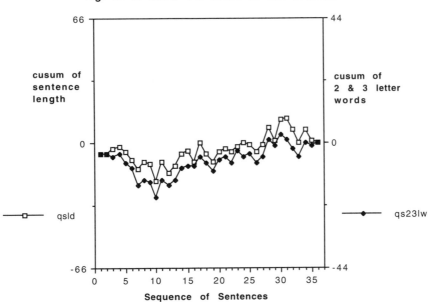

Figure V4-1: The occurrence of one of the simplest 'habits', that of using words that have two or three letters, in the sentences in the letter, the normal utterance of Voice 4.

and this defendant's acquittal was largely based on this, with some other evidence. The above chart, however, does demonstrate that Voice 4 is not an exception to the cusum technique.

The *23lw* habit was then tested on the statement alleged to be the utterance of Voice 4 and this is shown below.

The Chart of the Statement/Confession Purporting to be the Utterance of
Voice 4 After Cusum Analysis
Figure V4-2 very clearly shows that the habit is not consistent or homogeneous in this sample of utterance and is obviously the utterance of more than one person.

Again the technique of inserting the statement within the known utterance of Voice 4 was used to determine if the statement contained any utterance by the accused.

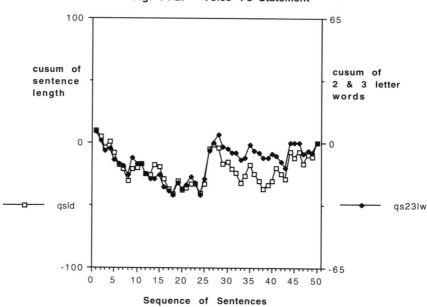

Fig. V4-2:   Voice 4's Statement

Figure V4-2: The occurrence of words with two or three letters in the statement/confession described above, consisting of fifty sentences purporting to be the utterance of Voice 4.

The Chart of the Statement/Confession Inserted in Middle of the Letters from Voice 4 to his Brother

Figure V4-3 shows the occurrence of words with two or three letters in the combined document described above: it consists of eighty-six sentences.

Figure V4-3 very clearly shows an insertion of the utterance of a person or persons other than that of Voice 4, which has even affected the parts known to be his utterance. Even given that some divergence was exhibited in Voice 4's known utterance, the divergence shown above can only be regarded as extreme.

It is doubtful if further subdivision and continued testing would have enabled the resolution of the authorship of any of the sentences in the statement to be shown to be the utterance of Voice 4.

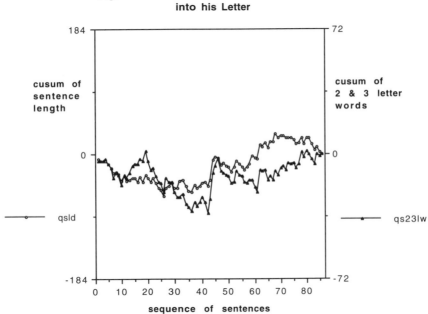

Fig. V4-3: Voice 4's Statement inserted into his Letter

Figure V4-3: Voice 4's statement inserted into the letter to his brother

Conclusions Reached for Voice 4

In this case it was easy to form an opinion and it was as clear cut as any opinion can be in cases of this nature. In my report to my instructing solicitor, my conclusion read: 'In my opinion the sentences in the alleged and disputed Statement, or Confession, purporting to be the utterance of Voice 4 cannot be accepted as the utterance of Voice 4 but is a mixed utterance by more than one person.'

Final Considerations

The result of cusum analysis on the four voices given above is interesting. Even though they all come from the same background, are of a similar age, upbringing, probably with similar schooling, and with the likelihood that they may well have been friends, nevertheless analysis of their language usage shows many differences.

There are differences associated with the 'habits' of each voice in that only two exhibit the commonest of 'habits' (that of two and three letters with initial vowel words, *23lw+ivw*); one was consistent with what is a quite uncommon 'habit' (two-, three- and four-letter words with initial vowel words, *234lw+ivw*); and finally, one was found to be consistent by the simplest pattern of all (that of two- and three-letter words, *23lw*). In addition, the voices demonstrate that whilst the tightness of the graph lines on a chart characteristically indicates consistency by the discriminating 'habit', the lines may also have divergences due to either confused sentence structure (i.e. poor use of language), or to low mental capacity. In short, it would be true to say that the differences displayed by cusum analysis are as many and as varied as that between different people.

The investigative techniques I have used follow a well tried and tested technique, but it is always necessary to confirm that the 'habit' being tested is the valid one for the person concerned. This is best shown by Voice 3 where the alleged statement by the accused was shown to be of a different 'habit' to that of his control document.

Certain other factors need to be borne in mind when carrying out expert witness work. Correct interpretation of the charts is absolutely vital: a single 'blip' may indicate an anomaly or may be due to imperfect language development. Only long experience of using QSUM, together with appropriate tutoring, will enable differentiation to be made with accuracy.

Testing takes time and it may be necessary to examine many documents for use as the 'control' to ensure that the right language 'habit' is selected. It is not uncommon to spend over fifty hours on one individual's documents. Additionally, this examination can not be carried out in continuous sessions; about the maximum for any one session will be of the order of three to four hours.

There have been, in my experience, as many occasions when QSUM has shown differentiation between the 'control 'and the witness statements as there have been where such differentiation has not been shown.

Finally, an expert witness has a duty to maintain an honest and impartial approach, as giving evidence under oath implies. A witness is acting in the interests of justice, and is at the service of the court rather than under any mistaken internal sense of loyalty to the instructing solicitor. The best interpretation of the evidence before the court, within legal constraints, must be the aim.

Above all, for an expert witness integrity is paramount.

Chapter 10

THE CRITICS ANSWERED

Michael Farringdon

Criticism of QSUM seems to fall into four distinct areas: firstly, that it does not agree with common sense.[1] Another cause for critical concern is that no theoretical basis for the technique has been advanced.[2] A frequent complaint is that no standard statistical measures to compare the two sets of data values have been used (in other words, the charge is that QSUM is subjective).[3] Lastly, critics have complained that it does not work.[4] These criticisms are dealt with in detail below.

However, a few words on the criticism that the technique is subjective are not out of place here. Many people are unhappy with numbers and mathematics and their minds appear to them to seize up when presented with, say, probabilities. For this reason, we often use diagrams and graphs to reduce the abstract to something more concrete (there is even, these days, a process called 'modelling' used in the teaching of reading in primary schools, whereby children are encouraged to convert text into different sorts of visual 'models' to aid comprehension). Most humanities' scholars, most of those who study the Bible, and most lawyers and jurors are uncomfortable, to put it mildly, with mathematical expressions and with numerical statistics any more sophisticated than the well known 'average'. As has been pointed out by Morton, the use of statistics such as multivariate analysis, catastrophe theory, or correlation-matrices and eigen analysis to analyse Shakespeare, the Gospel, the Book of Mormon, or Jane Austen, might be of use to literary, Biblical or theological scholars with a strong background in statistics, but such people are few and the great majority of those wishing to analyse biblical or literary texts for authorship are likely to find such statistics well beyond their understanding.[5]

Morton and Michaelson were concerned to find an authorship technique that would be readily understood by those not literate in statistics and that would also be usable by such people – provided they were willing to learn how to use it. Morton's QSUM is the result. However, as will be shown later in this chapter, the mathematics for a form of cusums, called weighted cusums, is already in place. Further statistical work has been done, initiated with QSUM, so that for those who object to the subjectivity of cusum analysis we can now offer probabilities and a *t*-test, as will be shown later in the chapter.

The Criticisms

The four published criticisms are by Canter, Hardcastle, Hilton and Holmes, and Sanford et al.[6] In addition, several reports written by Canter and by Hardcastle have been submitted as legal evidence in an attempt to counter QSUM-based reports already submitted in evidence and written variously by Morton, Baker, and Michael Farringdon. Before examining the criticisms in particular, it is worth noting that all the critics have missed a fundamental point concerning authorship attribution: that is, that the technique to be used depends on the size and simplicity of the problem. Various techniques have been briefly covered in Chapter 1. Suffice it to say that if one wishes to identify a volume of 400 pages, a newly discovered novel said to be by Charles Dickens, say, then one would use collocations of the word THE. For a chapter of a book containing a few thousand words and said to be by a single author, undoubtedly a smaller sized problem but still not inconsiderable, one would use a wider range of word counts and collocations. For small quantities of text where an intensive and precise examination is required, one would use QSUM. Only in very rare cases, such as the New Testament Gospels and Epistles where such an intensive examination might be considered appropriate, would the technique be used to examine a text of several thousand words or larger. The critics, somehow, seem to be unaware of the existence of different tools for different types of authorship problems.

The early published work on QSUM by Morton with Michaelson and Michael Farringdon was written for an audience of scholars and researchers who were already well versed and practised in authorship attribution, not for beginners or occasional enquirers. We knew that the audience we were aiming at would be fully conversant with such problems as the integrity of texts, for example, without our having to explain them. Unfortunately, the authors of the four critical papers appear to be only occasionally interested (at best) in authorship attribution, which, together with what seems to be their very superficial readings of the early QSUM publications, has led them into making erroneous judgements.

The Criticism: Cusum Analysis is Not Common Sense
Canter, a professor of behavioural psychology, in a report written for the Crown Prosecution Service (CPS), states that 'the basic propositions of "Cusum Charts" do not agree . . . with common sense'. Leaving aside, for the present, what Canter understands as 'the basic propositions of cusum charts', an appeal to common sense is hardly a scientific or academic judgement.[7]

Science and engineering would be much the poorer if this argument had been applied to, say, particle physics.

The Criticism: QSUM Has No Theoretical Basis

The fact that 'No published accounts can be found to indicate what the psychological or linguistic processes are that generate the "habit" that Cusum analysts claim to be so consistent' and 'the lack of a strong theoretical basis' is obviously worrying to Canter.[8] Hardcastle, closely echoing Canter, remarks that '. . . Morton identified no psychological or linguistic processes which might generate such habits' and 'Morton has advanced no theoretical basis as to why the features he examined should be consistent in a person's utterance, or why they should be characteristic in a person'.[9] Sanford et al. believe that they have shown 'the method to be without any reliable foundation' and they are also exercised by the suggestion that there is no distinguishable difference between the spoken and the written utterance of an individual.[10]

Cusum analysis is rather in the position of the use of fingerprints some seventy years before a scientific explanation was found for their being an identifier. It works, but no explanation is yet available. It is too early to provide a theoretical scientific reason as to why the technique succeeds. Similarly, Oliver Heaviside invented a calculus in the late nineteenth century, a calculus of which the Cambridge mathematicians were scathing, since they could not then prove it.[11] Notwithstanding, Heaviside's ideas and calculations were used to design and lay a telephone cable across the American continent, and the cable worked.[12] (The Heaviside Calculus was later 'proved' to the satisfaction of mathematicians.)

We would maintain that no explanation *can* yet be given because of the present stage at which the study of linguistics finds itself, and we are inclined to agree with Walker Percy's proposition that, 'Descriptive or structural linguistics cannot be regarded as a theory of language if the word *theory* is used as it is in other sciences.'[13]

In scientific evidence, what is required is that an experimental method be capable of being replicated by others. When cusum analysis is applied to the data under examination by other practitioners and identical results follow, then the evidence is verified. That is, utterance by one person will, under analysis, yield a consistent graph, and will separate from utterance by other persons. This is all that is required scientifically. I have no doubt that the reason the technique succeeds will be established. However, I would point out that it is not always necessary to advance a theoretical basis for a new scientific method for that method to be valid. Here we are helped by the nineteenth-century American philosopher, Charles Sanders Peirce: helped, that is, by Peirce's use of *ab*duction as the proper method to arrive at explanatory theory.[14]

Abduction is distinguishable from the other two components of the scientific method, induction and deduction.[15] No new truth can come from deduction or induction, only from abduction. Abduction starts from facts and seeks an explanatory theory. Peirce cites Kepler's theory of the elliptical form of orbit of the planet Mars as *the* classic example.[16] The observation of fact came first, the explanation was worked out by Kepler. In the case of cumulative sum analysis, what are the facts? The technique can be shown to work along the lines suggested by the current researchers – Andrew Morton, Jill and Michael Farringdon, and M. David Baker. (Jill Farringdon's demonstration that the technique works on children soon after learning to speak is surely of particular interest here.)[17]

I propose that proceeding by abduction meets Canter's and Hardcastle's objections that Morton puts forward no theoretical basis why the technique works. Morton has arrived at this method after some forty years of working on the problems of attributing utterance, and he works on practical lines: this technique is an end-product not a sudden invention.

Linguistics experts have to proceed as Kepler did, by observing how cumulative sum analysis works. Kepler made a guess as to what was happening from observations of the planet Mars, a knowledge of Ptolemaic theory and of Copernicus' hypothesis, then constructing a model, testing it, and modifying the model 'in such a way as to render it more rational or closer to the observed fact . . . when he finally reaches a modification...which exactly satisfies the observations', thus proving that the orbit of Mars is elliptical not circular.[18] Eventually, for QSUM, predictability should be possible – as it has already proved to be, in the broad sense that no individual tested by any of the researchers so far has proved to be an exception to the technique.

The Criticism: QSUM Uses No Standard Statistical Methods

Hardcastle objects to Morton not using 'standard statistical measures to compare the two sets of data values'.[19] It is a pity that Hardcastle did not contact either Morton or myself before going into print with this statement. Firstly, a number of statisticians have agreed that it would be non-trivial to find an appropriate statistical measure. However, we have successfully tested both a measure of probability for the cusums – the 'V_{max}-test' using 'weighted cusums' – and a t-test for comparing two text segments. These statistical measures are discussed later in this chapter. Their results have only served to confirm the analysis of comparing two cusum charts by eye.

'Weighted cusums' are similar to cusums described earlier, the main difference being that they take into account, in this context, the 'length', measured in words, of sentences. This idea has also been worked on by me at the suggestion, and with the help, of two professors of statistics. Using weighted cusums, long sentences are given more 'weight' than short sentences.

Also, the mathematics, developed by A. F. Bissell, was already in place to examine weighted cusum charts for anomalies, using the V_{max}-test.[20]

Hardcastle proposes an alternative method for presenting the data and draws histograms beneath his cusum charts.[21] Hardcastle's histograms are a step in the right direction since they take into account the different sizes of sentences, thus using the information given by the size of the sentences. However, Hardcastle's histograms also lose information: they would be improved by taking the weighted cusums of the histograms and plotting them at varying distances (proportional to the sentence size) along the horizontal axis; then they would be similar to the weighted cusum charts already tested and being used by me. As they stand, Hardcastle's histograms have lost information and are certainly not an improved alternative method.

Hilton and Holmes worry about 'the subjectivity of the technique in evaluating differences between pairs of superimposed cumulative sum charts'.[22] With the object of overcoming their uneasiness, they examine the use of weighted cusum charts and a *t*-test, along the lines described by Bissell. They start by making the assumption that 'a certain percentage of a person's words might be nouns, or perhaps be of only two or three letters in length'.[23] Nowhere do we propose this. What the cusum charts enable us to do is to match the *variation around the average* for sentence length and some other attribute of a sentence. This is very different from percentages or proportions. They have also missed the point that one examines control texts known to be the utterance of the target writer or speaker to find the appropriate test or tests to use before applying such tests to a possibly disputed piece of text. Without having checked which tests might be appropriate, Hilton and Holmes use three tests: initial vowel words, two- and three-letter words, and nouns. From our experience, the initial vowel word test is very rarely found to be appropriate; the two- and three-letter word test is certainly appropriate in a fair number of cases; the use of nouns is precarious. Asking a group of people to mark the nouns in the same piece of text, I have found that they usually come up with a number of different and conflicting versions; in other words, people find it difficult to recognize nouns in English. Nor is there (to my knowledge) a computer program able to recognize nouns with a high degree of accuracy.

Unfortunately, the sample texts used by Hilton and Holmes are not referenced beyond author and title, '*Colonel Sun* by Robert Markham (alias Kingsley Amis), and *From Russia With Love, Octopussy*, and *Chitty-Chitty-Bang-Bang* by Ian Fleming', so that I have been unable to check the samples either for integrity or for anomalies.[24] Similarly, the samples from the few Jane Austen works and Federalist papers that they tested are not identified. Although Hilton and Holmes appear to be using more sophisticated and objective criteria, both their data and their method of testing are suspect.

Canter wants 'a statistical calculation of the similarities between the two sets of Cusum values'.[25] He then states that 'Spearman's rank order correlation (often known as Rho) is an appropriate statistic to do this'.[26] A number of professional statisticians to whom I have shown his paper consider the use of Spearman's Rho an unsophisticated and inappropriate measure in this case. Anthony Kenny, a former Master of Balliol College, Oxford, in his book subtitled *An Introduction to Statistics for Students of Literature and Humanities* says 'Spearman's Rho is a comparatively crude coefficient of correlation' and does not recommend it for this type of work.[27]

Sanford et al. state that 'Morton (1991) does not specify a satisfactory method for determining deviation', by which they presumably mean that Morton does not give a *number* but, rather, asks us to compare, by eye, two cusum graphs.

The Criticism: QSUM Does Not Work

Canter states that his studies 'do not support the hypothesis that the variations [in the QSUM charts] are a consequence of mixed authorship'.[28] He further states that 'I have carried out my own studies on over 300 examples of text, including verbatim transcripts of recordings of personal accounts, letters, confessions, personal documents and formal writing'.[29] It takes those of us who are practised in the technique approximately ten hours' work, as a minimum, to examine and analyse a single piece of text; fifteen hours is close to the average. Thus, for those practised in QSUM, the analysis of 'over 300 examples of text' would represent somewhere between 3,000 and 5,000 hours work or, put another way, at least eighteen months solid work. It seems incredible that Canter, who first came across the technique only eighteen months previously, was able to do such a large amount of QSUM analysis in the available time. Were the 'transcripts of recordings' he mentions using checked for accuracy of transcription? It takes skilled transcribers about ten hours to transcribe one hour of recorded speech; were Canter's transcriptions made to such professional standards or were they made to lower standards, standards sufficient for Canter's psychological research? Were Canter's recordings in the form of interviews, and if so were there repetition of parts of the questions in the answers? And were any such repetitions edited? Did Canter check the integrity of the 'letters, confessions, personal documents and formal writing' that he used? These are circumstances in which the technique should not be undertaken without great caution; this 'health warning' was given when Morton, assisted by myself, presented the technique at Professor Canter's Investigative Psychology Conference on 4 July 1991. As has been shown in earlier chapters, one of the main problems in using QSUM is the intensive labour and experience required in using it. There are so many unanswered questions about Canter's own studies (and nowhere does Canter detail his work – rather he uses sweeping statements) that I have to treat his studies as highly suspect and unworthy of supporting any hypothesis.

In the paper by Hilton and Holmes, they conclude, 'We hypothesize . . . that authors do not follow habits as rigidly as is required for Cusum techniques to determine authorship correctly'.[30] For the reasons detailed in the previous section, that is, that both their data and their method of testing are suspect and based on erroneous assumptions about the technique, I conclude that they have not supported their hypothesis.

Several further points in Canter's, Hardcastle's and Sanford's papers are worth examining so that misconceptions therein may be laid to rest.

Canter's Paper

Canter asserts that in two cases Morton and I gave evidence that 'consists of the "stylistic" analysis of the statements'.[31] We have been very careful not to use the words 'style' or 'stylistics' when writing or speaking about QSUM, and with good reason. We do use the term 'stylometry' which has been defined 'as the use of numerical methods for the solution of literary problems'.[32] *Webster's Dictionary* defines 'stylistics' as 'the *literary study* that emphasizes the analysis of various elements of style (as metaphor and diction)', whereas the ending '-metry', as in 'stylometry' means the *'science of measuring'* (my italics).[33] QSUM does not describe or analyse 'style' in the literary sense, we do not use it to make a 'stylistic analysis' as Canter states, and no such claim has been made by those who use the technique. It follows therefore that his assertion of Courts being informed by Morton and myself that statements are 'not in the verbal style of the appellant' cannot be accurate.[34]

Canter describes the technique by asserting that 'usually the component used is the proportion of two- and three-letter words in any sentence (although the number of words starting with a vowel has also been used)'.[35] As the reader will be aware, by now, the test 'usually' found most useful is *23lw+ivw*. This often accounts for over 50 per cent of the text. Other tests involving three- or four-letter words, or nouns, and combinations of these, have also been successfully used. However, both here and later, we find that Canter has made a fundamental error that shows that he has completely misunderstood the technique. He asserts that 'this "habit" is proposed as a consistency, characteristic of each person, in the proportion of particular components of that person's utterance.'[36] Nowhere do we propose this. This misconception is the same as that of Hilton and Holmes and dealt with above.

In the first half of October 1992, a number of 'draft' copies of Canter's paper came into circulation or, as one journalist remarked, 'were leaked'; the leak to journalists and solicitors appeared so widespread that it took on the character of having been promoted. A copy of this 'draft' paper was also submitted in evidence in October 1992 by Canter, in rebuttal of a report made by me, to a retired High Court Judge, Sir Michael Davies.[37] This paper was published in the October 1992 issue (which was published in mid-November) of a new journal, *Expert Evidence*. There are a number of amendments in the printed version that are quite interesting considering some of the following criticisms, most of which Canter heard during evidence given by Morton in the Court of Criminal Appeal in London on 21 October 1992, in the case of Mr T. Clemmett.

The most interesting difference between the two versions of Canter's paper lies in two graphs. Canter claims to have produced divergent graphs based on pieces of his own text in his paper. The graphs presented in the later (published) version are quite different from those in the draft version, and I believe that the reason will soon become obvious. Canter makes great play with having taken samples from his paper to make the graphs: 'In fact, as indicated in detail in the notes to Figures 1 and 2, all the text is taken from the current paper, all being the definitive writing of one author' (both 'draft' and published versions of Canter's paper).[38] The following note is added in the published paper: 'The Cusum Charts in Figures 1 and 2 were derived from an early draft of this paper before editorial and reviewers' comments had been incorporated'.[39] In the figures, as printed in *Expert Evidence*, the notes are unreadable. However, in the draft version of the paper we can clearly read where the samples are taken from within the paper. I analysed the two texts indicated and find no divergence. (See my Figures C-1 and C-2, below.)

• **The samples chosen provide an *amazing example of precognition*, since the passages analysed for cusum inspection *contained detailed comments on the resulting figures.***

The text for Canter's Figure 1 (draft) starts at 'If most text shows the consistency . . .' through to '. . . whatever the level chosen'.[40] The text for Canter's Figure 2 (draft) starts at 'A comparison level of 0.9 is . . .' through to '. . . different authors were produced'.[41] In the text sample used to construct Figure 1 (draft), we find:

> For illustrative purposes it can be noted that the Rho value for Figure 1 is 0.93 and for Figure 2 is 0.74, showing that the relationship between the lines has more randomness in it for Figure 2 than for Figure 1.[42]

In the text sample used to construct Figure 2 (draft), we find:

> To illustrate this point with reference to Figures 1 and 2. The Rho value for Figure 1 is above the comparison level of 0.90 at 0.93. For Figure 2 it is below the level indicating a lack of consistency in the text. As already mentioned, both figures are based upon sentences drawn from the present paper, all written by the author. This one example does not support the central Cusum hypothesis.

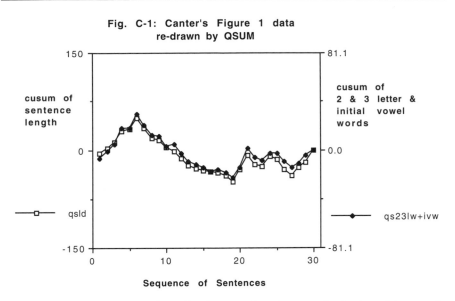

Figure C-1: The occurrence of words of two or three letters or beginning with a vowel in the sample of text used by Canter for his Figure 1.

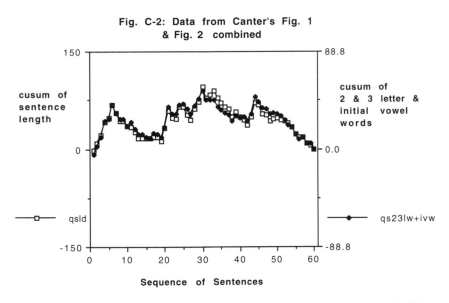

Figure C-2: The same habit in the two samples (combined) used by Canter in his Figures 1 and 2.

> To carry out enough empirical tests to see if the examples of Figures 1 and 2 were typical of Cusum analysis the writings of ten different authors were collected together.[43]

Although some sentences are radically incoherent, the text has been left intact, as in the draft paper (from which Canter drew his original graphs), and my QSUM charts using the same samples Figures C-1 and C-2. Figure C-1 shows a consistent habit running through this sample of utterance.

There is nothing in the charts of Figure C-2 to suggest that the combined sample is other than the homogeneous utterance of one person, that is Professor David Canter, indicating that Canter is not an exception to the technique. There are two blips, which overlaying transparencies indicate as being near sentences 31 and 45 of the combined sample. Sentence 31 contains repetition of a number of words, which is likely to give an anomaly, the full sentence being 'Texts that generate Rho values below this could be taken as indicating "multiple authorship" and texts above this value could be taken as from one author'. Sentence 45 is a typical list that we would expect to create an anomaly, namely:

> The material included letters, extracts from novels, papers to conferences, proposals submitted to university committees, dissertations, court transcripts and conference papers.[44]

Furthermore, a previous cusum analysis of writing by Canter had already produced homogeneous charts. These are shown in Figure C-3. Figures C-3 and C-4 confirm my opinion that Professor Canter is not an exception to the technique. The two sentences referred to above in Figure C-2 as creating an anomaly are at work here, too, at about sentences 55 to 60, and if deleted bring the charts back close together.

According to Canter, a research assistant was trained 'to make visual inspection of the Cusum charts'; few details are given, though Canter shows a gross underestimation of the experience necessary for efficient practice. In particular, I would draw attention to the fact that the research assistant was not 'allowed to study the actual text written'.[46] We make a point of stressing the need for reference back to the text. This may show that what looks like a separation is really an anomaly as, for example, the sentence referred to in Figure C-2 above. We stress that the charts illustrate observations; in other words, we are just illustrating a point so that reference can be made to the appropriate part of the text.

One criticism, in particular, that Canter makes has been repeated numerous times in the news media and in reports. This criticism, of Morton's work on authorship attribution in general, is that 'earlier theories and approaches . . .

Fig. C-3: Three samples of Canter's combined

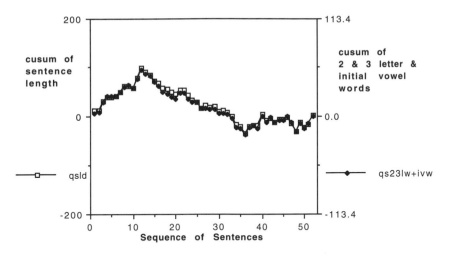

Figure C-3: Canter, three samples: (a) 'Fires', 1980 (22ss.) and (b) letter to AQM, 1991 (11ss.) and (c) Report Sect. 8 (19ss.).[45]

Fig. C-4: Canter's letter to Morton (11s.)
inserted into data for Fig. C-2

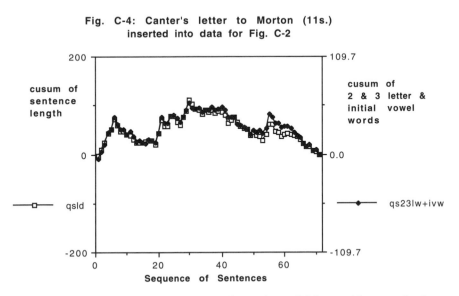

Figure C-4: The same habit with the letter from Figure C-3 inserted between the data for Canter's Figures 1 and 2 (draft version).

have been vigorously criticized for the quality of the methodology (Krippendorf, 1980; Smith, 1985)'.[47]

What are these criticisms that Canter refers to? He quotes Krippendorff, a professor of Communication, in his draft paper:

> After an analysis of the 15 [*sic*] Epistles attributed to Paul, Morton (1963) concluded that they were written by six different authors and that Paul himself had written only four. Ellison (1965) applied these constructs to texts of known authors; this led to the inference that *Ulysses* was written by five different authors none of whom wrote *Portrait of the Artist as a Young Man.* Even Morton's own article was found to be written in several distinct styles. This casts serious doubt on the utility of Morton's stylistic indices of an author's identity.[48]

It is a pity that Canter did not examine the source of this second-hand information. If he had read the Revd John W. Ellison's paper, 'Computers and the Testaments', he would have found that what Ellison actually wrote was, *I think that I could prove* at least five authors wrote James Joyce's *Ulysses* and that none of these wrote a *Portrait of the Artist as a Young Man*' (my italics).[49] Nowhere does Ellison claim to have done it, or even tried to, the reverse rather. Jacob Leed criticized Ellison in 1966:

> . . . it [Morton's 1963 work on the Epistles] cannot meanwhile be shaken in the way Ellison tries to shake it – by showing that Morton's own writings vary wildly in the rate of use of the word *and* (along with a few other items). Paul may use *kai* at a rate significantly different from other Greek authors and at a consistent rate within his own works, no matter how Morton uses *and*.[50]

Shortly after, in 1967, Ellison says, apropos of Morton's work in the Pauline Epistles,

> . . . I would like to get the routines that these people used. Then if I can obtain some letters that Thomas Jefferson wrote to his wife in June, 1776, *I think I might be able to prove one of two hypotheses*: one, that Thomas Jefferson did not write the Declaration of Independence, or two, that somebody else was carrying on a love-affair with his wife and signing his name! My hunch is that the literary style of these two things would be radically different [my italics].[51]

Ellison is still not saying that he has either made the tests or even tried them – he simply has a 'hunch'. Ellison also makes the mistake of thinking that what was being measured was 'literary style' when this was not the case – as the reader will by now be aware.

However, shortly after Ellison's 1965 paper, he was misquoted as having actually made these tests and had come to the conclusion that Krippendorff and Canter have accepted. In other words the secondary source rather than the original has been accepted by Krippendorff, Canter and others. It is puzzling that Canter, an academic, should quote a secondary source when the primary source is readily available. In the published version of Canter's paper the quotation has been deleted yet the reference is still given. (Typographically, there is plenty of spare white space on the page, more than enough to include the quotation.) I infer that the omission of the quotation from the published version must be intentional.

Canter also quotes Smith in the draft version and retains the reference in the published version. At a workshop on Authorship Studies organized by Sidney Michaelson and Andrew Q. Morton at Edinburgh University, 21–4 August 1984, which I attended, Smith took the extended opportunity to put his arguments, which he did robustly. I am not aware that they were found to be convincing. The late W. C. Wake (chief statistician at the Rubber and Plastics Research Association of Great Britain), who had worked on authorship problems since the early 1940s, demolished Smith's arguments in the workshop by pointing out that where Smith was using 42 degrees of freedom, there were actually only 3 degrees of freedom. The quotation from Smith is also omitted in the published paper.

To summarize, Morton, in evidence in Mr Clemmett's Appeal on 21 October 1992, with Canter present in the court, criticized Canter's draft paper in detail, including the points made above concerning the text samples used for the graphs, the misquoting by Krippendorff of Ellison, and the rejection of Smith's criticisms. The published version of Canter's paper, which appeared late, a month later, incorporated changes at these points.

To my knowledge, Canter has made no contribution to authorship studies and has no recognized standing in the area of authorship attribution. None of his papers over the past ten years seems remotely concerned with authorship studies and currently he appears on radio, television and in newspapers mainly speaking on 'offender profiling' or 'investigative psychology'. His publications include popular articles on crime (available in magazines on railway station bookstalls) and, more seriously, papers on behavioural psychology, such as 'Psychological aspects of nuclear war', 'A facet structure for nurses' evaluations of ward designs', and 'Psychologists and the media'. Canter's experience of cusum analysis appears minimal. When he was cross-examined by Mr Dermot Wright, QC in the case of Peter Mitchell in the Court of Criminal Appeal, Canter admitted that he had only made a small number of QSUM analyses himself, less than ten, and those with the help of an assistant;

when questioned on a QSUM chart he exhibited to the court he admitted that the analysis had been made by an undergraduate student – and was reminded that he was in the Appeal Court not in a Magistrates Court.[52]

Despite this lack of background and the superficial scrutiny just documented, Canter was still invited to act as critic and continued to criticize cusum evidence in a legal setting.

An especially obvious example of his lack of understanding came with his submission of a report (unpublished), dated 3 September 1993, to the Director of Public Prosecutions in Belfast in which he shows 'illustrations of the lack of validity of cusum'. He then displays two cusum charts 'produced from words and sentences that were generated completely randomly by computer'. The first five of the sixty sentences he uses will give the reader a flavour of Canter's test:

> [sentence 1] abacus aback it in top abash abate.
> [sentence 2] abatis abattoire the out abbreviate abdicate to abduce abduct abeam aberration to the so abide abject abjure him ablaze.
> [sentence 3] able ablepsy for him abnormal and abode do it if.
> [sentence 4] nor about above abrade pin abreast abreption an on abrupt put abscind it abscond in absolute absolve go absorb to abstemious.
> [sentence 5] no abstract abstruse the abundance abuse abyss academy for accelerate on accept access accessary accession accessory accidence set.

From sentence 31 through to sentence 60 Canter's random word and sentence generator has obviously got tired of words beginning with the letter 'a' and chooses instead (randomly, of course) words beginning with the letter 'b'.

Canter's list of data is absurd: the so-called 'sentences' are mere strings of words. A sentence is a linguistic structure unique to human beings, a semantic utterance constructed by use of syntax – and that this was allowed to stand as part of a submission to the court is its own comment on the procedure. Computer-generated strings of words are not sentences: therefore, no cusum analysis will cohere since such strings contain no pattern of language habits for analysis.

In the 'Note on [his] expertise' in this report, Canter states that 'he is internationally known for his expertise in statistical analysis of naturally occurring behaviour, including speech and other utterances, having published a widely cited text on this'.

Hardcastle's Paper

Hardcastle has a number of misconceptions of, and problems with, QSUM in common with Canter and Hilton and Holmes. He has certainly missed the essential attribute of the technique in that he omits any mention of the order and arrangement of words. His attempts at drawing cusum graphs often show them to be wrongly scaled, as can be seen easily by the naked eye in the published versions; in his reports and in his paper he shows only a single vertical scale on his graphs, where two vertical scales are required; on occasion he even has graph axes with no scales. This must cast doubt on the reliability of his competence in drawing these cusum charts.[53]

Hardcastle objects that 'Morton often employed the class of 'short words . . . such as "and", "of", "the", "to", etc., which are not related to the subject matter of the text' pointing out that 'a proportion of words of 2 or 3 letters in any text are subject-related but these are not specifically excluded'.[54] In other words Hardcastle objects that *all* two- and three-letter words are counted, including nouns. In practice, this presents no problem since the proportion of such nouns in ordinary vocabulary is relatively slight in comparison to vocabulary size.[55] Morton's 'filler' words are mainly connectives, pronouns, conjunctions and prepositions. It is hardly surprising that such heavy usage should prove to be a discriminating factor.

Hardcastle adds that 'words beginning with a vowel (other than those of two or three letters) are predominately subject-related, and the notion that occurrences of such words can distinguish authors is preposterous'.[56] The testing of words beginning with a vowel needs more detailed consideration than space allows here.[57] The exceptional noun that starts with a vowel need not detain us. Suffice to say that this *ivw* test has been used and does work well. The answer to Hardcastle's comment that the test is 'preposterous' is to point out that it works, and, in some cases, *works on its own without two- or three-letter words*. It is not for him to deny the evidence.

Where Canter uses 'proportion', and Hilton and Holmes use 'percentages', Hardcastle uses 'rates of use' as in 'Morton claimed that people can be consistent in their rates of use of particular classes of word'.[58] Whatever the synonym, the idea that cusum analysis is based on such consistency is erroneous and has been dealt with earlier in this chapter.

Hardcastle continues, 'Certain instances have been identified as the cause of anomalies: . . . sentences containing reported speech.'[59] It is not the case that 'reported speech' has been given by Morton as an anomaly. It is direct *quoted* speech (in inverted commas) which has to be deleted as being the words of somebody else.[60] A paraphrase will not cause an anomaly. Further, on the subject of anomalies, Hardcastle, continuing his list of types of anomaly with 'very short replies to questions and formal modes of address', complains that 'there is no comprehensive catalogue of such instances'.[61] Examples of anomalies that the researchers have noted have been listed earlier, and are routinely deleted.[62]

Hardcastle correctly points out that 'there are many linguistic differences between writing and speech'.[63] The most notable of these are to do with *manner* of physical utterance, since spoken utterance is naturally a mode of thinking aloud. Features of spoken utterance include: hesitation, pauses, repetition, tone, pace, pitch, and emphasis. Naturally, QSUM analysts edit their text to eliminate such features. Repetition of a sentence, or parts of a sentence, should be eliminated, as should filler-sounds, like 'um', [grunt] and 'er'.

Hardcastle is obviously exercised by these differences and gives a number of examples.[64] The rare half-sentence, 'Down the street and round the corner', can be eliminated along with the filler-sounds above. On the question of common contractions in speech ('I'm' for 'I am', etc.), consistency in the testing is all that is required. The analyst usually leaves the contraction as it is. Single word answers, like 'yes' and 'no' are not used in the analysis; the odd prefacing by the word 'yes' may be from preference, and is left in. The use of part of a question in a spoken reply is easily omitted, but it should also be noted that the subject need not necessarily make such a use.[65]

All that needs to be confirmed is that the analysts, who have been working with this technique since 1988, have already encountered all the problems that Hardcastle points out, with the éclat of a conjurer producing a rabbit from a hat. It is naïve and rather insulting to imagine that the professionals involved have been blissfully unaware of the rabbits all this time.

It is obvious that more recent studies of authorship attribution have escaped his attention. It is also a pity that Hardcastle, like many scientists, shows signs of antipathy to, and lack of understanding of, scholars in the humanities and their work.

I first met Hardcastle at the 1984 Edinburgh Workshop on Authorship Studies referred to above. He only attended the tutorial sessions on the first two days. The research discussions took place on the following two days. Hardcastle says that 'Smith [has] severely criticised Morton's statistical Stylometry procedures.'[66] It is regrettable that Hardcastle did not stay to listen to and participate in the research discussions since he would have heard Smith put his objections which were then demolished by Wake, as described earlier in this chapter. Hardcastle also states that 'The Stylometry method could only be applied to relatively lengthy texts of over 1,000 and preferably over 3,000 words.'[67] Hardcastle is wrong in stating this. The size of block samples was discussed in the tutorial sessions that Hardcastle attended at the Edinburgh workshop. Certainly I, and others, were successfully working with block samples of as little as 500 words at that time. Since one of the purposes of the workshop was to exchange this information, it would appear that Hardcastle gained little from attending it.

Like Canter, Hardcastle appears to have made no contribution to, or have any standing in the area of authorship attribution. If his published papers are a reliable indication, then his areas of expertise would appear to be in the examination of typewriter and word-processor print wheels, betting shop cameras, signature authentication and handwriting, the speed of writing, and ink, none of which seems remotely concerned with authorship studies. The only paper on authorship other than the paper under discussion here was published in 1987, and he is one of three co-authors.[68] This joint paper is descriptive – rather than critical in the academic sense of the word – of Morton and Michaelson's 1970s positional stylometry method.

Sanford's Paper

Sanford and his colleagues have similar misconceptions about the cusum technique to Canter, Hardcastle, and Hilton and Holmes. Somehow, they all appear to have brought assumptions and misconceptions from areas within which they themselves may work, and applied these to the cusum technique, the result being that they are able to show that what we have never claimed is unlikely to be true. Yet Sanford's group, certainly, had the opportunity of having these assumptions and misconceptions corrected. Firstly, they work in the Psychology Department at the same university, Glasgow, at which Morton is an Honorary Research Fellow in Computer Science; however, they made no attempt to contact Morton. Secondly, in 1993 I had a letter from one of Sanford's co-authors asking if I would work with her and Sanford on examining the 'merits [of QSUM] in the determination of authorship', even though I live and work 400 miles from Glasgow.[69] On receiving a copy of an unpublished paper of theirs together with the request that I might comment on it, I replied in detail explaining how their assumptions concerning the cusum technique were erroneous and that what they described as 'a major part of Morton's claim' had never been made by Morton.[70] In conclusion, I made it clear that I would be happy to talk further with them; no subsequent approach was made from Sanford's group.

Under the section heading 'Morton's claims', Sanford et al., speaking of the various word groups used in QSUM tests, say: 'Such habits are the ratios of various indicators to the number of words in each sentence of a discourse.'[71] 'Proportion', 'percentage', 'rate of use', and now 'ratio' (soon the critics will run out of words from a helpful thesaurus); this misconception has been dealt with earlier in the chapter.

Passing over the fact that the 'issues to be investigated' in the experiment are based on misconceptions, Sanford et al. then propose an experiment in which twenty 'subjects' – staff and students at Glasgow University – provided spoken and written samples of utterance. The spoken samples 'were tape-recorded and later transcribed'. While no mention is made as to the quality of the transcriptions, it is stated that 'full stops were inserted at what appeared to be sentence boundaries'.[72] If one examines the data in the Appendix to the paper, to illustrate the arithmetic for calculating cumulative sums, one finds that Sanford et al. give the sentence lengths for a sample of twenty-five sentences. Three of these sentences are extremely long, namely 127, 148, and 179 words, with another seven sentences having forty-eight words or more, while there are three short sentences of six, seven and eight words.[73] This does not sound like *natural* utterance. The problems with long sentences have been thoroughly examined earlier in this book and, of course, such long sentences lose information. In an experiment I carried out some years ago, I gave a sample of transcribed speech to nineteen people, staff and students at the University of Wales Swansea. I had deleted all punctuation from the sample and asked my 'subjects' to punctuate it sensibly. When comparing the various forms of the punctuated sample, I came to the conclusion that intelligent re-punctuation made no difference so far as the cusum technique was concerned. Thus, it would seem that Sanford and his group could have benefited from re-punctuating the long sentences in their appendix sample. Their method of punctuation thus appears strange, if not suspect.

The control material they used comprised 'three samples of each subject's written material . . . These samples consisted of essays or papers written in the academic context.'[74] It seems to me most naïve to believe that 'essays or papers written in the academic context' will be suitable for control material. The integrity of the utterance used in control material is of the utmost importance. In the academic context, essays, papers, and examination answers are very often riddled with quoted or copied material, often without attribution or quotation marks. Thus, it seems to me that both the design and the method of the experiment are flawed.

One of the 'issues to be investigated' which exercised Sanford et al. was based on 'scientific studies of differences in speech and writing [which] suggest that there should be differences'.[75] In 1992 I had the opportunity of examining both the spoken and written utterance of fifteen police officers. The officers were on a training course concerned with interviewing witnesses. The tape-recorded interviews had the utterance of the officers and the 'witness'. These interviews were transcribed for comparison with the witness statements written by the officers. With the comparisons so far made, there is no indication that QSUM can distinguish between the spoken and the written utterance of individual officers, but it does distinguish between officers.

The question of what people wish to distinguish between, or not, in text analysis is an interesting one. People have different requirements. Some, like myself, wish to distinguish between the utterance of different people. Others want techniques for distinguishing between genres but not between people; yet others wish to sort examples of utterance into chronological order, i.e. distinguishing between early and later utterance. No doubt others wish to distinguish between the spoken and written utterance of individuals. These, and similar problems, call for a number of different techniques, techniques that are suitable for the job in hand. The cusum technique suits problems in my area because I want it to be sensitive to differences between different people's utterance yet insensitive to differences in spoken and written utterance and to differences between genres for the same person's utterance. The fact that it is insensitive to chronology does not worry me.

In the published paper by Sanford's group, 'Discriminating one author from another etc.', they state their interest as 'modelling the development of an individual's writing style'. As explained earlier in the chapter, neither Morton nor I use the term 'style', deliberately. Certainly QSUM is not applicable to modelling the development of an individual's writing style. Scholars have long practised the recognition of authors by studying their 'style'. QSUM is a scientific method of attributing utterance: it does not describe or analyse style.

Like Canter and Hardcastle, Sanford appears to have made no contribution to, or have any standing in the area of authorship attribution. His published papers are in the area of psycho-linguistics and are unconnected with authorship studies.

Trial by TV

As already mentioned in Chapter 8, in 1993 Morton was contacted by a producer of a TV production company asking him to analyse, 'urgently', two short transcripts.[76] The result, three days later, was a six-minute report – heavily edited from two and a half hours of interview – in a British Channel 4 TV programme called *Street Legal*. The aim of the programme (or 'stunt' as one solicitor called it) seems to have been to disparage expert evidence in general and to discredit Morton in particular, by a quick sensational result purporting to show that QSUM was unable to distinguish between the language usage of two subjects, rather than to look seriously at a valuable forensic tool. This may impress the lay public but can have no scientific standing. A fuller discussion of this 'Trial by Television' is given in two articles by Richard Freeman and Morton in *The Expert*, the journal of The British Academy of Experts.[77] Detailed analyses of a transcript of the programme and the sample texts, carried out by Jill Farringdon and M. David Baker independently of each other in order to cross-check their results, showed how the wrong conclusion was drawn by the programme makers. If there is a lesson to be learnt it is surely that it is dangerous to take on, in good faith and without sufficient safeguards, a media commission by an unknown TV company without sufficient time for a thorough investigation.

Summary

Sadly, one comes to the conclusion that the above critics – the authors of the four published papers and the producer of the TV programme – had only read the published literature on QSUM superficially before making their experiments. None of these authors contacted the active workers in this field before coming to their 'conclusions'. In contrast, we have given advice, often in the form of tutorials, by mail, electronic mail, telephone, fax, and made personal visits to give lectures and workshops to individuals and groups who are serious enquirers.

A purist point of view of literary criticism, which is as valid for the criticism dealt with in this chapter, is considered by Tom Paulin in an article entitled 'The art of criticism: 3. Getting it wrong': 'To adapt Baden-Powell on personal hygiene, the good critic checks his or her references and quotations not once but several times', but goes on to add, 'But suppose time and money are short?'.[78] One may speculate that time and money were short for the critics of QSUM.

Oliver Heaviside recounts a scientific improvement made by chemists:

> One day our respected master informed us that it had been found out that water was not HO, as he had taught us before, but something else. It was henceforward to be H_2O. This was strange at first, and inconvenient, for so many other formulæ had to be altered, and new books written. But no one questions the wisdom of the change. The chemists . . . did not cry 'Too late', ignore the matter, and ask Parliament to legalise the old erroneous weights! They went and set the matter right.[79]

Will those self-appointed guardians of language likewise ignore QSUM?

Weighted Cusums and a *t*-test

Early in 1992, my statistician colleagues decided to take me in hand and help me to obtain a 'number' – a probability – which would give a measure of the separation of the cusum charts. One early approach investigated the use of aggregated Markov chains, but this was found inappropriate. Then Derek Bissell came to my aid. Professor Bissell was responsible for writing the British Standard on cusums and had recently published a paper on what he termed 'weighted' cusums.[80] With the cusum graphs as represented throughout this book so far, the distance representing each sentence along the horizontal axis is the same for all sentences. This even spacing accounts for the sudden steep rises of the cusum graph when a very long sentence is encountered, a sentence much longer than the average for the sample. It also accounts for some sudden drops in the cusum graph, not so pronounced, when a very short sentence, well below the average length, is encountered. Using weighted cusum charts, the distance between sentences on the horizontal axis is proportional to the length of each sentence. This means that there are far fewer pronounced steep rises or falls of the chart. It also means that only one graph is required, the sentence length information now being carried, in an indirect way, by the scale on the horizontal axis. The mathematics developed for weighted cusums by Bissell allows a probabilistic quantification to be made for sections of the chart which may appear to indicate a change of authorship. Further work by Bissell resulted in a monograph which sharpened his work on weighted cusums, with particular reference to text analysis, and produced some further statistics for use with text analysis, including a *t*-test (Welch's *t*).[81]

To use these probabilistic statistics, one first makes an initial hypothesis that the text being examined is the work of one author and therefore will be consistent in the habit. A low probability, less that 0.05, casts doubt on this hypothesis. There are two arbitrary points commonly used by statisticians, known as 'significant at the 5% level', and 'significant at the 1% level'. In statistics dealing with natural language, the 5 per cent level of significance is normally chosen, indicating that if the probability of a divergence is greater than 0.05, or odds of 1 in 19, then the sample could have come from a text used as a control, while if the probability is less than 0.05 the sample and control are not alike. It has been suggested to me by statisticians that even if the probability falls between the 5 per cent and 10 per cent levels, there is sufficient evidence to examine the text closely for lack of homogeneity.

As an example, consider Figure HK-9 from Chapter 7 (shown again on p. 260), where thirty-three sentences of Helen Keller's utterance is sandwiched between seventeen sentences and fourteen sentences of 'Katherine's' utterance. The 'equivalent' weighted cusum chart using the same sandwich of data is shown below in Figure HK-9a. There is a pronounced rise and fall of the weighted cusum chart from sentence 1 to sentence 29, peaking at sentence 21. This section looks worth testing for evidence of a divergence. Using the V_{max}-test the probability is well below 0.05; using Welch's *t*-test we again find the probability well below 0.05. In other words, both these probability tests indicate that serious doubt must be cast on the hypothesis that the sentences in the section examined are by the same author.[82] As the reader will probably have noticed, the horizontal scale in Figure HK-9a, the weighted cusum chart, is labelled 'Sequence of Words', rather than 'Sequence of Sentences'. Since the sentences are spaced along the horizontal axis in proportion to their lengths, it is relatively awkward, using a simple computer graphics package, to mark such a non-linear scale. However, the sentence numbers can be found from the linear scale of words. The following table (p. 261) shows the corresponding word and sentence numbers for the first twenty-six sentences in Figure HK-9a:

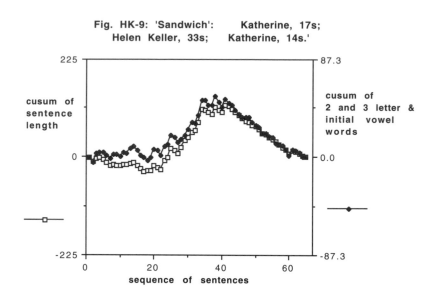

Figure HK-9

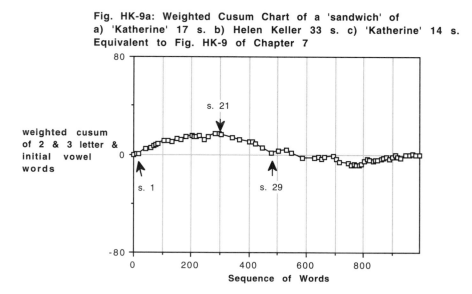

Figure HK-9a: Weighted cusum chart for the same habit as in Figure HK-9.

Sent# & ID	words Σw
1:	12.
2:	19.
3:	41.
4:	58.
5:	70.
6:	78.
7:	85.
8:	104.
9:	118.
10:	132.
11:	149.
12:	165.
13:	183.
14:	201.
15:	209.
16:	217.
17:	226.
18:	243.
19:	259.
20:	284.
21:	296.
22:	305.
23:	342.
24:	365.
25:	400.
26:	412.

Thus, for those critics who are not satisfied with examining Morton's QSUM charts by eye, there are tried and tested probabilistic quantifiers provided by Bissell, which should satisfy their call for 'standard statistical measures'. However, I have yet to find these measures giving a result that differs significantly from that found by visual inspection.

PART IV

A detailed account of the development of the cusum technique, illustrating the principles of scientific authorship attribution by the inventor of cusum analysis, A. Q. Morton

Chapter 11

THE QUESTION OF AUTHORSHIP

A. Q. Morton

When books were written and reproduced by hand, authors had no enforceable rights. Works could be copied freely, and any writer could use a text to suit his own purposes. He could quote, or plagiarize, without acknowledgement. As a result, there are many texts of uncertain authorship or integrity. Scholars have studied these and come to conclusions about the questions they raise. Unfortunately, there is no unanimity in their opinions. A simple example is the seventh letter of Plato. This contains biographical information which is important if authentic. But it is not difficult to compile three lists of names: the first of scholars, highly qualified and respected, who accept the letter as an authentic epistle of Plato; the second, equally lengthy, of scholars, also highly qualified and respected, who deny the letter to Plato. The third list would be rather shorter and contain the names of those scholars who argue that the epistle is composite, parts of it being from different hands.

Clearly it would be advantageous to have a method by which the authorship of a text could be determined. The historical stages by which this development has come about have been briefly indicated in Chapter 1, but some further commentary on that development is useful. With regard to Augustus de Morgan's suggestion described there, of the use of word length for attributing Pauline authenticity, in the simple form in which it was advanced, the suggestion is impracticable. It requires samples much larger than the Pauline Epistles.

The first test of authorship – it was also for writers of Greek prose – was established by an eminent industrial scientist W. C. Wake. Wake was doing a doctorate on the authorship of the *Corpus Hippocraticum* and, being a scientist, he examined a number of possible indicators of authorship, testing them on a range of texts and writers, before applying them to the disputed material. What Wake found, in simple terms, was that what de Morgan supposed might be true of *word length*, was true of *sentence length*. Sentences range in size from a single word to some hundreds of words, but the average length of sentence is a characteristic of the writer.[1]

In Greek prose, sentence length can be an effective test: the variations within writers are relatively small, the differences between them correspondingly large. In English, and other uninflected languages, it is much less effective: the variations within writers are greater and the variations between them much reduced.

However, there is a problem with sentence length distributions. Sentences do not come in a random sequence but tend to come in groups of long or short sentences. To represent a writer, the sample has to be large enough to contain these different groups. If sentences were random, the minimum sample would be about thirty sentences. In fact, it is about fifty sentences. Wake did his work 'BC', before computers, and when he first measured the bunching effect he did it by writing on a large number of cards the number of words in successive sentences of Greek prose. He then compared the results of dividing the large sample into smaller and smaller sub-samples with the results of taking the same number of sentences selected by random number tables. The statistics of the two sets of samples agreed well until the samples got below sixty sentences: they then diverged.

When G. H. C. Macgregor and the writer set out on the first systematic search for indicators of authorship in Greek prose, they decided to repeat and extend Wake's analysis with his advice and assistance. Wake devised a measure of serial correlation derived from the differential distribution of sentence length.[2] What this means is that by recording the pattern of differences between each sentence and the next, a coefficient can be calculated which showed that sentences did gather in groups. Having confirmed his earlier experiments, he joined with the writer in a further extension of the investigation. This turned to sampling methods.

In his first experiments, Wake had employed random samples. This meant using a set of random number tables to pick out sentences from a text in which all the sentences had been numbered in sequence. While important for some fundamental statistical purposes, random samples are ill-suited to literary problems. Wake then turned to spread samples and block samples.

A spread sample gives a picture of a large text and may be compiled by taking, say, the third sentence on every tenth page. If the problem is to compare two sizeable texts, as long as a volume of Dickens for example, a spread sample will give a quick result. But in Greek texts spread samples are not often appropriate.

Wake's main work was done using block samples. A block sample starts at any convenient point and carries on until it is long enough to represent the author. The complication of block sampling is to establish the minimum sample size below which the grouping effect comes into play. Any longer sample will give consistent results. The ideal sampling system would be one in which the text was read from first word to last and any sections which differed were isolated. Sequential sampling, in which a computer read not only from first word to last, but back again from last to first, was used by the writer in

1965.[3] The aim was to enable the minimum sample size to be determined with precision.

The chosen method was to use cumulative sum charts of sentence length. As will by now be clear, the method of making a cusum chart is simple enough. (The final step – adding the differences from the average in sequence – gives the chart its name, the cumulative sum of the differences, a title usually abbreviated to 'cusum'.) An application to (classical) Greek prose will give an illustration for another language.

In the Epistle to the Galatians, the first five sentences contain 30, 44, 1, 19 and 14 words. The average length of sentence in the epistle is 13.4 words and so the sequence of differences is +16.6, +30.6, -12.4, +5.6 and +0.6. Added in succession these give, 16.6, 47.2, 34.8, 40.4 and 41 as the first five points of the cusum chart of sentence lengths. Figure AQM-1 shows the whole chart for Galatians. There are some points to note about this chart.[4] First, it is based on Wake's definition of a sentence in Greek prose, namely, a sequence of words terminated by a full stop, a colon or an interrogation mark. Accepting the colon and the full stop means that any differences between texts are so small that they do not affect any conclusions based on the punctuation.

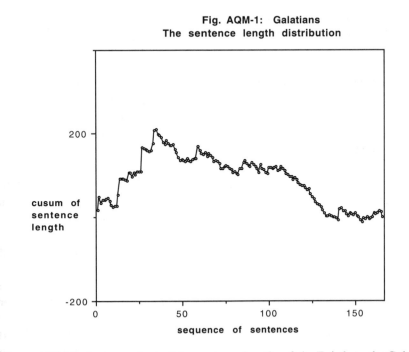

Figure AQM-1: A cusum chart of the sentence lengths of the Epistle to the Galatians.

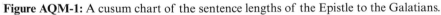

Characteristics of Cusum Charts

• **They end at zero – if they do not, some error has been made.**
Cusum charts need a target value, and the target value chosen in this technique is the average, which is appropriate because the data is 'historical', or complete. In a live industrial process, where one is looking for something abnormal occurring, a target value has to be estimated because the full range of values is not yet known. But when the target value is the average, then the cusum chart has to end at zero else an error has occurred: if your chart ends at zero, it is a proof that error has been avoided. Normally industrial cusum charts will appear to carry on its tendency at that point – the data is not a closed system.

Cusum charts do not often begin at zero: they only do so when the number of words in the first sentence and the average number of words in the sentences of the sample are the same.

• **Charts can take almost any shape**.
The only general feature is that they tend to have high peaks. If the average sentence length is ten words, the shortest sentence can only have nine less, but long sentences can run to ten times as many. From examples in previous chapters, the reader will recognize that the result of a long sentence is often a steep rise in the chart.

From Figure AQM-1 it is easy to see the cause of the trouble. The epistle begins with a sequence of long sentences running as far as sentence 35. To find whether or not these long sentences differ from the rest of the epistle, it is only necessary to drop a line from the peak to the base line, to the point P in the illustration Figure AQM-2; then measure the height of the peak, X-P, and the distance from the origin along the base line, O-P, and finally consult the tables to be found in all textbooks which deal with cusum methods. The result is not unexpected: the difference between the first thirty-five sentences and the rest of the epistle is too great to be accepted as due to chance variation.

The further advantage of using this chart is that to find the minimum sample to represent the writer, it is only necessary to move along the chart repeating the test. This shows the sample to represent the writer of Galatians to be forty-seven sentences. The bunching effect applies only to the opening group of sentences; for any later sample, the limit is set by the fact that below about thirty sentences it is rarely possible to separate one writer from another.

This illustration shows the problems of using sentence length for the determination of authorship in Greek prose. There is a statistically significant difference, due to the bunching of long sentences, between the first thirty-five sentences and the rest of the epistle and this is not likely to be due to any difference of authorship. Restricting comparisons to samples greater than the required minimum of forty-seven sentences not only means that short epistles such as Philemon cannot be tested, but also that, while a sample of fifty successive sentences may show some difference from other samples, it is not

Fig: AQM-2   Galatians
The sentence length distribution

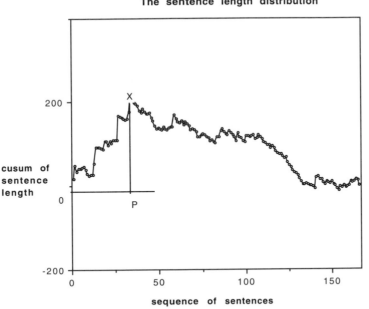

Figure AQM-2: Testing sample size in a cusum chart.

possible to say where within the sample the difference has arisen. A sample may be rejected when only part of the sample is from another source.

The other limitation is that intrusions into a text may well not show up. If the conclusions of modern historical scholarship are to be trusted, the Epistle to the Galatians is by Paul but has been extensively edited. It can be expected to show a relatively large number of small emendations but the only section of non-Pauline text comes at 5.13 and runs to 6.10.[5] This passage runs from sentence 134 to sentence 157 in the Greek text. In the cusum chart of sentence length, this sequence does not stand out. Recent developments in the interpretation of sentence length charts mean that, when the observations are weighted (i.e. when more weight is given to the longer sentences), it is possible to pick even single sentences from a sequence.[6] However, although this technique does show the interpolation in Galatians to differ from its surroundings, it does not resolve the dilemma, since not every statistically significant difference in sentence length implies a change of authorship. To enable decisions to be made about authorship or integrity another step must be taken.

The brief account of Udny Yule's work in Chapter 1 may here be expanded. When Yule looked on the *Shorter Oxford Dictionary* in the 1940s, he concluded that just over half the entries were nouns. Suppose that someone wrote a passage in which exactly half of every sentence was made up by the occurrence of nouns. If cusum charts were drawn, first of the sentence length distribution and then of the occurrence of nouns in the same sentences, what would the relationship of the two charts be? The answer is simple: the noun chart would be exactly the same shape as the sentence length chart but half the height. If the text ran to 1,000 words and contained fifty sentences, the average length of sentence would be twenty words. In the same fifty sentences, there would be 500 nouns, half the total number of words. So the average number of nouns per sentence would be ten. A sentence which had forty words in it would have twenty nouns. When it came to constructing the charts, the sentence length chart would rise by $40 - 20 = 20$ words. The noun chart would rise by $20 - 10 = 10$ occurrences. This relationship holds for every sentence: the noun chart moves in the same direction but half the distance. If the noun chart were to be doubled in size, or the sentence length chart to be halved, the two would be identical.

The result of a rigid habit, one in which every sentence had a fixed proportion of some class of words, would be two charts which were the same shape but different heights. If the habit of using the defined class of words included half the words of the sentences, the habit chart would be half the

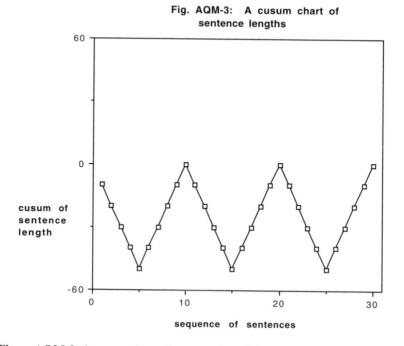

Fig. AQM-3: A cusum chart of sentence lengths

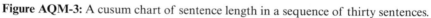

Figure AQM-3: A cusum chart of sentence length in a sequence of thirty sentences.

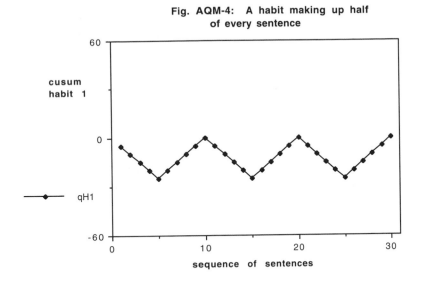

Fig. AQM-4: A habit making up half of every sentence

Figure AQM-4: A cusum chart of a habit (nouns) making up exactly 50 per cent of each sentence.

height of the sentence length chart. If it included one-third of the words in the sentences, the chart would be one-third the height of the sentence length chart.

It might seem unlikely that anyone has a perfectly rigid habit of this kind but the hypothesis makes a convenient starting point. The illustration begins with an alternation of five short sentences followed by five long sentences, and this pattern repeated three times. The first illustration is of the sentence length chart on its own (Figure AQM-3). There is little to be said about this chart; it is the comparison with others which is fruitful. The first comparison is of a rigid habit in which exactly half the words of every sentence fall into the defined class.

Figure AQM-4 shows that the cusum chart of this rigid habit is similar to the parent chart of sentence length, but it is not easy to make an accurate comparison of two separate charts. When the scale of the habit chart is changed to make the patterns the same height, the result is as shown in Figure AQM-5.

These charts have been made from sequences of short sentences (sentences of ten words) alternating with sequence of long sentences (sentences of thirty words). The average sentence length is twenty words and a habit which occurs as exactly half the words of every sentence means that the habit occurs five times in the short sentences, and fifteen times in the long sentences.

It may seem a fanciful assumption that such regularity would be

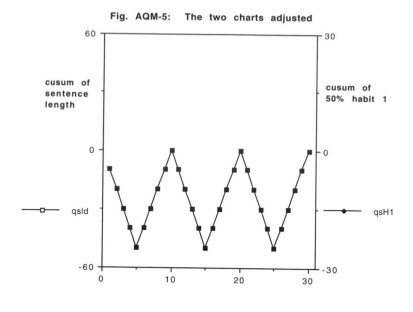

Figure AQM-5: The charts of Figures AQM-3 and AQM-4 adjusted and superimposed.

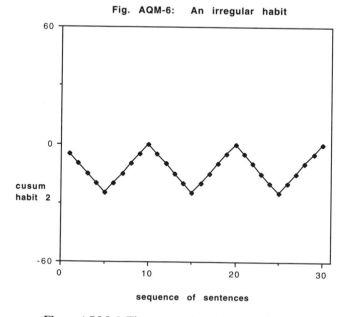

Figure AQM-6: The cusum chart of a non-linear habit.

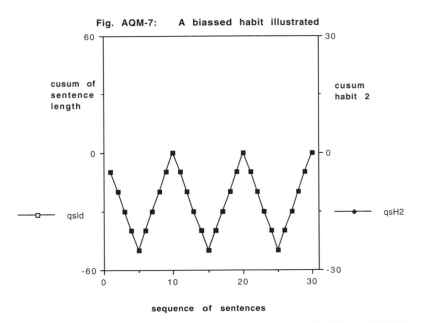

Fig. AQM-7:   A biassed habit illustrated

sequence of sentences

Figure AQM-7: The comparison of the habit shown in Figure AQM-5.

encountered in Greek texts. But the next step is to consider the effect of variations in the habit. Suppose that the short sentences contained more occurrences of the habit, six occurrences rather than five, and the long sentences also had a higher number, but relatively smaller proportional increase, sixteen occurrences against the previous fifteen. This would correspond to a habit which occurred more often in shorter sentences. The result is the chart shown as Figure AQM-6. As before, the shape of the chart looks much the same as the parent sentence length chart, but the similarity is more readily assessed by making the two charts the same height and superimposing them. This is shown in Figure AQM-7.

Suppose that the habit remained at the 50 per cent level in the long sentences and fell to only 40 per cent in the short sentences: the result is shown in Figure AQM-8. Again this looks rather like the familiar pattern of the parent sentence length distribution, but the comparison is better made by adjusting the two to be the same height and superimposing them, as in Figure AQM-9.

The point of interest in Figure AQM-9 is that the charts begin to separate. The evidence of their divergence is to be seen in the thickening of the lines around the lowest points. The divergence is not yet anything like a complete separation of the charts, even though the changes which produce it are very large if they refer to rates of occurrence of frequent words in a Greek text.

The final example of a habit which varies non-linearly with sentence length

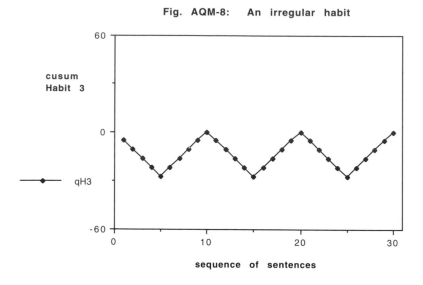

Figure AQM-8: An irregular habit. cusum Habit 3, qH3, sequence of sentences.

Figure AQM-8: Another illustration of bias in a habit.

is shown in Figure AQM-10. In this both the length of sentence and the occurrence of the habit are altered. Even with this double variation, the charts are closely similar. They just begin to separate at the bottom of the dips.

What these illustrations show is that if we record some component of sentences by making a cusum chart of the occurrence, adjusting the charts to be the same height, and superimposing them, they will coincide even when there are large variations, in terms of literary statistics, in the proportion of the component in different lengths of sentence. As long as the pattern of occurrence is consistent, the charts will be closely similar.

If the component occurs in a changing pattern, the charts will separate. This is shown in Figure AQM-11 in which the first set of ten sentences has a different pattern of habit from the next twenty (denoted by 'misqs'). In this illustration, the pattern of habit changes after sentence 10. In the early sentences, a short sentence, one of ten words, has six occurrences of the habit, as against five occurrences in the later sentences. The long sentences, sentences of thirty words, show fifteen occurrences in the initial group and sixteen in the later groups. The separation is quite clear: the first ten sentences differ from the remainder.

• **This suggests that cusum charts may have a role to play in the discovery and application of tests of authorship. A test of authorship is some habit which is shared by all writers and is used by each at a personal rate, enabling his works to be distinguished from the works of other writers.**

It is not to be expected that everyone will differ in a single habit, a battery of

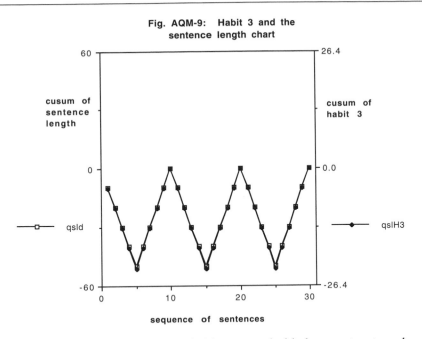

Figure AQM-9: Another irregular habit compared with the parent sentence length chart.

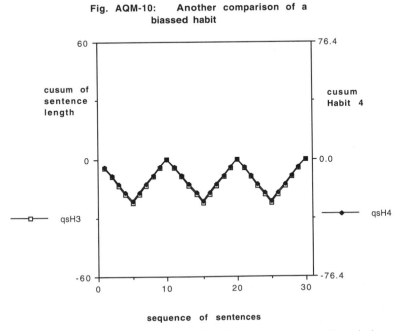

Figure AQM-10: A final example of habit and sentence-length variation.

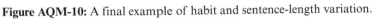

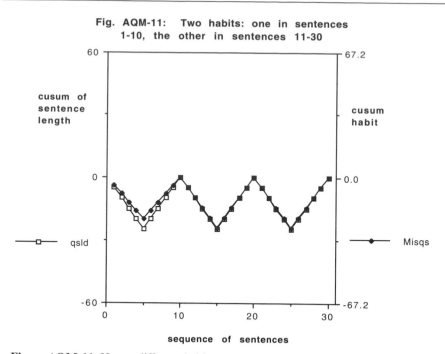

Figure AQM-11: How a different habit pattern causes a separation in a sequence of sentences.

suitable tests may be required. Tests of authorship will have some essential characteristics – for example, independence of subject-matter – and some desirable ones, such as frequency of occurrence. The desirable ones are first to be examined.

Desirable Tests of Authorship

The essential characteristic of any habit is consistency. The most desirable characteristic is frequent occurrence. Frequent occurrence is useful in different ways. The most obvious is to take as an example a text of 100 pages in which every element used in making a decision about the integrity, or origin, of the text has been underlined in red. What it is desirable to have would be a text pink on every page (i.e. a smooth blend of red and white). What is not to be desired, but is often found, is a text in which a few scarlet pages (i.e. with heavily predominant red marks) are separated by stretches of virgin white. To cover a text in detail, a habit must occur in every part: it is as simple as that.

Frequent occurrence is desirable for many reasons, but one other major one can be also be simply illustrated. The most frequent word form in Greek prose is the conjunction *kai*. The different forms of the article when combined,

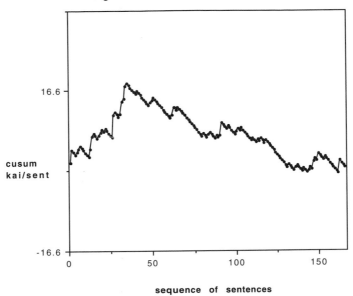

Fig. AQM-12: Galatians : kai in sentences

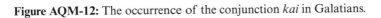

Figure AQM-12: The occurrence of the conjunction *kai* in Galatians.

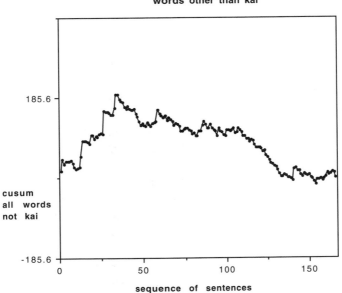

Fig. AQM-13: Galatians:
words other than kai

Figure AQM-13: A chart of all the words which are not occurrences of *kai*.

outnumber the occurrences of *kai*, but only rarely will any one form of the article be more frequent than occurrences of the conjunction. There are seventy-two occurrences of *kai* in Galatians, and Figure AQM-12 shows the cusum chart of these occurrences.

Of this illustration little needs to be said. While the chart has the same general shape as the parent sentence length chart, rising to a peak at sentence 35 and thereafter declining in a series of steps, superimposing the two reveals a large number of discrepancies. One obvious cause of differences is the relative scale of the charts. The range of the sentence length chart is 220 words The range of the *kai*-in-sentences chart is eighteen occurrences. So one occurrence of *kai* will appear equivalent to 220/18, about twelve words in a sentence. This makes the longer sentences, those which have two or three occurrences of *kai*, stand out. On its own, the chart of occurrences of *kai* suffers the same limitations as the sentence length chart. There is a statistically significant difference between the first thirty-five sentences and the rest of the epistle, which is not due to a difference of author, and the later intrusion does not show up as it should.

This does not mean that the occurrence of *kai* in sentences is not a reliable test of authorship. It does mean that the minimum sample size is subject to the same restrictions as apply to sentence length distributions.

If frequency of occurrence is important, it can be overdone, as a comparison of Figure AQM-12 and Figure AQM-13 shows. The occurrence of the conjunction *kai* necessarily implies a complementary chart of all the words in the same sentences which are not occurrences of *kai*. As there are only seventy-two occurrences of *kai* in the epistle, the number of occurrences of words *not kai* is the total, 2,229, less 72, 2,157. Not surprisingly, this chart very closely resembles the sentence length chart from which it was derived.

These illustrations show that

• **habits which occur infrequently are unlikely to prove profitable indicators of authorship and habits which are too frequent also lack power to discriminate.**

Habits which make up a substantial proportion of the words in sentences, but are not too frequent, seem the most promising to investigate.

If the occurrence of a word in a text were a mechanism similar to tossing a coin, the occurrence or non-occurrence being one of two mutually exclusive events, the probability of which did not change from trial to trial, the optimum proportion of occurrences for detecting any changes would be 50 per cent. The occurrence of one word in a group of words will not be a simple binomial event, but the average of the group, usually containing quite a large number of different words, will tend to behave more regularly than the individual words which make up the group, and the evidence suggests that the optimum rate of occurrence will not be far from 50 per cent. The range of variation, which differs from the rate of occurrence but is related to it, might well have a similar

Table 1: The occurrence of some classes of word in Galatians.

Defined class	Number of occurrences		Average rate per sentence	K
	No.	% of text		
All words	2229	100	13.43	
Kai	72	3.2	0.43	0.086
Article	272	12.2	1.64	0.153
Verbs	405	18.2	2.44	0.167
Nouns	523	23.5	3.15	0.267
23LW	811	36.4	4.89	0.351
IVW	1058	47.5	6.37	0.599
23LW+IVW	1507	67.6	9.08	0.775

Notes: (The classification of words by function is taken from *Analytical Greek New Testament*, Barbara and Timothy Friberg, Michigan, 1981.)

23LW denotes a word of two or three letters.

IVW, an Initial Vowel Word, denotes a word starting with a vowel.

Fig. AQM-14: The relationship of range to proportion

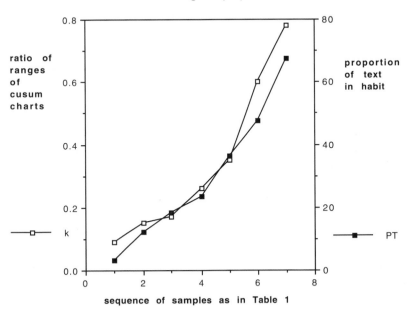

Figure AQM-14: The relationship of the proportion of occurrences of the habit to the range of variation in the QSUM-chart of the habits of Table 1.

characteristic, an optimum rate of about one half. To show what classes of word might make effective habits, Table 1 shows the rates of occurrence and the corresponding ratio, K, of the range of the cusum chart of the word class and the range of the parent sentence length distribution chart.

The relationship of the proportion of occurrences of the habit to the range of variation in the cusum chart of the habits of Table 1 is shown by Figure AQM-14. This illustration shows that while there is a close connection between the two variables, the proportion of words in the text which are included in a habit and the height of the cusum chart of the habit, the correlation coefficient is 0.954. This is not a simple equivalence. At the bottom of the scale, the occurrences of *kai* and of the definite article, the proportion is lower than the ratio; around the mid-values they are sensibly equal; at the higher values they again separate.

The most frequent words in a language have proved to be good discriminators between writers and speakers. The most frequent words in a language are mostly short words and so an obvious habit to examine is the use of words of two or three letters. This group of words will make up anything from 20 to 50 per cent of a Greek text. Included will be some rare words, usually nouns, but the number, and proportion, of these is too small to affect any judgement made using the occurrence of two- or three-letter words as a

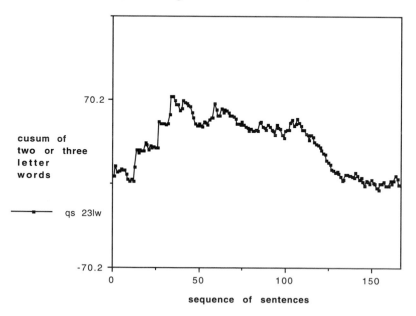

Fig. AQM-15:   GALATIANS

cusum of two or three letter words

qs 23lw

sequence of sentences

Figure AQM-15: The occurrence in *Galatians* of words of two or three letters.

habit. In any situation where this simple definition causes a problem, a computer can be given a list of words to count from which any troublesome elements are omitted. (For example, in Aeschylus' *Persians*, counting words which start with a vowel runs into a localized problem at the point where a number of Persian generals are named, all having names starting with the letter A.) Figure AQM-15 shows the occurrence in *Galatians* of words of two or three letters.

In this chart, the pattern is nearer to that of the parent sentence length chart than is the *kai*-in-sentences chart, but when the two are superimposed it is clear they do not match. Nor is it obvious that the mismatch could be due to the intrusion near the end of the text. To enable judgements to be made, it is necessary to go back to the beginning. It is essential to start with a sample of unquestionable authenticity. This means some text produced by the experimenter. While not everyone is as gullible as the man who chose a newspaper report of a football match as a specimen of homogeneous prose, many people have been surprised to find how little information they have about text they simply assumed to be homogeneous. So the starting point is a sample of the writer in person. This has been amply demonstrated in Chapter 2, 'Starting With Yourself', and a recapitulation by showing charts of Morton's utterance would add nothing new.

It is helpful, though, to clarify the practice of chart delineation used in the process of developing the method.

Identifying an Author: Morton's Conventions for Producing Cusum Charts (in his own publications)

The scale for a single chart is put down the left-hand edge. Sentence length, or other 'parent charts', are marked by black squares with a central white hole. Other habits are marked by different symbols. When there are pairs of charts, the sentence length chart has its scale down the left hand edge of the diagram, the habit chart down the right-hand side. In the reference notes, which show the marks used, the parent chart is uppermost, and the habit chart marking is below.[7]

The choice of scale is determined by a number of factors. When single charts are made and traditional tests of significance are used, the standard deviation of the data is the basis of the scale. For this purpose, it is of greater value to be able to see clearly what it is important to see.

There are three factors to take into account. One is ease of interpretation. Much research has been done on the relation of human beings to machines and, as it affects this use, a diagram which fills a space of about one half to one third of the vertical space has been found most effective. This rule does not apply to either very long sequences, or very short sequences, of sentences.

Another consideration is what information it is valuable to have. When stock market prices are being displayed, the smallest change which is of interest is something just below the cost of buying or selling a share and the scale is usually in pence or cents. Currency dealers on the other hand are interested in small fractions of a penny, or a cent. They quote prices to one ten-thousandth of a penny, or cent, in transactions involving billions of pounds or dollars. It is impossible for words to occur in fractions, so one limit to the scale used is set by the change produced by recording the occurrence of one word.

A consequential change is made by rounding off the figures to the nearest unit. The average number of words per sentence in a sample may well be a fractional figure, 12.4 and, in every difference which goes to the making of the cusum chart, the result is either a difference ending in 0.4, or in its complement 0.6. These fractions are rounded off to the nearest whole number. The dimension of this effect will shortly be illustrated.

The third factor to be taken into account in presenting cusum charts is the nature of the hypothesis being examined. If an insertion of 50–60 sentences has been suggested, a chart which would show such a sequence should be made: for example if the supposed insertion was five or ten sentences, something more detailed would be required.

• **Decisions of this kind come with experience.**

The results obtained from applications of the method to Morton's own utterance were sound, as in the **JMF** examples, and suggested that a general principle may be at work:

• **To validate a test of authorship based upon it, a range of texts and authors must be examined**.

It is not possible to examine a representative number of writers, or speakers, of Greek or English; many millions, if not billions, of samples would be involved.

The testing moves therefore in two directions: the first is to look at a number of samples and individuals. Should the results be consistent, then it is fair to call on Laplace's law of succession: if an experiment has worked N times, the best estimate that a similar experiment will work next trial is $(N+1)/(N+2)$. After a few hundred successful trials, a claim to general application can reasonably be made.

The other route for testing is to take extreme instances. If works written fifty years apart show consistency, it is difficult to argue that smaller intervals can explain a difference. If a series of illnesses, misfortunes and upheavals cause no change in a habit, it becomes difficult to argue that some lesser alteration in a career will do so.

All this work has been done and the results have been in print for some years now.[8] Of the habits in Table 1, only verbs are unsuited to this technique. The reason is that while the other classes of word occur in samples most frequently

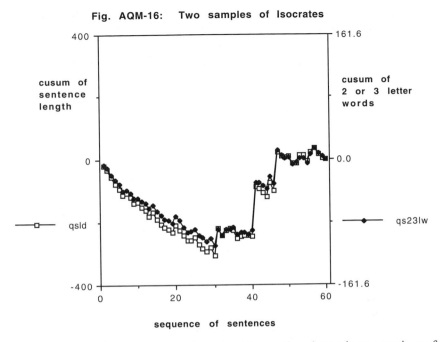

Fig. AQM-16:   Two samples of Isocrates

Figure AQM-16: The occurrence of words of two or three letters in two orations of Isocrates.

at rates near to the average value, and departures from the average become rarer the further they move from the average, this is not true of verbs. Verbs seem to occur either rather more often than average; or rather less often than average. The pattern for verbs is U-shaped: there are relatively few samples near to the average of all the samples, and more as you go further from the central value. The pattern of averages for the occurrence of verbs is rather like the pattern of clouds in the sky: either you find lots of cloud, or very little; a balance of 50 per cent cloud and open sky is rare.

An interesting illustration of this resulted from analysis of two samples of Isocrates. Regarded by many as a model stylist, his works were preserved free from the historical emendations required to adopt the teaching of a philosopher to changed circumstances. He started his career writing forensic orations and ended with the grand patriotic epideictic *Oration 12*. Figure AQM-16 shows a habit in a forensic oration and in *Oration 12*. These orations present not only a contrast in literary form: they are separated by more than sixty years. For all that, the habit runs consistently through both. It was earlier pointed out that two charts of this type cannot completely coincide as the charts are drawn in units and the data from which they are constructed is often

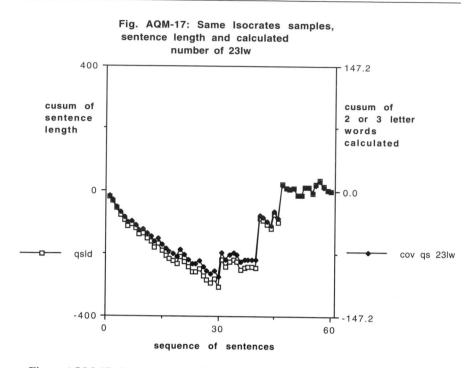

Fig. AQM-17: Same Isocrates samples, sentence length and calculated number of 23lw

Figure AQM-17: A comparison of actual and calculated values in cusum charts.

fractional. The rounding off applies to both components, the sentence lengths and the occurrence of words of two or three letters.

From this illustration it can be seen that most of the differences between the charts visible in Figure AQM-17 arise from the rounding off of the values.

• **One question always asked by beginners is how does one decide if two charts are similar?**

The reply is that experience serves to bring confidence in making this judgement, but just as the first step recommended to beginners taking up the technique is to make a pair of charts of a sample of known origin – the result should be a good match – the next step is to make a pair of charts showing how much of the differences which do appear are due to the rounding-off effect.

• **Validation of a technique of this kind is done in stages.**

The first is an examination of a range of writers, and speakers, an examination covering contrasts in literary form, differences in subject matter, changes in mood, differences in any aspect of composition which might be supposed to affect such habits. When this examination has confirmed that people do have consistent habits by which they might be identified, the next step is to show that they differ enough in these habits to make the technique useful in separating writers.

Identifying a Mixed Text

The first example of a mixed text is a sandwich in which some sentences of James McLeman are placed between sentences of A. Q. Morton. This illustration has a background. Editors from our first two publishers, dealing with our joint publications, confessed that they could not tell our writings apart, nor whose writing any chapter had been. A number of our New Testament colleagues who claim to distinguish a single sentence of Paul from one of Timothy, written in a foreign language nearly two thousand years before, proved unable to separate two contemporaries known to them. While we share the same outlook, we are quite different in many respects in expressing our viewpoint. But many scholars cannot separate the substance from the mode in which it finds expression.

To make this illustration, the first fifteen sentences of Morton from a book written in 1961 were taken, together with the fifteen sentences which begin this chapter, sentences composed more than thirty years later.[9] These two

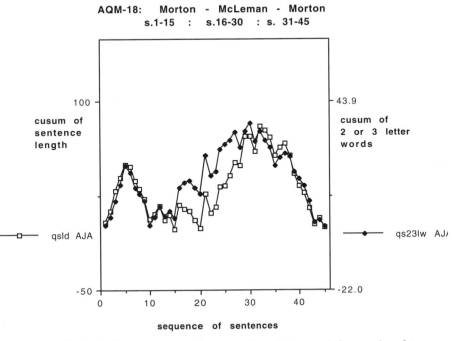

AQM-18:   Morton - McLeman - Morton
s.1-15   :   s.16-30   :   s. 31-45

cusum of sentence length

cusum of 2 or 3 letter words

qsld AJA

qs23lw AJ/

sequence of sentences

Figure AQM-18: The occurrence of two- or three-letter words in samples of two writers.

sequences were separated by fifteen sentences of McLeman from his first chapter in *The Genesis of John*. Clearly the two charts separate, dividing near to sentence 15 and coming together again near to sentence 30. The diagram might well indicate the difference of authorship with some precision; a difference which could be confirmed by excising the central section and showing that the remainder produced charts which closely coincided, and also the central section placed into a sample of McLeman showed homogeneity.

But not many examples are as simple as this one, and it is better to look at some general principles before embarking on the interpretation of cusum charts.

Some Principles in Interpreting Cusum Charts

If two samples are much the same size they can be expected to affect each other to much the same extent.

• **But if one sample is much smaller than the other, the large sample will be relatively unaffected by the intrusion of the smaller one, while the smaller one will be greatly affected by the large one.**

Figure AQM-19 shows the result of inserting five sentences of one writer, Thomas Hardy, into a sample of fifty sentences of Sir Walter Scott. If the

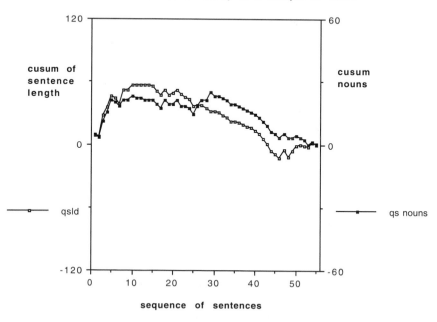

Figure AQM-19: The result of inserting five sentences of Thomas Hardy into fifty sentences of Sir Walter Scott.

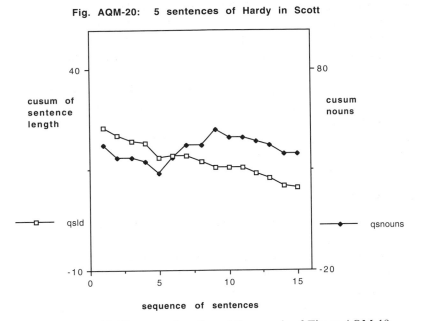

Figure AQM-20: The central section of the sample of Figure AQM-19.

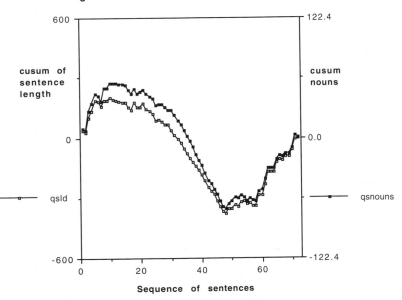

Figure AQM-21: The insertion of twenty-two sentences of Hardy into Scott.

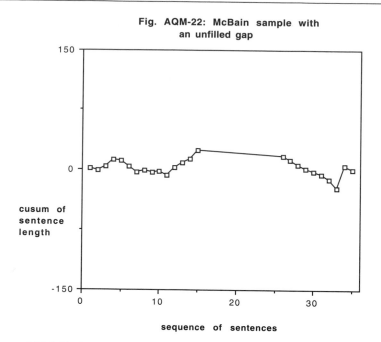

Figure AQM-22: A sequence of sentences from Ed McBain's *Killer's Payoff*, with a section cut.

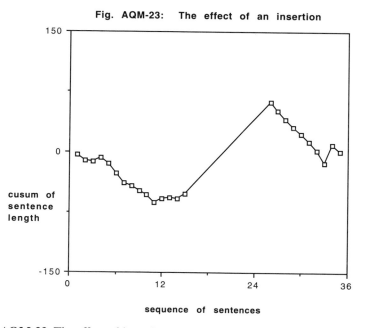

Figure AQM-23: The effect of inserting ten sentences into the sample of Ed McBain.

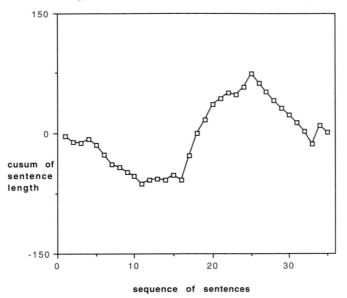

Figure **AQM-24:** The sentence lengths of the combination of writers.

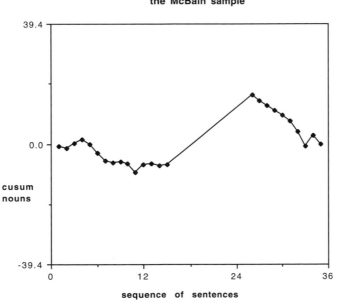

Figure **AQM-25:** The occurrence of nouns in the combined sample.

charts were printed individually, one on transparent material, it would be easy to show that the first part of the Scott charts had hardly changed, nor had the second part, and the insertion was responsible for the separation of the charts. (This could be confirmed showing the central part of the combined sample on a larger scale.)

In these charts the pattern is similar but there is a displacement due to the five sentences which have been inserted. Overlaying the charts shows that the insertion has little changed the original charts.

That the difference is confined to sentences 6 to 10 of this Figure AQM-20 (the five sentences of the insertion) is not difficult to see. (Note that as this illustration is extracted from the previous chart, the rule of ending at zero does not apply.) How much easier it is than judging the start and finish of a large insertion, using samples of the same writers, can be seen in Figure AQM-21 which shows the result of inserting twenty-two sentences of Hardy between the Scott samples.[10]

From this illustration it is not any easier to delimit the insertion even though it is so much larger. The reason for this is now to be explored. The first step towards understanding the necessity, and the virtues, of superimposing charts in making comparisons, is to see what the result of an insertion will be. Figure 22 shows a sequence of sentences from a popular detective story, *Killer's Payoff,* by the American writer Ed McBain.[11] In the diagram the sequence has been cut and the observations moved apart far enough to allow ten sentences of another writer to be inserted following sentence 15.

The next chart, Figure AQM-23, shows the consequence of inserting into this gap ten sentences from page 121 of Nicolas Utechin's *Hellbirds*.[12] The sentences from Utechin are much longer and so the points lie along a line sloping sharply up. To accommodate the change, the first sequence of McBain sentences has to be depressed and the second sequence starts from a higher position.

The new chart of the sentence lengths of the combined sample of the two writers is shown in Figure AQM-24. Given only this chart, there is no indication that the sample is composite. But the noun chart has suffered a corresponding, but not identical, twisting and as soon as the noun chart is laid over the sentence length chart it is obvious that the sequence is not homogeneous. The noun chart of the composite sample is Figure AQM-25.

The change in the noun chart looks similar to the change in the sentence length chart but the central section, the insertion, is tilted at a different angle. This means that, given only one chart, it could not be discovered that there was any insertion but as soon as both charts are superimposed, it becomes clear. The two charts, Figures AQM-26 and AQM-27, show the complete track of the noun chart and both sentence length and noun charts together. If the two charts are drawn by a computer program, they will be adjusted to start and finish together. The result is shown in Figure AQM-27.

Fig. AQM-26: New insertion in McBain.

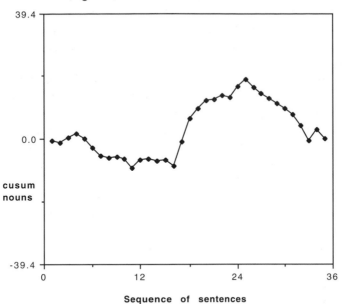

Figure AQM-26: The occurrence of nouns in the combined sample.

Fig. AQM-27: McBain with an insertion

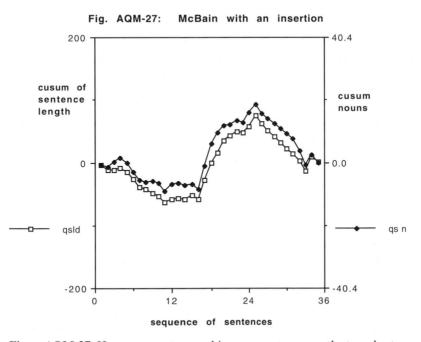

Figure AQM-27: How a computer graphics program arranges the two charts.

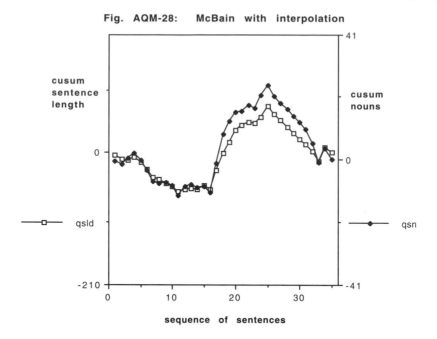

Figure 28: The sentence length and noun charts compared.

Figure AQM-27 is not easy to interpret. But when a tracing (or transparency) of the noun chart is overlaid on the sentence length chart some regularities appear. When the initial observations are aligned and the noun chart is rotated a little clockwise, there is a good match running up to sentence 16. When the final points are aligned, a good match runs back to sentence 25. The central section, the insertion, gives a good match for pattern, but seems to start one observation after it does. The insertion is sentences 16 to 25, but the separation is not clear until sentence 17.

  • **This illustrates a principle of the technique: it is not realistic to expect that an insertion can be precisely defined.**

There is always a small area of uncertainty at any point of transition: an indication that sentences 101–10 are separate from their context, means that some difference very near to ten sentences in size begins and ends near to these points. This point is confirmed in Figure AQM-28. In this a trace of the sentence length chart is overlaid on the noun chart. The separation of the two is not difficult to see: they diverge from 16 onwards.

In Figure AQM-28, the noun chart has been rotated until it lies along the sentence length chart. The match from the first point as far as the sixteenth is good. The charts then diverge showing that the points now range above and

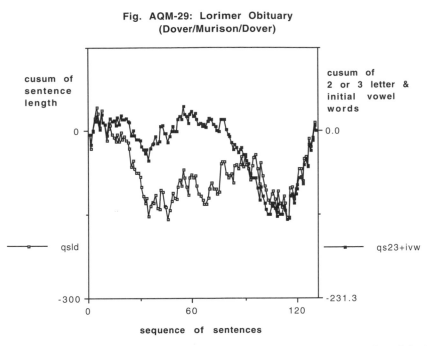

**Fig. AQM-29: Lorimer Obituary
(Dover/Murison/Dover)**

Figure AQM-29: Combined sample of 131 sentences from an obituary written jointly by Sir Kenneth Dover and Murison.

below a line revealing a change in the average value for this part of the series. The charts could again be rotated and the match would run further. It might seem that the process could hardly be simpler: the charts are overlaid and rotated to reveal the successive matching sequences. In principle this is the case, but there are some other things to be taken into account. In the overlay, the first point of the insertion looks more likely to come from the initial sequence than the central section to which it belongs.

 • **The true location of the insertion can be confirmed by reading the text. It must never be forgotten that the examination begins and ends with the utterance. The cusum charts are only guides to what is to be found in the sample of utterance.**

It might seem that the larger the samples, and the larger any difference between, then the easier it will be to see the divergence of the cusum charts. This is generally true, but there is an important limitation now to be illustrated. When Sir Kenneth Dover contributed an appreciation of his late colleague, W. L. Lorimer to the Proceedings of the British Academy, he included three paragraphs supplied by Murison, the editor of the *Scottish National Dictionary*.[13] In the tribute, the first seventy-one sentences are Dover, the next thirty-three are Murison and the final twenty-seven are again Dover.

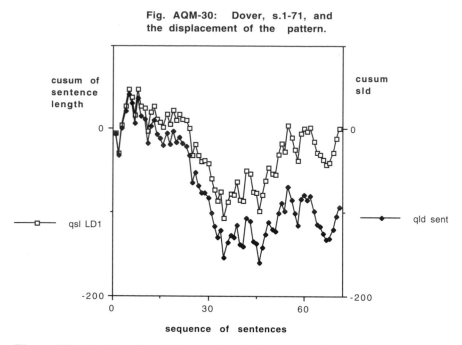

Fig. AQM-30: Dover, s.1-71, and the displacement of the pattern.

Figure AQM-30: The effect of the insertion by Murison on Dover's first seventy-one sentences of the combined sample.

There is a large difference in habit between the two contributors. Figure AQM-29 shows the occurrence in the text of words having two or three letters or starting with a vowel.

Superimposing copies of these charts is not going to reveal the change-overs from one writer to the other with any precision. The reason can be seen in Figure AQM-30 which shows how the first part of the sentence length chart is altered by the insertion. In this illustration the black points are the cusum chart of the first seventy-one sentences, Dover's, on their own. The open points show the change brought by adding to these seventy-one sentences, the following thirty-three sentences, of Murison. The new path lies along a line from the first observation down to a point ninety-four units below the original track. The pattern, which originally ran for seventy-one units, now tilts down and runs to 118 units, an increase of nearly two-thirds. Added to this is the distortion due to the use of a combined average value covering the whole sequence. In most cases, an insertion will make little alteration in the overall average, and the only changes in the charts will be that observations which ran a short way up, or down, might be reversed in direction. The effect on the whole pattern, and in the range of values, will be limited. When the change in average is relatively large, the general appearance of the chart will also change and, for anyone without experience of chart interpretation, it is much more difficult to match the two charts. Should the chart of the habit also show a large difference but in the opposite sense, longer sentences with fewer occurrences or shorter sentences with more, the problem becomes doubly difficult, the comparison is now of two charts both pulled out of shape.

The problem is readily resolved, and in shorter samples it will not arise. In this example the text offered a logical choice of possible transitions: sentence 72, for instance, began the description of an aspect of Lorimer's work quite different from what preceded or followed.[14] A sample of forty sentences centred on sentence 71 show the first transition very clearly and a second sample of forty sentences, from sentence 80 to sentence 120, shows the second with complete accuracy.

Where the text offers no indication of a likely change, it is then necessary to start a logarithmic search, dividing a large sample into halves, quarters, eighths and so on. This is much less trouble than its description might suggest. Very rarely will a second set of charts fail to resolve the question and a third set be required.

• **It is important to note exactly what is being said at this point. Cusum charts do not fail to work on long sequences of sentences, but they can give a confusing first impression and do so when the differences in the text are large rather than small.**

In such a case it is better to confine analyses to sequences of around fifty successive sentences. The progressive deformation, which occurs in all charts, does not make matching difficult until sequences of more than fifteen sentences are involved. Samples no more than three or four times this size are also convenient for the detailed study of Classical texts.

The Example of Galatians Re-examined

If we now return to the example of Galatians, the dual challenge is that cusum charts should not give a false indication for the opening sequence of long sentences, nor fail to pick out the later insertion. Figure AQM-31 shows the first fifty sentences of Galatians. In this comparison there is a good match and no sign that sentences 1–35 differ from those which follow. The minor separation to be seen at sentences 10–20 is the result of the inclusion of a quotation in sentence 19, (l. 23) in the text.

The tracing of this habit through the sequence of sentences generates no false signal due to the presence of the longer sentences. The automatic compensation provided by the cusum chart removes the disability from the sentence length distribution. This conclusion has been borne out by many examples.

Within the final sequence of sentences in the epistle, sentences 124–66, the

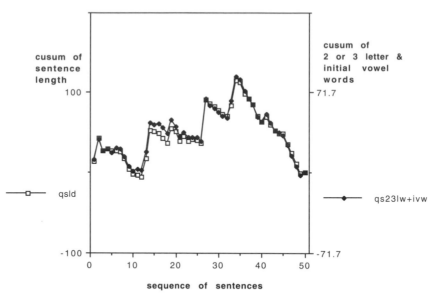

Figure AQM-31: A frequent habit in the first fifty sentences of Galatians.

insertion, 5.13–6.10, runs from sentence 10 to sentence 34. The insertion is not likely to homogeneous; it consists of a number of paragraphs arranged in a loose sequence. The first question is whether or not it shows up in the comparison of charts. Figure AQM-32 shows the occurrence of words of two or three letters in the sequence. This figure demonstrates a separation of the charts starting near the right place, sentence 10 of the sequence, but ending after sentence 22. When the same diagrams are reproduced in a form which allows superimposition, the start is confirmed to be at sentence 10 and the ending is most likely to be at sentence 27. The more frequent habit, adding to words of two or three letters those which start with a vowel is shown in Figure AQM-33.

In this comparison the start of the insertion is again clear, but the ending could be at sentence 30. Superimposing the charts suggests an insertion from sentence 10 to sentence 29 or 30. Adding nouns to the already combined habit of using words of two or three letters and words starting with a vowel, makes little difference, the separation is very much as in Figure AQM-33 and the insertion would run from sentence 10 to sentence 30.

This example not only shows that cusum charts offer a sensitive test of heterogeneity, it demonstrates two fundamental principles of this type of analysis.

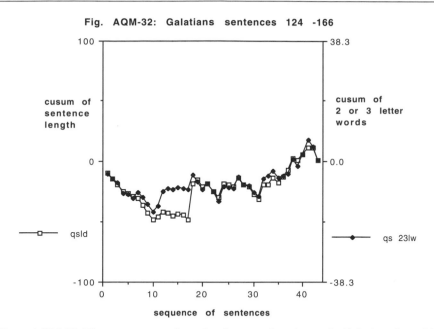

Figure AQM-32: The occurrence of words of two or three letters in Galatians from 5.7 to the end.

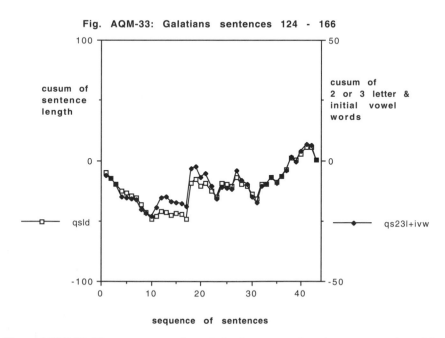

Figure AQM-33: The occurrence of words having two or three letters or starting with a vowel in the same sequence of sentences.

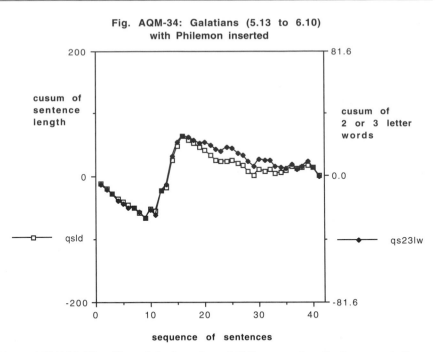

Figure AQM-34: The effect of the insertion of Philomenon in a Pauline sample from Galatians.

- **The first is that there must be a testable hypothesis to examine.**

In this case what is being tested is J. C. O'Neill's hypothesis that 5.13 to 6.10 of Galatians is an addition to the text. The passage is a series of proverbial statements unlikely to have come from a single source. The evidence is consistent with this hypothesis.

It is true that the final four sentences do not differ from the body of the text, but this is a reminder of the second principle.

- **The second principle is that in this kind of comparison only differences offer positive proof.**

A man with blue eyes and a man with brown eyes cannot be one man, but two men with blue eyes need not be the same man.

Not only is it necessary to have a testable hypothesis, it is essential to have a proper description of the samples being tested. A man serving a prison sentence asked for his confession to be examined. He supplied samples of his authentic utterance and samples of the police officers who might have produced the confession as well as a version of his supposed confession. As first tested, it appeared that the confession was not the utterance of the accused but of one of the officers. This started a move to have the verdict overturned. The first step was repeat the analysis using certified and accurate transcriptions and not the typescript supplied by the accused. The second analysis completely reversed the results of the first. The sources of the samples had been completely misrepresented, and if only the charts appeared in the report of the analysis it might well have gone undetected.

• **An important feature of this technique is that it is often possible to confirm a conclusion by further testing.**[15]

In this case some sentences in Galatians have been denied to the titular author. This can be confirmed in two ways; (a) the passage which is not Paul can be put into another piece of Paul to show that it does not fit, and (b) a genuine piece of Paul can be inserted in the position left vacant by the excision. Figure AQM-34 shows the replacement of the passage by the brief letter to Philemon, a text generally accepted as Pauline but too short to test by other methods. The superimposition of the charts confirms that there is no significant difference between them.

In Greek prose texts cusum analysis is most convenient with samples of around 50–60 sentences. In samples of this size, intrusions are likely to show up without the distortion which can attend longer sequences.

• **Such charts often bring to light a new phenomenon, the presence of small anomalies.**

These have always existed; it is only with cusum charts that they stand out. The habits which are the basis of the analysis are those used in free composition. But not all our utterance is made in that mode. Most of the anomalies are single sentences, but at times two or three may be involved.

Kinds of Anomaly

Anomalies have already been discussed in Chapter 2. They can here be further explored with the emphasis on fuller explanation and probabilities.

• **The first cause of an anomaly can be chance variation.**

Most statistical testing is designed to show whether or not chance variation can be excluded as the cause of some observed difference. To indicate how unlikely chance variation could be as an acceptable explanation, the probability that such variation would reach the observed level is calculated and cited. It may be that chance would only explain the difference once in 100, or once in 1,000 trials. However, we all compose many hundreds of sentences each day. In a year we may well make up more than a hundred thousand sentences. So we will produce, from time to time, a few strikingly different sentences and properly conclude that they would be found in our normal utterance very rarely. But they are part of our utterance: One example, which struck the writer on reading a record of court proceedings, was this reply to a question: 'No, it was not six of the ten of us, nor two of the six of us, it was one of the two of us.' This sentence has twenty-five words, all of two or three letters, and would stand out in a cusum chart of the utterance of the witness who had a normal rate of using such words of just over 20 per cent and so who would have five such words in an average 25-word sentence. This is an unlikely sentence to find but it *did* occur as one of the large number of sentences composed by the individual.

  • **A second cause of anomaly is when something is incorporated into a sentence.**

The sentence above (starting 'One example, which struck . . .') has produced a sentence very unlike this writer's normal rate of using two- or three-letter words. The compound sentence has forty-four words, thirty-two of which are words of two or three letters; the writer's average rate would be less than half as many. Quite often, a quotation will take the form of a sentence embodying parts of two or three short sentences from another person.

  • **The most frequent cause of anomalies is the inclusion within a sentence of a list of some kind.**
The list may result from an internal constraint, as when someone suggests there should be not ten commandments but twice as many and goes on to list them; or it may be the result of an external constraint, as when a person is asked to describe a journey down a sequence of city streets, or name the twenty best tunes of the last ten years, or describe, in detail, a large and complex building.

Anomalies are a striking feature of some Classical texts. They are either explanatory notes added by an editor to make clear to later generations something which would have needed no explanation to the first generation, or they are the stitching needed to join two sources. This can produce the kind of sentence which still affords amusement as when a TV news reader tries to warn of a change of subject with a sentence supposed to carry the viewer smoothly across what proves to be an unbridgeable gap. Biblical examples are Mark 7:1–5 and John 4:1–3.

Some scholars find it difficult to accept that a technique can isolate a single sentence as not being the composition of the author under examination. But this does happen and it can be confirmed, as was suggested above, by taking the anomalous sentence and inserting it into a sample of the writer from which it has come, where no difference will appear, and also by taking a comparable sentence from his work and showing that when inserted into the text sequence it produces a similar disturbance.

An example of this has been in print for some time.[16] In this, one paper in the *Federalist* series is shown to have been enlarged by the insertion of two descriptive passages, leaving a single original sentence, a rather long one, between them. The single sentence interrupts the sequence of the expansions and, when these are removed, it fits in both literary and stylometric contexts. When the sentence is placed in a sample of the writer of the expansion, it is clear that it differs from his utterance. This ability to confirm by experiment adds a new dimension to historical and analytical criticism.

Like every technique, cusum analysis has its limitations. It will give no useful result if the sample is a sequence of very short sentences. There is simply not enough variation in such sentences to separate one person from another. The extreme example would be a series of 100 questions to which the only replies could be 'Yes' or 'No'. No matter who was replying, the samples would be identical, 100 one-word sentences, each having one two- or three-letter word, no words starting with a vowel, and no nouns. Such a configuration is unlikely to occur, but sequences of sentences having fewer than five words are not rare.

The most taxing situation arises from redaction. A sample may contain material from one person or be a mixture of more than one person. Should a sample be two sequences from different people this will usually be clearly indicated. If the same texts had been alternated two or three sentences at a time, it would not be practicable to separate them. There would be clear indications that the text is heterogeneous but resolving it into such small components would become too uncertain. If a scholar had suggested the sample was composite and used traditional criteria to separate the text into its component sources, these could be tested for homogeneity.

Of course, there are always going to be borderline decisions to be made. In one chart of a section of the Gospel of Mark two sentences are rather out of line. The standard text shows that both sentences contain extensive references, printed in bold face, to the Greek Old Testament. This is a satisfactory explanation of the anomalous appearance of the chart. But had the reference been to some unknown text, it is to be doubted that the uncertainty could have been resolved. One scholar might suggest a connection with some other text, a colleague could reject this hypothesis and there is no experiment which could resolve the difference.

Cusum analysis is a useful technique but it is not some isolated touchstone of authenticity. Cusum analysis should be used by those who have some understanding of the type of text being examined, the nature of sentence length distributions and the occurrence of different kinds and classes of word, in addition to an appreciation of the role cusum analysis can play. Cusum analysis is not difficult to learn, but the beginner must start at the right place and acquire some practical skill. It will take some time and application, but so does learning to drive a car, or to type by touch. For the effort, the return can be very much worthwhile.

For the reader who has some statistical background, an alternative approach, based on the same material and in almost every application reaching the same result, has been developed by Professor Derek Bissell. (The paper describing this was printed by the Royal Statistical Society in 1995.)[17]

What he has done is to make one graph and not two. The habit, such as the number of words of two or three letters, is recorded, as before, in the vertical scale, but the horizontal scale is no longer equal divisions each representing a sentence in the sequence. Now each division is proportional to the length of each sentence so that the cell, on the horizontal scale, is ten times as wide for a sentence of fifty words than it is for a sentence of ten words.

Each version of the technique can have an advantage in certain circumstances, but most readers whose training has not been scientific will find the original technique, as described in this book, the easier to use.

NOTES

Notes to Chapter 1

[1] The two critics who have examined cusum analysis in a legal context have been Professor David Canter (University of Liverpool), and Dr Robert Anthony Hardcastle. Dr David Holmes (University of the West of England) and Dr Michael Hilton (University of South Carolina) have also attempted to disprove the method in a joint published paper. The most recent attempt to assess cusum analysis, one which ends in denying its validity as a forensic tool, is that of Professor Anthony J. Sanford (University of Glasgow) *et al.* Details of all these critical reports and papers and of the points raised in them are discussed and rebutted in Chapter 10.

[2] For example, see Robert Matthews, 'Linguistics on Trial', in *New Scientist,* 139, No. 1887 (21 August 1993), 12–13, which relies heavily on Professor Canter's account of the method.

[3] Details of the samples of Helen Keller's language analysed in both charts are given in Chapter 5.

[4] For a fuller account of this particular analysis of letters by Helen Keller and its implications, see Chapter 5.

[5] Andrew Q. Morton, MA, BSc, BD, FRSE, is recognized as the foremost forensic expert on authorship attribution studies. Sir Kenneth Dover, a past president of the British Academy, and long acquainted with statistical authorship attribution, has commented on the cusum technique, 'I have no doubt about the validity of the method, but "proof" is a strong word and I prefer to think in terms of the accumulation of probabilities.' (From his autobiography, *Marginal Comment* [London, Duckworth, 1994], 121).

[6] These included about half a dozen academics, and others, known by Morton to have both interest and experience in this field.

[7] Walter Hooper (ed.), *The Dark Tower and Other Stories,* (London, Collins, 1977). A. Q. Morton was asked to make an analysis of the disputed text by Kathryn Lindskoog, editor of *The Lewis Legacy*, the newsletter of the C. S. Lewis Foundation for Truth in Publishing). Subsequently, Morton's analysis of other posthumous work attributed to Lewis appeared, namely, 'Ascertaining Disputed Authorship Today: The Disunion of "Christian Reunion"'. Kathryn Lindskoog gives an account of Morton's work on Lewis in her latest book, *Light in the Shadow Lands* (Lindskoog, East Mayfair Ave, Orange, Ca. 92667, US, 1994), 246–51.

[8] Augustus de Morgan, letter to Revd W. Heald, 18 August 1851, printed in his sister's *Memoir of Augustus de Morgan* (London, 1882), 214–16.

[9] The practice of *counting*, of course, has had an established and respectable place in literary criticism for some time: see Farringdon and Farringdon, 'Literature and Computers', in *Poetry Wales*, 17, No. 1 (Summer 1981), 53–60.

[10] G. Udny Yule, *The Statistical Study of Literary Vocabulary* (Cambridge University Press, 1944).

[11] Farringdon and Morton, *Fielding and the Federalist* (University of Glasgow, Department of Computing Science, 1990). See also Chapter 7.

[12] Interested readers are referred for further details to Professor Robert Oakman's *Computers in Literary Research*, (Athens, University of Georgia Press, 1980), 142 *et seq.*

[13] See the Preface to Bernard Shaw's play, *Saint Joan*. This attitude is strong, of course, in the thought of the Neoplatonic 'Sophia Perennis'.

[14] All references to legal appearances by Morton and others appear in **Part III** of this book.

[15] See the bibliography for titles of a selection of Morton's many attribution studies of the New Testament.

[16] Andrew Q. Morton and Sidney Michaelson, *The Qsum Plot* (University of Edinburgh, April, 1990); updated by Morton the following year as *Proper Words in Proper Places* (University of Glasgow, October, 1991).

Morton's sweeping statement regarding 'style' and 'precision', (*Proper Words in Proper Places*, 23 – *scientific* precision is implied), could, of course, be challenged by more than one attempt to define style very precisely indeed, e.g. Enkvist *Linguistic Stylistics* (Hague/Paris, 1973),136: '. . . our definition of style as the aggregate of significant differences between a text and a contextually related norm'. (I am indebted to Sir Kenneth Dover for drawing my attention to this, and other, definitions.)

Morton claims (ibid.) that there is common awareness of linguistic change in our speech/writing 'but the assertion that such changes affect *stylometric* habits has not yet been supported by any evidence' (my italics). As far as I am aware, assertions as to *stylometry* – the quantitative analysis of utterance – do not normally play any part in describing varieties of language. Evidential support would therefore be irrelevant.

[17] This revelation came in conversation with broadcaster Brian McGee, in a BBC television series, *Philosophers Talking*, later published as a book (London, BBC Publications, 1978).

[18] Examples of the Iris Murdoch study appear in Morton's *The Qsum Plot*, 26–8, cited above (see note 16).

[19] In Chapter 4.

[20] Eur.Ing. Dr Michael Farringdon FBCS, lectured in computing in the European Business Management School at the University College of Swansea (a constituent college of the University of Wales). The only other expert witness qualified to use QSUM is M. David Baker FBCS, a computer information systems consultant, who has submitted legal reports and given evidence in cases in Northern Ireland 1993–4, and who writes in Chapter 9.

[21] Andrew Q. Morton, *The Authorship of the New Testament Epistles* (University of Glasgow, Department of Computing Science, 1993).

[22] Publication pending in 1996 by Mellen Biblical Press, Georgia, USA

Notes to Chapter 2

[1] Although the sentence is overwhelmingly the unit used for analysis, the use of the poetic line has, on occasion, been successfully used by Morton as a basis for analysis.

It should further be noted that description of textual preparation in this chapter relates to analysis in English: Greek texts, for example, use different punctuating conventions with regard to the use of the semicolon, and require slightly different text-processing.

[2] On the graphs/charts, the abbreviation *qs* stands for 'cusum'; but the sentence length distribution is designated *qsld* in order to avoid the clumsiness of *qssld*.

³ A SPITBOL program, designed to run on an Apple Macintosh computer, was designed and written by Michael Farringdon for the contributors to this book (copyright M. G. Farringdon and A. Q. Morton).

⁴ The sentence given as an example uses the first person pronoun 'I'. Questions about using the test of words starting with a vowel, and misgivings with regard to use of the indefinite articles ('a', 'an') or the first person pronoun ('I'), is common, and is addressed later (see 'A note on the "habit" and linguistics' in this chapter). At this stage, it will be enough for the reader to trust the utility of this test by proven experiment.

⁵ An example is shown in Chapter 3, where the thirteenth sentence of the sample from Lawrence's *Sons and Lovers* causes just such a 'jump' in the graph-lines.

⁶ That is, in Chapter 5.

⁷ This is the Results File for the illustrative graphs and charts **JMF-1** to **JMF-3,** which follow later in the chapter.

⁸ *New England Review/Bread Loaf Quarterly*, Middlebury College, Vermont, X, No. 4 (Summer 1988), 381–402.

⁹ This can be confirmed by further tests using the more sophisticated statistical method of *weighted cusums* discussed in Chapters 10 and 11. But the beginner will be reassured to know that removal of three of the anomalous sentences will remove the 'blip' by the standard analysis and QSUM-chart.

¹⁰ It is proper to note here that opening sentences (or sometimes passages) can often cause problems: they seek to catch the reader's attention by characteristic devices, and serve to introduce a subject. Thus, when selecting a sample, caution should be exercised: it is preferable not to choose any sample from the beginning (or ending) of works, since this may be abnormal utterance for your subject. In the present case, though, to reduce the sample of the theatre review below its full length would have been undesirable: it deserved to be used in its entirety as a sample of the writer's writing in 1967.

¹¹ For the full text of this review (where all the anomalous sentences are indicated), the *NER/BLQ* sample, and the reference for the sample from this book, see Appendix One .

¹² For details (Huxley sample) see note 9 to Chapter 3.

¹³ An illustration of this point occurs in discussion of the results of the *Craftsman* essay, in Chapter 7.

On the general question of the use of transparencies, this is the recommended method for enquirers with a serious attribution method to solve (for example, in legal work). It is not suggested that the reader attempt to make transparencies for use with the examples shown here; and it is difficult to illustrate what can be seen by using a transparency, since this involves rotating the two cusum lines to find the exact overlay and the discrepancy. For a more detailed description on this point, with further illustration, see Morton's Chapter 11.

¹⁴ A 'sandwich' is a useful test: as its name indicates, it is a procedure whereby a new sample of sentences is inserted into utterance already tested and found to be homogeneous – in this case, the 1967 and 1988 samples already combined in Figure JMF-4.

¹⁵ 'Finer points' refers to the marking used to delineate each separate sentence on the graph visually. A computer graphic display will allow a variety of symbols to mark the graph points – boxes (as used by the writer), or circles, crosses, or any other kind on different computers. 'Finer points' here means a smaller box, thus showing the position

of sentences in greater detail. Each side of the graph shows the exact size, shape and colour-density of the graph symbols used to mark the points of the two lines, *qsld*, and *qs23lw+ivw* (cf. the two symbols in Figures **JMF-1** and **JMF-2**, where one is a darker box than the other so as to show up differences by the use of a transparency).

[16] The Prosecuting Counsel in question, a barrister in the Republic of Ireland, who made this query in the Central Irish Criminal Court, Dublin, could equally well have queried the use of the more familiar words 'dog' and 'cat', perhaps.

[17] Dr A. D. Hardcastle: 'An assessment of the cusum method for the determination of authorship', in *Journal of Forensic Science Society*, 33, No. 2 (1993), 95–106. (This critique will be fully refuted in detail in Chapter 10.)

[18] The Ladybird series is a children's 'reading scheme' published in the UK, and the *Key Words to Literacy* information, for the use of teachers, is part of this scheme.

[19] Any innovative lecturer using such a negative illustration need only take care that one of Her Majesty's Inspectors of Schools should not misread the example as showing that the process of cloze procedure was being misrepresented to the student teachers, as I once discovered to my cost.

Notes to Chapter 3

[1] *Everyman* (London, Dent, 27 June 1913), 325.

[2] Jonathan Rose, 'Lawrence for Everyman: An Undiscovered Short Story?', *D. H. Lawrence Review*, 22, No. 3 (Fall 1990), 267–73.

[3] The biography mentioned is *D. H. Lawrence: the Early Years, 1885–1912* (Cambridge University Press, 1991). John Worthen, formerly Professor of English Literature at the University College of Wales, Swansea, is now Professor of D. H. Lawrence Studies at the University of Nottingham.

[4] See note 7 to Chapter 1.

[5] The standard CUP edition of D. H. Lawrence provided the final sentences from *Sons and Lovers*, the two letters from *The Collected Letters* (to Louie Burrows, 38, and to Edward Garnett, 550–1), and the opening of 'New Eve and Old Adam' was taken from *Love Among the Haystacks*, 161–2. 'German Books: Thomas Mann', came from *Phoenix*, ed. E. D. McDonald (New York, 1936), 308–9. Further information on the texts (also indicating the reduced twenty-sentence samples), are given in Appendix 1. It should be noted here that John Worthen's selected passages included the *opening* of a short story (**NE**) and also of the critical essay (**TM**), and the *ending* of a novel (**SL**). Although this project was fortunately successful in proving homogeneity for D. H. Lawrence, researchers should be warned that, on the whole, it may be more advisable to choose samples from within the body of texts. Often, beginnings and endings are subject to special rhetorical effects and constraints, and so may not be typical of the normal utterance of an author.

[6] QSUM's indifference to time has already been demonstrated in the **JMF** figures in Chapter 2, especially Figure JMF-7.

[7] That is, statistically insignificant when measured by the use of the more sophisticated statistical testing discussed in Chapter 10, i.e. the use of weighted cusums for authorship attribution, as suggested by Professor Derek Bissell (who has written a monograph on the subject – see Bibliography). Professor Bissell is the statistician responsible for providing the British Standard 5703 for Cusums.

[8] The 'sandwich' test has already been described – see Chapter 2, note 11. In the

present case, the Lawrence letter previously inserted into two other letters by him is inserted into two samples of different genres of his writing.

9. Aldous Huxley, *Letters of D. H. Lawrence* (Heinemann, London, 1932), xiii–xiv.

Notes to Chapter 4

[1] Letter to the author (1992) from Dennis Jackson, editor of the *D. H. Lawrence Review*.

[2] The quotation is from a letter by Jim Jackson, published in *Matrix* 9 (see note 30, Chapter 7); Dr Jackson is a lecturer in French and Quebec Studies, Trinity College, Dublin.

[3] See Chapters 5 and 7.

[4] There is no reason why Shakespeare should be an exception to the technique, and indeed early experiments have proved very encouraging. The student newspaper referred to (*Bad Press*) is a publication at University of Wales, Swansea, and the article was written in support of a lecturer in dispute with the college authorities.

[5] Dr A. D. Hardcastle, 'An assessment of the cusum method for the determination of authorship', in *Journal of Forensic Science Society*, 33, 2 (1993), 95–106. (See also Chapter 2, Note 14.)

[6] See 'A note on the habit and linguistics' in Chapter 2, pp. 45–8.

[7] Cf. Farringdon and Farringdon, 'Literature and Computers', *Poetry Wales* (Summer 1981), 53–60. This opens: 'Literature is addressed to human readers: poems, novels and plays are created as particular kinds of aesthetic experience. The computer is a counting machine, associated with programmed robots, and sometimes assuming in the popular mind a dominance not unlike that of Frankenstein's monster . . . The humanist instinct might well be to assume, as a matter of course, that literature and computers could – and should – have nothing to with each other . . . Yet any reader who has remarked on the "preponderance" of, say, imagery of disease in *Hamlet*, or pondered the significance of the "number" of questions in *Macbeth* is making rudimentary quantitative judgments about literary questions. She, or he, is counting.'

[8] Blake Morrison: review of *W. H. Auden: Juvenilia* (London, Faber, 1994), in the *Sunday Independent*, 25 July 1994.

[9] William Golding, *A Moving Target* (London, Faber & Faber, 1982), 197.

[10] Quoted in Jay Tolson, *Pilgrim in the Ruins* (New York, Simon & Schuster, 1992), 389 and 387.

[11] Ursula LeGuin, 'From Elfland to Poughkeepsie', in *The Language of the Night* (London, The Women's Press, 1989), 81.

[12] The projected book became the co-authored *The Qsum Plot*.

[13] Ibid., 26–8, for a report of the results of the analysis of Iris Murdoch's writing.

[14] See Chapter 6 for subsequent research on children's language.

[15] *Twentieth Century*, Autumn 1961, 58–63.

[16] *The Comforters*, 1957; *Robinson*, 1958; *Memento Mori*, 1959; *The Bachelors*, 1960; and *The Ballad of Peckham Rye*, 1960. Editions of Spark novels used for this research were all Penguin Books (Harmondsworth, UK).

[17] *The Go-Away Bird*, 1958, and *Voices at Play*, 1961. (Harmondsworth, UK, Penguin); and *Collected Poems I* (London, Macmillan, 1967, incorporating Muriel Spark's first book of verse, *The Fanfarlo*, London, Hand and Flower Press, 1952).

[18] Morton, in *Proper Words in Proper Places*, 23. (See note 16 to Chapter 1 for an objection to Morton's position on defining style).

[19] 'My Conversion', *Twentieth Century*, 62.

[20] Chapter 1, p.12.

[21] 'Is Nothing Sacred?', in *Granta*, No. 31 (London), 108. The lecture was delivered for Salman Rushdie by Harold Pinter in February 1990.

[22] Muriel Spark, *John Masefield*, (1953), 86–9; *Collected Poems I*, (London, 1967, incorporating *The Fanfarlo*, 1952), 19–22; the 'The Seraph and the Zambesi', 1951, reprinted in *The Go-Away Bird and Other Stories* (Penguin Books, 1958), 159–60.

[23] Morton, op. cit., 22.

[24] 'The First Year of My Life', in *The Secret Self*, ed. Hermione Lee (London, Dent, 1987), 267–8.

[25] Spark, *Curriculum Vitae* (Harmondsworth, Penguin, 1993), 164.

[26] [Spark, Muriel], *Argentor I* (London, n.d.), 147–54, signed by William Llewellyn Amos.

[27] The forty-two sentences started 'During the fifteenth and sixteenth centuries, when the influences of the Renaissance were sweeping across Europe . . .' to '. . . Sandro was apprenticed to the master, Fra Fillipo Lippi', 147–50, with the omission of paragraph 3 which listed artist's names and dates). The Masefield sample was identical to that used in the earlier analysis (25s.) in the chapter.

[28] The 25-sentence sample from the article start 'He had already begun to study painting' to '. . . he finally found his true medium was painting'. The twenty-five sentences from *A Far Cry From Kensington* are the same as those used earlier in the chapter.

Notes to Chapter 5

[1] Sir Kingsley Amis, *Memoirs* (New York, Summit Books, 1991), 237.

[2] Rowan Williams, *After Silent Centuries* (Cambridge, Perpetua Press, 1994), 8.

[3] Wells, J. E., 'Henry Fielding and the History of Charles XII' in *Journal of English and Germanic Philology* (1912), 603–13; also, Wilbur L. Cross, *The History of Henry Fielding* (New Haven, Yale University Press, 1918).

[4] See Farringdon and Farringdon, 'A Computer-aided study of the prose style of Henry Fielding and its support for his translation of *The Military History of Charles XII*' ', in *Advances in Computer-Aided Literary and Linguistic Research* (Birmingham, University of Aston, 1979), 95–105.

[5] Martin C. Battestin, *New Essays by Henry Fielding, with a Stylometric Analysis by Michael G. Farringdon* (Charlottesville, University of Virginia Press, 1989).

[6] See Chapter 7 for a QSUM attribution of a *Craftsman* essay.

[7] 'Finer graph points': see note 11 to Chapter 2.

[8] It should, in fairness, be noted that if the previous three QSUM charts had also been redrawn using finer graph points, even the novice would have been able to see some degree of separation. However, the lesson drawn in this chapter stands as an instructive one.

[9] Creating 'alternate sample' tests can be a fairly tedious and lengthy text-processing chore, so it always an additional procedure rather than a standard approach; it is rarely necessary in normal circumstances.

Notes to Chapter 6

[1] The substance of the first part of this chapter appeared initially, in a slightly

altered form, in the *Swansea Review*, Department of English, University College of Swansea, Wales, No. 12 (1994), 30–40.

[2] Professor David Canter, 'An Evaluation of the "CUSUM" Stylistic Analysis of Confessions', *Expert Evidence*, 1, No. 3 (October, 1992), 93–9. This critical evaluation is fully considered in Chapter 10.

[3] Helen Keller, *The Story of My Life* (London, Hodder & Stoughton, 1908). Prior to her illness, Helen had already learnt to say one or two words – including the crucial *water*.

[4] Walker Percy, 'The Delta Factor', in *The Message in the Bottle* (New York, Farrar, Straus and Giroux, 1975), 3–45. Percy's views on the 'triadic nature of language' (based on the thought of Charles Peirce, an American philosopher of the nineteenth century) received mixed responses from those working in professional linguistics. Hugh Kenner (*National Review*, 12 September 1975), was enthusiastic, suggesting that Percy had 'probably made a breakthrough . . . If he has – such is the importance of the subject – *The Message in the Bottle* may one day rank with *De Revolutionibis Orbium Coelestium* . . .', i.e. with Copernicus: quoted in Jay Tolson's biography of Percy, *Pilgrim in the Ruins* (New York, Simon and Schuster, 1992), 401. Since Helen Keller had already learnt a few words before the illness that left her without sight or hearing, her 'breakthrough' into the triadic nature of language may have occurred before the age of one, and her experience at the Tuscumbia well be a recapitulation of the earlier process. This does not invalidate Percy's hypothesis, but confirmation of the process of acquiring 'triadic' language from those deaf-mute from birth would be useful.

[5] Keller, op. cit., 149–51.

[6] Ibid., 154–5 and 159–61.

[7] Ibid., 164–5.

[8] Ibid., 278–9.

[9] Ibid., 192–3.

[10] Ibid., 316–17.

[11] This approach is suggested by Walker Percy in his essay 'Towards a Theory of Language', op. cit., 320 *et seq*.

[12] Keller, op. cit., 400.

[13] Ibid., 401. (Margaret Canby's story was first published in a collection of children's stories, *Birdie and his Friends*, in 1873).

[14] Ibid., 64.

[15] Ibid., 401.

[16] Ibid., 402.

[17] Ibid.

[18] Ibid., 403–6.

[19] Ibid., 192–3 (letter of 10 November 1890).

[20] It will be recalled from many other examples that the point of insertion in a mixed text is not always the point of visual separation, and that the alien segment sometimes disturbs the whole chart.

[21] See Canby's letter, Keller, op. cit., 402.

[22] Ibid. 406–13.

Notes to Chapter 7

[1] Mark Twain, *Huckleberry Finn* (Harmondsworth, UK, Penguin English Library, 1966): the three samples used are from pp. 97–8, 112–13, 168–9.

[2] Anthony Burgess, *A Clockwork Orange* (Harmondsworth, UK, Penguin Books, 1972).

[3] Ibid., 132–4.

[4] Ibid., 85–6 .

[5] Tom Stoppard, *Arcadia* (London, Faber & Faber, 1993).

[6] Ibid., 53.

[7] Ibid., 19.

[8] Ibid., 62–3.

[9] Emily Dickinson, *Collected Poems*, II (Cambridge, Mass., Harvard University Press, 1955), 644.

[10] Stoppard, op. cit., 15 and 18.

[11] Ibid., 15, 19 and 41.

[12] Martin Battestin, *New Essays By Henry Fielding* (Charlottesville, University of Virginia, 1989), xi.

[13] Stephen Copley, in *Year's Work in English Studies*, 70 (1989), 381.

[14] Ian A. Bell, review in *British Journal for Eighteenth Century Studies* (Autumn 1992) 226–7.

[15] Harold Love, review in *Journal of English & Germanic Philology*, 90 (July 1992) 432–5.

[16] Battestin, op. cit., 287–91.

[17] Farringdon and Morton, *Fielding and the Federalist* (University of Glasgow, Department of Computing Science, 1990),

[18] Ibid., 22.

[19] Ibid., 28.

[20] The whole of the final account, based on the three projects carried out, was (at some 46 pages) too long to publish here.

[21] Letter to Dr M. G. Farringdon, 30 March 1992, from RADHARC TV (Republic of Ireland).

[22] Robert O'Driscoll and Lorna Reynolds (eds.), 'Black '47: A Summer of Sorrow', in *The Untold Story: The Irish in Canada*, I (Toronto, Celtic Arts of Canada, 1987).

[23] Later found to be Wolfhound Press, Dublin.

[24] Mr Don Mullin is Director of Action from Ireland, a charity based in Dublin and devoted to famine relief in Africa.

[25] This article, referred to in Don Mullin's letter and supplied by him, was by Dr Jim Jackson, a lecturer at Trinity College, Dublin, and was printed in the *Irish Times*, 14 September 1991.

[26] Dr Padraig O'Laighin, of Montreal, was the academic who chose and supplied further textual extracts from Sellar's *The Tragedy of Quebec* and *The Diary of Gerald Keegan*.

[27] The use of the word 'fingerprint' to denote the consistent habit demonstrated in a control text used in cross-matching can be a little misleading if readers expect an exact analogy with a physical fingerprint. It is a convenient popular tag to convey the ability of cusum analysis to act as a recognition system, but it should not be imagined that it is like a real fingerprint in having *one invariable pictorial image* of a person's utterance.

[28] The two fifteen-sentence samples were as follows: **TRGQ/Sample 1**, pp. 48–51, from '. . . could not help contrasting the easy circumstances . . .' to '. . . the friendly alliance of the two people that was'. **TRGQ/Sample 2**, pp. 129–32, from 'In every one of the four opportunities . . .' to '. . . in tracing the causes which have led to the dying'.

[29] The sample from the diary, **D3** was taken from p. 127, starting 'All that the cheating villain had done . . .' to 'I knew was a serious offence in the eyes of the law, and so did Aileen'.

[30] This debate involved Ms Marianna O'Gallagher, publisher at Carraig Books, Quebec; Dr Robert Hill, a Canadian academic who had written a doctoral thesis on Robert Sellar and therefore knew his work well; and Dr Jim Jackson, of Trinity College, Dublin. Dr Jackson's letter in *Matrix*, already mentioned in Chapter 4, is of particular interest, since it refers to Dr Farringdon's first report on the disputed diary. Dr Jackson wonders about the 'stylistic features which make up Keegan's and Sellar's distinct fingerprint', and goes on to make the comment already quoted in Chapter 4: 'Going by Morton's published book on the subject, these may be *nothing more than the frequency of three and four letter words*' (my italics). Such a judgment of the efficacy of QSUM is, of course, perfectly understandable coming from a layman who has not had the opportunity to study the technique's applications in detail. But it does serve to point up the general lack of awareness of the importance of the syntactic filler-words which this book is now addressing. Few academics have ever thought syntax or word-length of great importance in attributing authorship.

[31] This was the 1992 reprint of *Famine Diary*.

[32] Textual references for the four new diary samples provided by Dr Padraig O'Laighin is given in the full-length report referred to in note 20 above.

[33] This example misled many credulous viewers, some of them distinguished lawyers, who were prepared to believe that a six-minute report in a TV legal 'magazine' programme was a valid scientific test. What misled many of these was possibly a matter of vocabulary – Morton's use of, and firm repetition of, the word 'indistinguishable': this was, and is, as modern linguistics might describe it, part of the 'language of the subject' of cusum analysis, with a specific meaning for the scientific discipline.

See further on the use of this word in Chapter 8. Thorough testing according to the correct QSUM procedure would have involved control samples and data that was not mixed, i.e. corrupt in terms of the test.

Notes to Chapter 8

[1] Professor Sidney Michaelson (1925–91) founded the Computer Science Department at Edinburgh University. From the early 1960s he collaborated closely with A. Q. Morton on 'his last passion . . . the stylistic analysis of literary texts . . . he used computers to analyse disputed authorships and chronologies of both literary works and modern criminal "confessions".' (From his obituary in the *Independent*, 27 February 1991.)

For a description, with examples relating to English, of the positional stylometry technique see S. Michaelson, A. Q. Morton, N. Hamilton-Smith, *To Couple is the Custom* (University of Edinburgh Department of Computer Science Report CSR-22-78, October 1977). An application of positional stylometry in Swedish is described in S. Michaelson, A. Q. Morton and N. Hamilton-Smith, *Justice for Helander* (University of Edinburgh Department of Computer Science Report CSR-42-79, July 1979). A further description of an application to some eighteenth-century English essays may be found in Martin C. Battestin, *New Essays by Henry Fielding, With a Stylometric Analysis by Michael G. Farringdon* (Charlottesville, University Press of Virginia, 1989), 551–91.

[2] The Steven Raymond case is described in A. Q. Morton, *Literary Detection* (NY, Charles Scribner's Sons, 1987), 204–6.

[3] Bryan Niblett is a barrister and Emeritus Professor of Computer Science at the University of Wales, Swansea. In 1975, when he gave expert evidence in the Steven Raymond case he was Reader in Law and Computing at the University of Kent at Canterbury. See B. Niblett and J. Boreham, 'Cluster analysis in court', *Criminal Law Review* (March 1976), 175–80. Reprinted in *Jurimetrics Journal*, 17 (Fall 1976), and in *Computer Law Service*, 3, Sec. 5-4.2., Art. 4.

[4] In the Pennsylvania case, all the expert evidence was excluded by the judge, and a compromise settlement made on the will when the case reached appeal.

In the Supreme Court of Victoria, Australia, in the case of *R.* v. *Tilley*, 16 and 19 November 1984, Morton's evidence was heard by the judge on *voir dire*. The judge held that 'Stylistic analysis of documents is a science and, in appropriate cases, expert opinion based on such analysis may be received in evidence when disputes arise concerning the authenticity of documents . . .', but considered that 'In the present case, it would be inappropriate to receive M's evidence', because 'what was in dispute were the oral answers given by the accused . . . [and] There was no evidence establishing the proposition that an individual's manner or style of speech is the same as his manner or style of writing. Such a finding would be contrary to human experience.'

In Queensland, Australia, in the case of *R.* v *Finch* at appeal in 1985 Morton's evidence was again disregarded. Finch and another had been convicted in the Supreme Court, Brisbane in October 1975 of a firebombing. The Crown's case rested solely on an unsigned record of interview which, as the judge said, constituted a 'full admission by Finch of every element of the offence of murder'. What actually happened is elucidated in a feature article by Bruce Stannard, 'How we got Finch' (*The Bulletin*, 22 November 1988), 39–40, and 44. Stannard recounts an interview with one of the police officers involved in arresting Finch, and says, 'According to the details of the former detective, Finch was telling the truth when he said he had made no statement and that he had remained silent despite a police attempt to beat a confession out of him in the Brisbane Watch House.' The former detective is quoted as saying, 'It didn't matter whether you were a copper in Queensland, New South Wales or Victoria – verbals were a fact of everyday life. Fabrication of evidence was something we all took for granted . . . Finch did it. We all know that for sure. That's why we had no hesitation bricking the bastard. We were very careful not to get too specific in the statement, not to give too many details because they might be challenged in court. It was agreed that we would all put our names to it. Christ, I mean, it was the word of six coppers, from three states, up against a convicted fucking criminal. Who do you think the jury was going to believe? So long as we stuck together, we had the bastard cold.'

[5] No.90/1256/Y2 in the Court of Appeal (Criminal Division), London, Wednesday, 10 July 1991, before Lord Justice Taylor, Mr. Justice Ian Kennedy and Mr Justice Morland (*The Queen* v. *Thomas McCrossen*).

[6] A. Q. Morton has given QSUM evidence in the following additional cases: in November 1991 concerning a number of statements in the trial of Frank Beck (child abuse) in Leicester Crown Court; in October 1992 in the Family Division of the Crown Court, Chatham; in October 1992 in the case of Mr Clemmett at the Court of Appeal, London.

[7] On 15–20 November and 16–17 December 1991 Michael Farringdon presented the technique and gave evidence in the trial of Vincent Connell at the Central Criminal Court, Dublin.

Michael Farringdon has given QSUM evidence in the following additional cases: on 4 March 1992 in the trial of Joseph Nelson-Wilson at the Central Criminal Court, London; on 12 May 1992 in the 'Phoenix Park Murder' trial of John Francis McAllistair and Richard McDermott at the Central Criminal Court, Dublin; on 12 June 1992 in the re-trial of Joseph Nelson-Wilson at the Central Criminal Court, London; on 17 December 1992 in the trial of Andrew Bourke at the Central Criminal Court, London; on 18 December 1992, 11 January 1993 in the case of Mr Peter Mitchell in the Court of Appeal, London. [No.82/2419/E2 in the Court of Appeal (Criminal Division), Friday 26 March 1993. Before Lord Justice Russell, Mr Justice Blofeld and Mr Justice Latham. *The Queen* v. *Peter Mitchell*.]

[8] M. David Baker has given 'QSUM' evidence in *The Queen* v. *James McGee*, Central Criminal Court, Belfast, in March, 1993, and in *Regina* v. *Stephen Hill* and another, Central Criminal Court, Belfast, June, 1993.

[9] The recent availability of relatively inexpensive scanners with their associated software means that, so long as one has a good printed copy text, transforming that text into a word-processor computer file is relatively simple and fast compared with having to enter it manually by typing at the computer keyboard. Expect a few mis-read characters per page and be prepared for the software trying to be clever and inserting its own suggestion for a word it does not recognize; also, it usually does not recognize words such as place-names.

[10] The CusumChart program, mentioned earlier in Chapter 2, reads a text file and does all the counting of the various classes of words, makes the cusum calculations, and produces a file containing these suitable for use with a graphics program package, such as Cricket Graph™, with which one can draw the cusum charts.

[11] This statement should not be taken as an admission of a failure of the QSUM technique. No analyst is in a position to *assert* authorship of a piece of utterance presented to her/him. However, if the technique cannot distinguish between the control and the disputed text, while the control could readily be shown to separate from another person's utterance, the weight of the evidence points heavily towards one conclusion.

[12] John S. James, *Stroud's Judicial Dictionary of Words and Phrases* (5th edition, London, 1986); John Burke, *Jowitt's Dictionary of English Law* (2nd edition, London, 1977).

Notes to Chapter 9

[1] Peter Trudgell, *Accent, Dialect and the School* (London, Arnold, 1975).

[2] Cf. the Irish novelist Roddy Doyle's Booker prize-winning novel *Paddy Clarke Ha Ha Ha*.

[3] Cf. the QSUM-chart HF-1, in Chapter 7, where two anomalous sentences distorted the whole chart.

[4] Cf. Figure EFL-3 (of the non-national EFL speaker) above, where the same habit was found to produce the positive discriminator.

[5] Cf. the thirty-two sentences analysed in the QSUM-chart of the utterance of a young girl, the seven-year old 'Katherine', in Chapter 6.

Notes to Chapter 10

[1] Under the heading 'Evaluation of the cusum approach', David Canter, in his report to the Crown Prosecution Service (CPS) in the *Case of Peter Mitchell* (Court of Criminal Appeal, London – undated but late December, 1992, or early January, 1993), p. 2, states that 'The basic propositions of "Cusum Charts" do not agree either with common sense, or with well established principles derived from the careful study of spoken and written language.'

[2] In his paper 'An evaluation of the "Cusum" stylistic analysis of confessions', in *Expert Evidence*, 1, No. 3 (October, 1992), 95, Canter states that 'No published accounts can be found to indicate what the psychological or linguistic processes are that generate the "habit" that Cusum analysts claim to be consistent.' Also, Robert Anthony Hardcastle, in his paper 'Forensic linguistics: an assessment of the CUSUM method for the determination of authorship', *J. Forensic Science Society*, 33, No. 2 (1993), 96, states that '. . . Morton identified no psychological or linguistic processes which might generate such habits'. This is curiously similar to Canter's wording (although Hardcastle makes no reference or acknowledgement to Canter's paper). Anthony J. Sanford, Joy P. Aked, Linda M. Moxey, and James Mullin, in their joint paper 'A critical examination of assumptions underlying the cusum technique of forensic linguistics', *Forensic Linguistics*, 1, Issue 2 (1994), 165, claim that QSUM is 'without any reliable foundation'.

[3] Hardcastle (op. cit., 98) states 'He [Morton] made no use of standard statistical measures to compare the two sets of data values . . .'; Michael L. Hilton and David I. Holmes, in their paper 'An assessment of cumulative sum charts for authorship attribution', *Literary and Linguistic Computing*, 8, No. 2 (1993), 75, consider that 'the subjectivity of the technique in evaluating differences between pairs of superimposed cumulative sum charts does give cause for concern'; while Canter ('An evaluation', 96) says 'a measure is required that reflects the correlation between the relative Cusum values within the two sets of numbers'. Sanford et al. (op. cit., 165) say that 'Morton (1991) does not specify a satisfactory method for determining deviation'.

[4] Canter ('An evaluation', 98) says 'The studies that have been reported here do not support the hypothesis that the variations are a consequence of mixed authorship.' Hilton and Holmes (op. cit., 80) say 'We hypothesize . . . that authors do not follow habits as rigidly as is required for Cusum techniques to determine authorship correctly'. Sanford et al. (op. cit., 165) conclude that 'until the method [QSUM] receives more adequate support, it should not be entertained as a forensic technique'.

[5] See (a) T. B. Horton, *The Effectiveness of the Stylometry of Function Words in Discriminating between Shakespeare and Fletcher* (Ph.D. thesis, University of Edinburgh, 1987). Horton uses multivariate analysis.

(b) Colin L. Griffiths, *Numerical Correlation of Data in the Synoptic Gospels* (M.Phil. thesis, University of Wales, 1987). Griffiths uses catastrophe theory.

(c) D. I. Holmes, 'A stylometric analysis of Mormon scripture and related texts,' in *J. Royal Statistical Society*, Series A, 155, Part 1 (1992), 91–120. Holmes uses multivariate analysis.

(d) John Frederick Burrows, *Computation into Criticism: A Study of Jane Austen's Novels and an Experiment in Method* (Clarendon Press, Oxford, 1987). Burrows uses correlation-matrices and eigen analysis, amongst other statistics, not only for authorship attribution but also to examine the 'interrelationship of characters'.

[6] (a) Canter, 'An evaluation', (b) Hardcastle, 'Forensic linguistics', (c) Hilton and Holmes, 'An assessment', and Sanford et al., 'A critical examination'.

[7] Canter, evidence in *Case of Peter Mitchell*.

[8] Canter, 'An evaluation', 95-6.

[9] Hardcastle, 'Forensic linguistics', 96.

[10] Sanford et al. 'A critical evaluation', 165.

[11] See the Foreword by Sir Edmund T. Whittaker, 'Oliver Heaviside' in Oliver Heaviside, *Electromagnetic Theory*, I (Chelsea Publishing Co. New York, 1971), XXV.

[12] Ibid., XXIII.

[13] See the chapter 'A theory of language' in Walker Percy's *The Message in the Bottle* (New York, Farrar, Straus & Giroux, 1975), 302.

[14] Peirce also uses 'Hypothesis' and 'Retroduction' for what he calls 'Abduction'.

[15] Abduction is described by Peirce in paragraph 68 in the first volume of *The Collected Papers of Charles Sanders Peirce* (ed. Charles Hartshorne and Paul Weiss, Harvard University Press, Cambridge, Mass., 1931–58, 8 vols.). References to the *Collected Papers* will be of the form 1.68, signifying volume 1, paragraph 68.

[16] Peirce, *Collected Papers*, 1.71–4

[17] Jill Farringdon, 'The cusum technique and young language', *Swansea Review*, No. 12 (1994), 30–40.

[18] Peirce, *Collected Papers*, 1.73–4.

[19] Hardcastle, 'Forensic linguistics', 98.

[20] A. F. Bissell, 'Weighted cusums – method and applications', *Total Quality Management*, 1, No. 3 (1990), 391–402.

[21] Hardcastle, 'Forensic linguistics', 98.

[22] Hilton and Holmes, 'An assessment', 75.

[23] Ibid., 73.

[24] Ibid., 77.

[25] Canter, 'An evaluation', 96.

[26] Ibid., 96

[27] Anthony Kenny, *The Computation of Style* (Oxford, Pergamon Press, 1982), 79.

[28] Canter, 'An evaluation', 98.

[29] Canter, *Case of Peter Mitchell*, 2

[30] Hilton and Holmes, 'An assessment', 80

[31] Canter, 'An evaluation', 93

[32] See S. Michaelson and A. Q. Morton, 'Positional stylometry', in A. J. Aitken, R. W. Bailey and N. Hamilton-Smith (eds.) *The Computer and Literary Studies* (Edinburgh, Edinburgh University Press, 1973), 69–83.

[33] *Webster's Ninth New Collegiate Dictionary*, (Springfield, Mass., Merriam-Webster, 1983).

[34] Canter, 'An evaluation', 93.

[35] Ibid., 93.

[36] Ibid., 93.

[37] Canter's covering letter, accompanying the 'draft' paper, to Michael Cohen at University College of Swansea, is dated 14 October 1992. Sir Michael Davies was appointed by the Privy Council in 1992 to enquire into and write a report on a dispute within the Philosophy Department at the University of Wales, Swansea.

[38] Canter, 'An evaluation', 94.

[39] Ibid., 94–5.

⁴⁰ In Canter's published version of his paper, the text for his Figure 1 (draft version) starts on p. 96, paragraph 2, finishing at the penultimate paragraph on p. 96.

⁴¹ For Canter's Figure 2 (draft version), the text sample starts on p. 96 final paragraph, finishing in the first paragraph of the second column on p. 97 in the published version. However, the published version has been slightly rewritten.

⁴² In the published version this passage may be found on p. 96 column 2, at the end of the third paragraph.

⁴³ This is quoted from the draft version; in the published version it appears in a slightly rewritten version on p. 97 in the second and third paragraphs.

⁴⁴ This sentence may be found in paragraph 3 of p. 97 in the published version.

⁴⁵ The three samples are taken from the 'Foreword' to a book on *Fires and Human Behaviour* by Canter, a letter of invitation he wrote to Morton to give a paper at a conference, and from Canter's report on the Morton and Farringdon reports in the UDR4 appeal.

⁴⁶ Canter, 'An evaluation', 98.

⁴⁷ Ibid., 99.

⁴⁸ Quoted by Canter in his 'draft' version of 'An evaluation'. The quotation is from Klaus Krippendorff, *Content Analysis: An Introduction to its Methodology* (Beverly Hills & London, Sage Publications, 1980), 42. Krippendorff's contemporary publications were concerned with sociology, journalism, mass media, and communication content.

⁴⁹ J. W. Ellison, 'Computers and the Testaments', in *Computers for the Humanities?*, (New Haven, Yale University Press, 1965), 64–74.

⁵⁰ See Jacob Leed's book review of *Computers for the Humanities?* in *Computers and the Humanities*, 1, No. 1 (September 1966), 12–14.

⁵¹ J. W. Ellison, 'Computers and the Testaments', in Edmund A. Bowles (ed.), *Computers in Humanistic Research* (Englewood Cliffs, Prentice-Hall, 1967), 160–9.

⁵² Canter was cross-examined by Mr Dermot Wright QC on 11 January 1993.

⁵³ See Hardcastle, 'Forensic linguistics': (a) Figure 6, for example, on p. 102, where the graphs are obviously wrongly scaled; there are numerous other examples in his report submitted in the UDR4 Appeal case; (b) For single instead of two vertical scales, see Figures 2, 3(a), 4(a), 5(a), 6(a) and 8(a), pp. 98–103; (c) For no scales, see Figures 3(b), 4(b), 7(b) and 8(b), pp. 100–3.

⁵⁴ Ibid., 96.

⁵⁵ See Chapter 2.

⁵⁶ Hardcastle, 'Forensic Linguistics', 96.

⁵⁷ See previous comment in Chapter 2.

⁵⁸ Hardcastle, 'Forensic linguistics', 96.

⁵⁹ Ibid., 96

⁶⁰ See Chapter 2.

⁶¹ Hardcastle, 'Forensic linguistics', 96.

⁶² See Chapter 2.

⁶³ Hardcastle, 'Forensic linguistics', 97.

⁶⁴ Ibid., 97.

⁶⁵ See Chapter 2.

⁶⁶ Hardcastle, 'Forensic linguistics', 96.

⁶⁷ Ibid., 97.

⁶⁸ R. N. Totty, R. A. Hardcastle and J. Pearson, 'Forensic linguistics: the determination of authorship from habits of style', *J. Forensic Science Soc.*, 27, No. 1 (1987), 13–28.

[69] Letter to me dated 16 February 1993, from Joy P. Aked, Research Assistant in the Psychology Department of Glasgow University, 'writing on behalf of myself and Professor Sanford'.

[70] My letter to Ms Aked, dated 10 March 1993, made enquiries concerning an unpublished paper by Sanford, Aked, Moxey and Mullin entitled 'Discriminating one author from another through simple habits of expression: an empirical analysis'. A paper bearing this title is referred to as 'in press' in Sanford's paper under discussion here.

[71] Sanford et al. 'A critical examination', 152.

[72] Ibid., 155.

[73] Ibid., 166–7.

[74] Ibid., 155.

[75] Ibid., 154.

[76] Letter dated 28 May 1993, from Robert Moore, producer, of Baobab Productions of London NW1, to A. Q. Morton.

[77] Richard Freeman, 'Trial by Television: discussion of the *Street Legal* programme', *The Expert*, 1, No. 2 (Winter, 1994), 17–18 and Andrew Morton, 'A reply to Trial by Television', ibid.,19–21.

[78] *Independent on Sunday*, London, 22 January 1995.

[79] Heaviside, *Electromagnetic Theory*, Vol. I, unnumbered (last page of Preface).

[80] See British Standard 5703, *Data Analysis and Quality Control using Cusum Techniques. Part 2: Decision Rules and Statistical Tests for Cusum Charts and Tabulations* (London, British Standards Institution, 1980), and A. F. Bissell, 'Weighted cusums – method and applications', *Total Quality Management*, 1 (1990), 391–402.

[81] See Derek Bissell, *Statistical Methods for Text Analysis by Word-Counts* (Swansea, European Business Management School, University of Wales Swansea, 1995). I have been using Bissell's first draft of his monograph since 1993, initially testing both the weighted cusums and the t-test against results obtained with Morton's cusum charts for known text combinations. Later in 1993, after I was convinced that the results were consistent with known controls, I included probabilities from weighted cusum charts and the t-test in legal reports.

[82] It should be noted that the calculations involved are non-trivial. However, in Bissell's monograph, *Statistical Methods for Text Analysis by Word-Counts*, there is sufficient information given with which to write a computer program for carrying out the required calculations. For the V_{max}-test, the reader will find it useful to have a nomogram (such as the one given in British Standard 7503: Part 2:1980) for reading off the probability.

Notes to Chapter 11

[1] W. C. Wake, 'Sentence length, distributions of Greek authors', in the *Journal of the Royal Statistical Society*, (London, 1957), 331–46.

[2] Ibid., 331–46.

[3] M. Levison, A. Q., Morton, and W. C. Wake, 'On certain statistical features of the Pauline Epistles', in the *Philosophical Journal* (1966), 129–48.

[4] Readers should note that the illustrations in this chapter appear in a slightly different format, since they were produced on a different model of the Apple Macintosh computer. This reminds potential users that graphic illustrations may vary slightly in format according to the machine used.

(Note, too, that Morton uses the 'habit' description two- **or** three-letter words, not two- **and** three-letter words, as it appears in other illustrations in this book; but exactly the same principle is being applied, namely, the habit of using, within sentences, words of two letters and/or three letters and words starting with a vowel.)

[5] J. C. O'Neill, *The Recovery of Paul's Letter to the Galatians* (London, SPCK, 1972).

[6] A. F. Bissell, 'Weighted cusums for text analysis using word counts', in the *Journal of the Royal Statistical Society* (1995).

[7] Note that this is different from the **JMF** conventions used throughout this book, where, on all the charts shown, sentence length is delineated by the white square and the habit by the dark diamond.

[8] Sidney Michaelson and Andrew Q. Morton, *The QSUM Plot* (University of Edinburgh, April, 1990), updated by Morton, as *Proper Words in Proper Places* (University of Glasgow, October, 1991).

[9] G. H. C. MacGregor and A. Q. Morton, *The Structure of the Fourth Gospel* (Edinburgh, 1961).

[10] Another example of the same point occurs in Chapter 6, where an insertion of eight sentences in sixty-three sentences of Helen Keller is contrasted with the same insertion in her letter of eighteen sentences – see Chapter 6. (Ed.).

[11] Ed McBain, *Killer's Payoff* (Harmondsworth, UK, Penguin Books), 1958.

[12] Austin Mitchelson and Nicolas Utechin, *Hellbirds* (NY, Tower Publications, 1976).

[13] *Proceedings of the British Academy*, 12 (1967), 437–48.

[14] This reference to the content has nothing to do with the effect – or, rather, lack of effect – of new subject-matter: we are here trying to anticipate, from ordinary reading of the text, where it might be logically obvious to separate a joint piece of writing. (Ed.)

[15] A case in point is demonstrated in the case of *The Diary of Gerald Keegan* in Chapter 7, where analysis of new samples confirmed that an author, Robert Sellar, was not an exception to the technique.

[16] Farringdon and Morton, *Fielding and the Federalist* (University of Glasgow, Department of Computing Science, 1990).

[17] See note 6 above.

SELECT BIBLIOGRAPHY

Battestin, Martin C., *New Essays by Henry Fielding, with a Stylometric Analysis by Michael G. Farringdon* (Charlottesville, University of Virginia Press, 1989).

Bissell, Derek, *Statistical Methods for Text Analysis by Word-Counts* (Swansea, European Business Management School, University of Wales Swansea, 1995).

Bissell, A. F., 'Weighted cusums for text analysis using word counts', *Journal of the Royal Statistical Society* (1995) 158, Part 3, 525–45.

Canter, David, 'An Evaluation of the "CUSUM" Stylistic Analysis of Confessions', *Expert Evidence*, 1, No. 3 (October, 1992), 93–9.

Dover, Sir Kenneth, *Marginal Comment,* (London, Duckworth, 1994).

Ellegard, Alvar, *A Statistical Method for Determining Authorship: The Junius Letters, 1769–1772* (University of Gothenberg, 1962).

Farringdon, Jill, 'Confessions of an Anglo-Welsh reader', *New England Review and Bread Loaf Quarterly* (Middlebury College, Vermont) No. 4, Summer 1980.

Farringdon, Michael and Farringdon, Jill, 'A Computer-aided study of the prose style of Henry Fielding and its support for his translation of *The Military History of Charles XII*', in *Advances in Computer-Aided Literary and Linguistic Research* (Birmingham, University of Aston, 1979).

Farringdon, Jillian and Farringdon, Michael, 'Literature and Computers', *Poetry Wales*, 17, No. 1, Summer 1981.

Farringdon, Michael, *Cusum Counter Manual* (and QSUM program, copyright, 1992).

Farringdon, M. G. and Morton, A. Q., *Fielding and the Federalist* (University of Glasgow, Department of Computing Science, 1990).

Hardcastle, R. A., 'Analysis of Confessions', *Expert Evidence,* 1, No. 3 (October, 1992), 93–9.

Hardcastle, R. A., 'An assessment of the cusum method for the determination of authorship', *The Journal of Forensic Science Society Journal* , 33, No. 2 (1993), 93–9.

Hilton, Michael L. and Holmes, David I., 'An assessment of cumulative sum charts for authorship attribution', *Literary and Linguistic Computing*, 8, No. 2 (1993), 73–80.

MacGregor, G. H. C. and Morton, A. Q., *The Structure of Luke and Acts* (New York, Harper & Row, 1964).

Milic, Louis, *A Quantitative Approach to the Style of Jonathan Swift* (The Hague, Mouton & Co., 1967).

Morton, A. Q., *Literary Detection: How to Prove Authorship and Fraud in Literature and Documents* (NY, Charles Scribner's Sons, 1987.)

Morton, A. Q., *Proper Words in Proper Places* (University of Glasgow, October, 1991).

Morton, A. Q., *The Authorship of the New Testament Epistles* (University of Glasgow, Department of Computing Science, 1993).

Morton, A. Q., *The Making of Mark* (Georgia, Mellen Press, 1996).

Morton, A. Q., 'Ascertaining Disputed Authorship Today: The Disunion of "Christian Reunion" ', in *The Lamp-Post* (the Southern California C. S. Lewis Society, March, 1993), 4–7.

Morton, A. Q., and McLeman, James, *Paul, the Man and the Myth, A Study in the Authorship of Greek Prose,* (Hodder & Stoughton, London, 1966).

Morton, A. Q., and McLeman, James, *The Genesis of John* (Edinburgh, St Andrews Press, 1980).

Morton, Andrew Q. and Michaelson, Sidney, *The Qsum Plot* (University of Edinburgh, Department of Computer Science, 1990).

Mosteller, Frederick and Wallace, David, *Inference and Disputed Authorship: The Federalist* (Reading, Mass., 1964).

Oakman, Robert, *Computers in Literary Research* (Athens, University of Georgia Press, 1980).

Percy, Walker, 'The Delta Factor', in *The Message in the Bottle* (New York, Farrar, Straus & Giroux, 1975), 3–45.

Sanford, Anthony J., Aked, Joy P., Moxey, Linda M. and Mullin, James: 'A critical examination of assumptions underlying the cusum technique of forensic linguistics', in *Forensic Linguistics*, 1, No. 2 (1994), 151–67.

Wake, W. C., 'Sentence Length, Distributions of Greek Authors', *Journal Royal Statistical Society*, Ser. A, CXX, III (1957), 331–46.

Yule, G. Udny, *The Statistical Study of Literary Vocabulary* (Cambridge, Cambridge University Press, 1944).

INDEX